IRON ROAD TO THE WEST : AMERIC

D0378889

DATE DUE

DE 19'80			
MY 7'82	JA 7'82		
NOV 2 83	MY 24		
JA 13'85			
DE 13'86	NO 8'96		
MAY 25'86			
SEP 9'90			
JA 11'01			
AP19'01			

HE2751
S73

RIVERSIDE CITY COLLEGE
LIBRARY
Riverside, California

JAN   1988

IRON ROAD TO THE WEST

AMERICAN RAILROADS IN THE 1850s

IRON ROAD
TO
THE WEST

AMERICAN RAILROADS IN THE 1850s

JOHN F. STOVER

COLUMBIA UNIVERSITY PRESS
New York *1978*

Riverside Community College
Library
4800 Magnolia Avenue
Riverside, CA 92506

Library of Congress Cataloging in Publication Data

Stover, John F.
  Iron road to the West.

  Bibliography: p.
  Includes index.
  1. Railroads—United States—History.   I. Title.
HE2751.S73   385'.0973   78-9588
ISBN 0-231-04046-6

New York   Columbia University Press   Guildford, Surrey

Copyright © 1978 Columbia University Press
All rights reserved
Printed in the United States of America

For Marjorie, once more

Contents

Illustrations

Maps

Introduction

IT HAS long been my belief that no decade was more important in the history of American railroads than the antebellum 1850s. What was little more than a scattering of short lines stretching from Maine to Georgia at mid-century became by 1860 an iron network serving all the states east of the Mississippi. As the rail mileage of the nation more than tripled during the decade, the expanding rail industry fully shared in the optimism and prosperity which appeared with the discovery of gold in California. Few other economic institutions of that day did business on so vast a scale, found financial support from such a variety of sources, or employed the numbers of men of diverse skills. By the eve of the Civil War the westward growth of the railroad had nearly reached the moving edge of the frontier in mid-America.

As more than 20,000 miles of new line were built in the decade, railroads helped the national economy achieve a new orientation and posture. American agriculture, especially that of the Old Northwest and the Upper Mississippi Valley, experienced several significant changes because of the expanding iron network. The first maturing of American industry accompanied this rapid construction of new lines, while the merchants in large eastern cities gave a new attention to their growing domestic trade with western states. The major rail construction in the trunk line region between the mid-Atlantic states and the Upper Mississippi Valley soon resulted in a new east–west trade axis which replaced the earlier north–south trade of the Ohio and Mississippi steamboats. This shift in the direction and mode of commerce goes far in explaining the loyalty of the Old Northwest to Lincoln and the Union during the Civil War.

Many people have helped make this book possible. In the early planning of the volume I received excellent advice from my long-time friend, Professor Richard C. Overton of Manchester Center, Vermont. Helpful suggestions were also given by two Purdue colleagues, Professors Donald J. Berthrong, and Harold D. Woodman. Much assistance was provided by the staff of the Purdue University Library, especially by Helen Q. Schroyer. John H. White, Jr., Curator, Division of Transportation in the National Museum of History and Technology, Smithsonian Institution, made several excellent suggestions after reading portions of the manuscript. He and his staff also provided me with a number of pictures for the book. Anne O. Bennof and John McCleod, both of the Association of American Railroads, were generous in furnishing other photographs and maps, many from the files of several American railroads. Other pictures were furnished by Albert M. Rung and J. M. Hagen of the Burlington Northern, Gayle Thornbrough and Tom Rumer of the Indiana Historical Society Library, and Ira Bartfield of the National Gallery of Art.

Copies of several contemporary railroad maps of the early 1850s, provided by Andrew M. Modelski of the Geography and Map Division, Library of Congress, helped in the preparation of the railroad maps of 1850. The works of such authors as Frederick L. Paxson, Robert C. Black, III, Irene D. Neu, and George R. Taylor were very useful in making the maps for 1855 and 1860. Also I wish to thank Bernard Gronert and Joan McQuary, both of Columbia University Press, for their advice and counsel in bringing the book to final publication. Finally, I want to acknowledge the services of several competent secretaries: Joyce Good, Grace Dienhart, Dorothy Mays, Tracy Reeves, and Kathryn McClellan.

JOHN F. STOVER

West Lafayette, Indiana
February 1, 1978

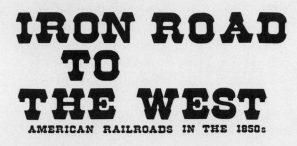

IRON ROAD
TO
THE WEST

AMERICAN RAILROADS IN THE 1850s

CHAPTER ONE

The Iron Horse at Midcentury

IN THE early days of March 1849, while a new president, Zachary Taylor, was getting settled in the White House, a 40-year-old former congressman was preparing to return to his law practice in Illinois. Even though his wife was back in Springfield, Abraham Lincoln did not immediately return home. On a stormy and snowy March 5, a Monday, Lincoln attended the inauguration of President Taylor. Later, at an inaugural ball, he lost his hat and was forced to return bareheaded to his boarding house. On Wednesday he was admitted to practice law before the Supreme Court of the United States, and later in the week he applied at the Patent Office for a patent for an improved method of lifting vessels over shoals. In a few more days he was all packed and ready to start home.

While the records are sketchy, Lincoln probably took eleven or twelve days to return to Illinois, going by railroad, stagecoach, and steamboat. Lincoln no doubt took the Washington Branch Baltimore & Ohio train, leaving the capital at 6:00 A.M., either on March 20 or March 21, 1849. The train connected at the Relay House, 7 miles west of Baltimore, with the B. & O. "Great Western Mail," bound for Cumberland, Maryland, 178 miles west of Baltimore. The train was due at Cumberland at 5:30 P.M. The fare to Baltimore was $1.60, and the ticket to Cumberland an additional $7.00. Cumberland had been the "end of track" for the Baltimore & Ohio for several years, and the lanky Illinois lawyer had to transfer to one of the numerous stage lines that terminated

at the Potomac river town and gave through service west to
Wheeling. The grades were steep northwest of Cumberland
since the National Road went over successive ranges up to
the divide on Little Savage Mountain, but travel was easier
once the road crossed into Pennsylvania. The 130-mile trip to
Wheeling took about twenty-four hours, and a ticket in the
nine-passenger, Concord-type coach cost the homeward-
bound congressman another $4.00 to $5.00.

At Wheeling Lincoln boarded a steamboat for the nearly
1,100-mile journey down the Ohio to Cairo and up the Mississippi to Saint Louis. At midcentury the Ohio river traffic
was heavy, and each week Saint Louis had an average of
eight or nine steamboat arrivals from the Ohio. Past Louisville the shore line may have reminded Lincoln of his earlier
boyhood in Kentucky and Indiana. As a youth back in the
mid-1820s, he had earned occasional pocket money rowing
passengers from the Hoosier shore out to passing steamers.
In 1828 he had embarked from Gentry's landing for a flatboat journey down to New Orleans. His return trip by Mississippi steamboat had given the youth a passing fancy to
become "a steamboat man." Lincoln's three or four days on
the Ohio and Mississippi rivers was faster and far more comfortable than the earlier stage journey over the Alleghenies
into Wheeling. The returning congressman reached Saint
Louis by March 26, 1849, and a few days later he was home
in Springfield.[1]

Several weeks earlier another river journey on western
waters had taken the president-elect to the nation's capital.
Early in February the military hero of the Mexican War,
General Zachary Taylor, had left his Louisiana home to
travel by steamboat up the Mississippi and Ohio rivers.
Although his journey was halted by numerous receptions and
celebrations, Taylor arrived in Washington on the evening of
February 23. The retiring president, James K. Polk, had left
Washington more quickly than Abraham Lincoln. Haggard
and worn out by four busy years in the presidency, Polk
departed on March 6, 1849, traveling south chiefly by
railroad to Richmond and on to Wilmington, North Carolina.

Coastal steamers took him to Charleston and Savannah, and he continued by railroad and stage on to Montgomery, Alabama. Again river and coastal steamers carried Polk to Mobile, New Orleans, and Memphis before the final stage journey home to Nashville.

In the leisurely and needlessly indirect journey of more than three weeks, Polk had ridden over a major portion of all existing railroads located in the southern states. Lincoln and Taylor, however, had taken the best and most expeditious routes and modes of travel then available. All three men had traveled much more by boat or road than by rail. This was unavoidable, since the nation's railroad system was then chiefly located in the Northeast. Only 40 percent of the total railroad mileage at midcentury was found in the twenty-one states south and west of Pennsylvania. Only ten of the twenty-one states had 100 miles of line. In 1850 Lincoln's home state had just over 100 miles of railroad. Louisiana, Taylor's home, had only 80 miles in operation, and Tennessee had but 9 miles.

James K. Polk was to die in mid-June 1849, and President Taylor died early in July a year later. But the 1850s were to be years of expanding legal and political activity for Lincoln, and in 1860 he was nominated and elected to be the sixteenth president of the United States. Three weeks before his inauguration, the president-elect left his hometown for the nation's capital. Early on a drizzling Monday morning he boarded a special train at the Great Western Railway depot in Springfield to start a twelve day inaugural trip to Washington. Traveling entirely by rail via Indianapolis, Cincinnati, Columbus, Pittsburgh, Cleveland, Buffalo, Albany, New York City, Philadelphia, and Baltimore, Lincoln journeyed through eight states over twenty different railroads—a total distance of more than 1,900 miles. In the major cities and dozens of smaller towns and villages more than a million Americans saw and heard the president-elect during those twelve days. The prolonged and roundabout journey to Washington was aimed more to generate political good will than to ensure Lincoln's speedy arrival in Washington.[2]

The *Daniel Nason* was built for the Boston & Providence Railroad in 1858 by that line's longtime master mechanic, George S. Griggs. Note the inside connection (cylinders located inside the frame) as well as the six-wheel tender, a type favored by Griggs. (COURTESY, SMITHSONIAN INSTITUTION.)

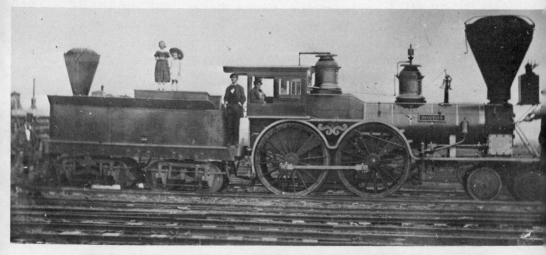

The *Boston*, built in 1843 for the Western Railroad (Massachusetts), like the *Daniel Nason* was an inside connected wood-burner. Early locomotives were often permanently assigned to engine crews, and the children on the tender no doubt shared their father's pride in the well-maintained locomotive. (COURTESY, SMITHSONIAN INSTITUTION.)

Had he wished to, Lincoln in February 1861 certainly could have traveled by rail to his inaugural far more easily and quickly than he was able to journey from Washington a dozen years earlier. The rail distance in 1860 was much shorter. If the president-elect had changed his route at Cincinnati to take the Marietta and Cincinanati to a Baltimore & Ohio connection at Parkersburg, he could have reached Washington with a railroad trip of only 966 miles as compared with the nearly 1,500 miles he had traveled by rail, stage, and steamer back in March 1849. The rail route just described would have taken a little more than two days as contrasted with the eleven or twelve days consumed in the earlier trip. When the two presidents and the congressman had journeyed to and from Washington in 1849, not a single railroad crossed the Pennsylvania-Ohio border, the Ohio-Indiana border, or the Indiana-Illinois border. When Abe Lincoln went east to become the nation's chief executive in February 1861, he could have taken any of seven east–west rail lines that crossed the Indiana-Illinois border, any of the seven that crossed from Indiana into Ohio, and any of five that crossed from Ohio into Pennsylvania or western Virginia.[3]

In 1850 about 9,000 miles of railroad were in operation in the United States, with each of the twenty-six states east of the Mississippi having at least a bit of line. The four states located west of the Mississippi—Iowa, Missouri, Arkansas, and Texas—could not yet claim the iron horse at midcentury. Americans were proud of their expanding railroads, but it was still a broken and scattered network. Only eighteen states had as much as 100 miles of line. Claiming about 60 percent of the total mileage, the New England and mid-Atlantic states dominated the railroad. Boston had a connection with Buffalo, and one could travel, with only minor breaks, from Maine to North Carolina by rail. Most eastern seaports still had no rail connections with western markets. West of Pennsylvania all the states of the Old Northwest together had fewer than 1,300 miles of railway. Below the Potomac and Ohio rivers most of the southern mileage was found in

Virginia and Georgia. By 1850 about $300 million had been invested in American railroads, but much northeastern commerce continued to move by canal. West of the mountains in the Mississippi Valley the river steamboat was clearly dominant.

In 1850 slightly more than 62 percent of American rail mileage was located in the northeastern region—that is, the six New England states plus the mid-Atlantic states (including Delaware and Maryland). New England had 2,507 miles of line; 3,105 miles of line were located in the adjoining five states to the south and west. Some of the details of the 5,612-mile network located in these eleven states are shown in Table 1.1.[4]

It is not easy to be certain of "firsts" when rival states, communities, or companies each sometimes claim to have built or operated the "first railroad." The several "first railroad" dates in Table 1.1 refer to regular and permanent rail service, rather than to early track laid or service of a peculiar or temporary nature. In February 1825, Colonel John Stevens entertained venturesome house guests when he let them ride on his 16-ft. "Steam Waggon" locomotive running at a speed of 12 miles an hour around a circular track laid on the grounds of his Hoboken, New Jersey, estate. A year and a half later Gridley Bryant, Massachusetts civil engineer and inventor, opened his broad-gauge Granite Railway at Quincy to transport granite for the Bunker Hill Monument. And in 1829 in Honesdale, Pennsylvania, Horatio Allen, resident engineer with the Delaware & Hudson Canal and Railroad Company, had experimented with the *Stourbridge Lion,* but found the seven-ton English-built engine too rigid and heavy for American track.

But regular and permanent railroad service for the public was introduced by the Baltimore & Ohio Railroad, a line incorporated in 1827, and started on Independence Day, 1828. By late May 1830, 13 miles of track were completed out to Ellicott's Mills, Maryland, and horses pulling "rail wagons" were providing regular freight and passenger service. (That was three months before the famous race between the little gray horse and *Tom Thumb,* the small experimental

T A B L E 1.1
R A I L R O A D S   I N   N E W   E N G L A N D   A N D   M I D - A T L A N T I C   S T A T E S   (1 1   S T A T E S)

State	First Railroad	1840 Mileage	1850 Mileage	1850 Pop.	Area Sq. Miles	One mile of R.R. (1850)	
						to Pop.	to Sq. Miles
Connecticut	1838	102	402	370,792	5,009	921	12
Delaware	1831	39	39	91,532	2,057	2,347	53
Maine	1836	11	245	583,169	33,225	2,380	135
Maryland	1830	213	259	583,034	10,577	2,251	41
Massachusetts	1834	301	1,035	994,514	8,257	961	8
New Hampshire	1838	53	467	317,976	9,304	681	20
New Jersey	1831	186	206	489,555	7,836	2,376	38
New York	1831	374	1,361	3,097,394	49,576	2,276	36
Pennsylvania	1832	754	1,240	2,311,786	45,333	1,872	37
Rhode Island	1835	50	68	147,545	1,214	2,170	18
Vermont	1848	0	290	314,120	9,609	1,084	33
Total (11 states)		2,083	5,612	9,301,417	181,997	1,657	32
Total (U.S.)		2,808	9,021				

locomotive built by Peter Cooper, glue-maker and part-time inventor from New York City.) Thus regular service on the B. & O. had predated the *Best Friend of Charleston* (December 25, 1830) by more than six months, and the *DeWitt Clinton* in upstate New York by over a year (August 9, 1831).

The mid-Atlantic states easily maintained their leadership during the first decade of railroad history. The five mid-Atlantic states in 1840 could claim 1,566 miles of track, well over half the national total. Pennsylvania was a trailblazer and her 754 miles in operation in 1840 were more than twice the mileage of any other state. New York was second, Massachusetts third, Maryland fourth, and New Jersey fifth among the states with some railroad mileage in 1840.

In New England during the 1830s, only Massachusetts made much headway in railroad development. Worried about the commercial success of New York City, the Boston merchants wisely rejected the notion of more canals and chose railroads instead. By 1835 three lines out of Boston were in operation—one north to Lowell, a second west to Worcester, and the third south to Providence. Other routes were also added in the decade, and by 1840 Massachusetts had 301 miles of completed railroad line. However, the rest of New England was much slower to adopt the new mode of transport, and the total for the six states in 1840 was only 517 miles. Of the other states only Connecticut had more than 100 miles of line in 1840, and Vermont had no mileage at all.

Between 1840 and 1850 the pace of construction accelerated rapidly in New England. Almost 2,000 miles of additional line were constructed, for a total mileage of 2,507 at midcentury. The railroad system in New England seemed fairly complete, and each of the six states, except Rhode Island, had considerably more than 200 miles of line. Three states, Massachusetts, New Hampshire, and Connecticut, each had half the mileage in 1850 that they would have in the mid-twentieth century. They were far better supplied with railways, both on a basis of population and area, than any of the other states in the entire nation.

During the decade Boston even obtained a transsectional line, the 150-mile Western Railroad, running from Worcester, via Springfield and Pittsfield, to Albany. When the road was completed through the rugged Berkshires to the Hudson River and Albany, the city fathers of Boston and Albany celebrated by making the first round trip in December 1841. The Boston delegation returned home on December 28 with a barrel of Rochester flour, which was used to bake bread for the evening's celebration. Boston now had a rail connection with the busy Erie Canal, but she would never obtain much of the traffic destined to go down the Hudson to New York City. Most Bostonians had to agree with Charles F. Adams, Jr., who would later write that the Western Railroad was built upon "the fallacy that steam could run up hill cheaper than water could run down."[5]

During the 1840s the five mid-Atlantic states did not match the rate of construction in New England but kept well ahead in total mileage. Relatively little new line was added in the three smaller states of Delaware, Maryland, and New Jersey, but construction was pushed in Pennsylvania and New York. The Empire State added mileage at an especially rapid rate, taking over first place in the nation from Pennyslvania as it more than tripled its trackage to a total of 1,361 miles in 1850. Much of the construction in New York was on the New York and Erie Railroad, which was being built through the southern part of the state to Dunkirk on Lake Erie.

During the 1830s and 1840s the major seaports north of the Potomac had all sought to obtain rail connections with western markets. In the early 1840s Boston had obtained a rail connection with Albany and Buffalo, but the new route brought little additional traffic to the "Hub of the Universe," as Oliver Wendell Holmes termed Boston. In 1850 New York City, Philadelphia, and Baltimore still lacked completed rail connections with either the Great Lakes or the upper Ohio. Early in the 1850s four important rail routes would be completed to the western markets: the New York Central and the Erie both connected New York City with Lake Erie; the Pennsylvania gave Philadelphia a rail route to Pittsburgh on the Ohio; and the Baltimore & Ohio provided comparable service between Baltimore and Wheeling, also on the Ohio.

South of the Potomac and Ohio rivers railroads were much less common than in the northeastern states. In 1850 the South (here defined as the eleven Confederate states plus Kentucky) could claim 2,133 miles of railroad, or a bit more than 23 percent of the national rail system. The details of the rail network in the South are shown in Table 1.2.[6]

More than half of the southern states projected and built their first railways during the 1830s. The first southern line was in South Carolina, where the South Carolina Canal and Railroad Company hired Horatio Allen, the man who had found the English-built *Stourbridge Lion* unsuitable for American track, to build their road from Charleston to Hamburg, South Carolina, just across the Savannah River from Augusta, Georgia. When the American-built, $4,000, four-ton *Best Friend of Charleston* pulled a short passenger train out of Charleston on Christmas Day, 1830, it became the first American railroad to use steam power in regular rail service. Six months later the engine was destroyed in a fatal accident when the annoyed fireman tied down a noisy safety steam valve. When the 136-mile line was finished in 1833, it was for a short time the longest railroad in the world.

At least six other southern states built railways during the decade, but by 1840, three southern states—Georgia, South Carolina, and Virginia—were by far the most ardent supporters of the new mode of transportation. In 1840 the three coastal states together had 469 miles of line, or nearly three-quarters of the regional total. This domination continued in the following decade, with the most rapid construction taking place in Virginia and Georgia. At midcentury Georgia (643 miles) ranked fourth in rail mileage among all the states, and Virginia (481 miles) ranked sixth.

Four railroads—the Petersburg; the Richmond, Fredericksburg and Potomac; the Seaboard and Roanoke; and the Virginia Central—each of about equal length, made up three-fifths of Virginia's rail mileage in 1850. The four lines

TABLE 1.2
RAILROADS IN THE SOUTH (12 STATES)

State	First Railroad	1840 Mileage	1850 Mileage	1850 Pop.	Area Sq. Mi.	One Mile of R.R. (1850) to Pop.	to Sq. Miles
Alabama	1832	46	183	771,623	51,609	4,216	282
Arkansas	1857	—	—	209,897	53,104	—	—
Florida	1836	(22)*	21	87,445	58,560	4,164	2,788
Georgia	1837	185	643	906,185	58,876	1,409	91
Kentucky	1834	28	78	982,405	40,395	12,595	520
Louisiana	1831	40	80	517,762	48,523	6,472	606
Mississippi	1837	(25)*	75	606,526	47,716	8,087	636
North Carolina	1833	53	283	869,039	52,586	3,071	185
South Carolina	1830	137	289	668,507	31,055	2,313	107
Tennessee	1842	—	(9)*	1,002,717	42,244	—	—
Texas	1853	—	—	212,592	267,339	—	—
Virginia (+West Virginia)	1831	147	481	1,421,661	64,998	2,956	135
Total (states with r.r.)		636 (7 states)	2,133 •(9 states)	6,831,153 (9 states)	454,318 (9 states)	3,203	212
Total (U.S.)		2,808	9,021				

*While the Poor *Manuals* and the U.S. Census for 1860 both indicate otherwise, there is considerable evidence that Florida and Mississippi each had some rail mileage by 1840, and also that Tennessee had some by 1850. However, these three state mileage figures have not been included in the seven-state total for 1840 or the nine-state total for 1850.

served Richmond and southeastern Virginia, with two of the roads reaching Weldon, North Carolina. In Georgia at midcentury the total mileage was shared exclusively by four major lines: the Central of Georgia (190 miles), the Georgia (213 miles), the Macon and Western (102 miles), and the Western and Atlantic (138 miles). These four roads served the northern half of the state, connecting Savannah and Augusta with Macon, Atlanta, and Chattanooga, Tennessee. A Quaker from Pennsylvania, J. Edgar Thomson, helped build the Georgia Railroad, the longest of the four lines in the state. Trained by his father to be a civil engineer, Thomson had helped survey the Camden and Amboy before spending fifteen years (1832–1847) as the chief engineer of the Georgia Railroad. Later he returned north to build the Pennsylvania across the Alleghenies.

Southern states at midcentury did not begin to have a serviceable or coordinated rail network like that found in the Northeast. The railroads of Virginia connected with lines in North Carolina serving Raleigh and Wilmington. And the network in Georgia was connected with the South Carolina Railroad giving service to Charleston. In the other southern states the rail lines formed only disconnected bits and pieces, with Alabama being the only other state in 1850 with more than 100 miles of road. A comparison of Tables 1.1 and 1.2 reveals this contrast. Of the twelve southern states in 1850, only Georgia possessed rail mileage and service at all comparable with that of the Northeast. On a basis of population, the eleven northeastern states had twice as much railroad as the South, and on a basis of area the difference was more than six to one in favor of the North.

Railroads in the West at midcentury were even scarcer than in the South. The 1,276 miles of line in the western states (the Old Northwest plus California, Iowa, Minnesota, Missouri, and Oregon) constituted about a seventh of the national mileage in 1850. The early railroad development in these ten states is shown in Table 1.3.[7]

Quite naturally railroads had been slower to appear in

TABLE 1.3
RAILROADS IN THE WEST (10 STATES)

State	First Railroad	1840 Mileage	1850 Mileage	1850 Pop.	Area Sq. Mi.	One mile of R.R. (1850)	
						to Pop.	to Sq. Miles
California	1856	—	—	92,597	158,693	—	—
Illinois	1838	(24)*	111	851,470	56,400	7,671	508
Indiana	1838	(20)*	228	988,416	36,291	4,335	159
Iowa	1855	—	—	192,214	56,290	—	—
Michigan	1836	59	342	397,654	58,212	1,163	170
Minnesota	1862	—	—	6,077	84,068	—	—
Missouri	1852	—	—	682,044	69,686	—	—
Ohio	1836	30	575	1,980,329	41,222	3,270	72
Oregon	1862	—	—	13,294	96,981	—	—
Wisconsin	1850	—	20	305,391	56,154	15,269	2,808
Total (states with r.r.)		89 (2 states)	1,276 (5 states)	4,523,260 (5 states)	248,279 (5 states)	3,537	194
Total (U.S.)		2,808	9,021				

*While the Poor Manuals indicate otherwise, there is considerable evidence that Illinois and Indiana had some railroad mileage by 1840. These two state mileage figures, however, are not included in the two-state total for 1840.

the western states. All but one of the eleven mid-Atlantic and New England states had started their first railways by 1838. Three-quarters of the southern states had railroads before 1838, and two of the twelve started construction only in the middle 1850s. Among the ten western states, only four had railroads by the mid- or late 1830s, with the other six waiting until 1850 or after. As a consequence, western railroads in 1840 were limited to only 89 miles, or only about 3 percent of the national total.

All of the western mileage, both in 1840 and 1850, was located in the Old Northwest, with Ohio and Michigan possessing about three-quarters of the total. The railroads in Michigan ran west from Detroit and Toledo toward Lake Michigan and Chicago. The 575-mile rail network in Ohio placed her fifth among all the states in 1850, below New York, Pennsylvania, Massachusetts, and Georgia. In Ohio the railroads ran north and south connecting the two Lake Erie ports of Cleveland and Sandusky with Columbus in the central part of the state and Cincinnati on the Ohio River. Alfred Kelley, Cleveland's first lawyer and a long-time member of the state legislature, was the president of two of Ohio's five railways in 1850. Earlier, in the 1820s and 1830s, Kelley had been the prime mover in building the Ohio system of canals, a network of waterways that reached a total of 744 miles by 1840. By the late 1840s Kelley had shifted his allegiance to railroads, a change in policy that would be fully justified by economic developments in the following decade.

A comparison of Table 1.3 with Table 1.2 shows that the Old Northwest in 1850 was about as well served by railroads as was the South. On a basis of both area and population, the railroads in both regions were quite comparable, and both were much inferior to those in the Northeast. The railroad investment in 1850 per mile of line was also fairly equal in the two regions: $19,600 per mile in the West and $21,100 per mile in the South. In the eleven northeastern states there was an investment of $43,000 per mile of road.[8]

The 9,000 miles of railroad operating in the nation in 1850 represented a total investment of about $300 million, or an average of roughly $33,000 per mile of road. At midcentury the railroads were the major "big business" on the American scene. Few other segments of the national economy did business on so vast a scale or financed themselves in such a variety of ways. Few other industries in America employed so many men in such diverse capacities. Few other business leaders had the optimism expressed by railroad promoters as they entered the 1850s. An editorial "Are we Building Too Many Railroads?" appearing late in 1850 in the *American Railroad Journal* expressed this spirit:

> The construction of railroads is, probably the most engrossing subject now occupying the attention of our people. Every portion of our country is aroused to their importance. In the West, the feeling in their favor amounts almost to a mania, and every farmer there is contriving how he shall secure one within convenient distance. Their influence, as instruments of wealth, are now thoroughly appreciated, and the social advantages which they confer, are scarcely less valued. . . . People will have railroads. . . . This is a settled fact, and their construction will go on til every section of the country is penetrated with them. . . ."[9]

Certainly American railroads by 1850 were quite successfully competing with earlier modes of transportation. In the twenty years prior to 1850, canals and later railroads had brought economic ruin to most of the important turnpikes in the Northeast. By the 1840s most turnpikes still in operation were no more than feeder lines to other forms of transport.[10] The canals too were suffering as shown by the relative plateau in canal mileage after 1840. In 1830 canal mileage exceeded railroad mileage by a margin of 1,277 miles to 73. In 1840 canals were still ahead, 3,326 miles to 2,808 miles. But in 1850 railroads were well ahead, with 9,021 miles of railway to only 3,698 miles of canal.[11] River steamboats, especially those on western waters, were much slower to fear the competition of the railroad. In 1849, no railroad was operating within 50 miles of Saint Louis, and that city was dependent upon the river steamer: more than 2,750 steamboats, with a total weight of 590,000 tons, arrived in Saint Louis that year. Many observers saw the decade of the 1850s as the golden age of steamboating on the Mississippi, but in reality western railroads by the eve of the Civil War had proven that they possessed several competitive advantages over side-wheeler and stern-wheeler.[12]

The long decade between the Mexican War and the firing on Fort Sumter was to be a period of dynamic growth for America and the national economy. The census takers in 1850 counted a population growth of more than 6 million above the 1840 figure, a result of the high birthrate and growing immigration. The 1850 official figure, of just over 23 million, represented an increase for the decade of almost 36 percent, the highest growth rate in forty years. The nation was growing in area as well: with the end of the Mexican War, "Manifest Destiny" was a reality, and Americans were proud to note that their borders now extended fully to the far Pacific and the Rio Grande.

The decade was prosperous both for farm and factory; the nation enjoyed an unparalleled expansion of its material wealth and resources. The value both of manufactured goods and farm products roughly doubled. Foreign trade was expanding in the fifties, but the internal commerce grew even faster. In the Northeast industrial production was booming. In the South the planters and growers of cotton were proud that their region seemed hardly touched by the Panic of 1857. And midwestern farmers were experiencing an agricultural revolution as new or improved plows, reapers, and threshing machines greatly increased their total farm production.

All these factors hastened railroad construction, and between 1850 and 1860 rail mileage in the nation increased from 9,021 to 30,626 miles[13]—the United States, with only 5 percent of the globe's population, was building railroads about as fast as the rest of the world together. Early in 1857 the *American Railroad Journal* reported that the United States had 24,500 miles of line out of a world total of 51,000 miles.[14] Well behind were the other nations with major rail mileage: England and Wales (6,400 miles), France (3,700 miles), and Prussia (2,300 miles).

The growth and development of American railways during the decade was widely reported in several commercial papers. The most important coverage was given by the weekly *American Railroad Journal.* In 1849 Henry Varnum Poor gave up his modest practice of law in Bangor, Maine, and moved to New York City to become editor of the *Journal,* which for seventeen years had been serving the railroad industry. Poor soon had expanded the circulation from 1,200 to nearly 5,000. Long before his retirement in 1861, Poor had become a major spokesman for the railroads of the nation. Early in the decade he eagerly promoted western rail construction, but by mid-decade his editorials were stressing corporate restraint and warning against the dangers of over-construction. His paper gave quite complete reports of railroad stock and bond prices. Two other journals that helped promote the growing rail industry during the antebellum years were *Hunt's Merchant's Magazine and Commercial Review,* also published in New York City, and *DeBow's Commercial Review of the South and West,* published in New Orleans by that ardent advocate of slavery and secession James Dunwoody Brownson DeBow.

The American railroads that Poor and DeBow were describing were experiencing changing traffic and revenue patterns at midcentury. During the first years of railroad operation, most railways had much larger passenger than freight revenues. By 1850 passenger and freight revenues were about equal on most roads, and by the eve of the Civil War freight receipts were generally well ahead of passenger receipts.[15] This trend would accelerate after the Civil War as the nation experienced its rapid industrialization. During the early 1850s those railroads that competed with canals often had larger passenger revenues, while other railroads without such competition depended to a greater extent upon their freight business. Thus the New York Central, even after the 1851 repeal of New York state laws favoring the Erie Canal over the railroad, had passenger revenues much larger than those from freight. In contrast, typical Baltimore & Ohio annual reports showed freight receipts four to five times as large as passenger revenue.[16]

BOSTON & MAINE RAILROAD.

WINTER ARRANGEMENT,

COMMENCING JANUARY 1, 1850.

Trains will run FROM BOSTON, as follows, viz:

For PORTLAND, at 7, A. M., and 2½, P. M.
For GREAT FALLS, at 7, A. M., 2½, and 3½, P. M.
For HAVERHILL, at 7, and 9½; A. M., 2½, 3½, and 5½, P. M.
For LAWRENCE, (South side,) at 7, and 7½, A. M., 2½, 3½, and 4½, P. M.
For LAWRENCE, (North side,) at 7½, and 9½, A. M., 12, M., 4½, and 5½, P. M.
For READING, at 7, and 9½, A. M., 12, M., 2½, 3½, 4½, 5½, 7¼, and 9¼††, P. M.

Trains will run TO BOSTON, as follows, viz:

From PORTLAND, at 8½, A. M., and 4, P. M.
From GREAT FALLS, at 6¾, and 10¼, A. M., and 5¾, P. M.
From HAVERHILL, at 7, and 8¼*, A. M., 12*, M., 3, and 7½*, P. M.
From LAWRENCE, (South side,) at 8¾*, A. M., 12¼*, and 7¾*, P. M.
From LAWRENCE, (North side,) at 7¼*, 8¼†, 11¾†, A. M., 3¼*, and 4¾†, P. M.
From READING, at 6¾, 7¾*, and 9_4*, A. M., 12¼†, 12¾*, 3¾*, 5¾, 8††, and 8¼*, P M.

*Or on their arrival from the East. †Or on their arrival from the North.

The 7 1-2 A. M. and the 4 1-2 P. M. trains from Boston, and the 8 1-4 A. M. train from Lawrence do not stop between Lawrence and Boston; The 4 3-4 P. M. train from Lawrence stops only at Andover.

MEDFORD BRANCH TRAINS.

From BOSTON, at 7, and 9¼, A. M., 12¾, 2¾, 5, 6½, and 9¼††, P. M.
From MEDFORD, at 6¾, 8, and 10, A. M., 2, 4, 6, and 7 P. M.

††On Wednesday evenings these trains will be two hours later; on Saturday evenings, one hour later

Passengers are not allowed to carry Baggage, above $50 in value, and that PERSONAL, unless notice is given and an extra amount paid, at the rate of the Price of a Ticket for every $500 additional value.

December 25, 1849. **CHA'S MINOT, Sup't.**

Dearborn, Printer, 1 Water Street, Boston.

Schedule of Boston & Maine trains for Boston. Charles Minot, who later would work for the Erie, was providing ample north-bound rail service for Boston in 1850. (COURTESY, BOSTON & MAINE RAILROAD.)

At midcentury all passenger trains were on faster schedules than freight trains. In freight service cheaper rates were more important than faster schedules, since rail freight at almost any speed had a great time advantage over the canal boat and the Conestoga wagon. A study made of an 1852 issue of the *American Railway Guide* on the speed of the "swiftest trains" on 113 different railway lines in all parts of the country gave a range of from 9 miles per hour to 35 miles per hour for passenger service. The study was based upon the total running time, including station stops, over routes ranging in length from 20 to 328 miles. Average speed for all the runs was about 22 miles per hour, with actual running-time speed being somewhat higher. Northern lines in general had faster schedules than those in the South or the West. One of the fastest passenger schedules in the early 1850s was the 144-mile trip (made in four hours and five minutes) on the Hudson River R.R. between New York City and Albany. Competing river steamers, much like those earlier operated by those fierce rivals Commodore Cornelius Vanderbilt and Daniel Drew, took eight to nine hours for the trip, but charged less than half the fare of the railroad.[17]

At midcentury there was also quite a range in the passenger fares charged by the several railroads. In 1850 the fares charged by over 125 lines in some twenty states ranged from a low of 1.33 cents per mile to a high of 6.25 cents per mile. Only two lines had fares of less than 2 cents, and only five roads had fares about 5 cents a mile. The average fares for the entire group of lines was about 3 cents a mile, with the higher fares generally being found in the southern states.[18]

Railroad freight rates varied about as much as passenger fares. In the early 1850s they ranged between 2 cents and 8 cents a ton mile, with most rates averaging between 3 and 4 cents a ton mile on the typical railroad. Heavy freight such as coal moved at rates well below the average. In all cases rail freight cost two to three times the rates charged on well-managed canals. However, railroads remained competitive with canals because there were faster, open all year, and generally available over a wider geographic area.

By midcentury many improvements had been made on railroad motive power. In 1850 most railroad presidents or general managers were buying 4–4–0 (a swiveled four-wheeled truck in front plus four drivers under the fire box and cab) locomotives. This type of engine, after the Civil War called the American type, in the early years of the decade almost certainly used cord-wood for fuel, cost $8,000 to $10,000 when purchased new, had total operating expenses of well under a dollar a mile, carried a name rather than a number, and was the pride and joy of the engine crew assigned to it. The range of engine names was wide: *Ajax, Cyclone, Frugality, Hiawatha, Lightning, Samson,* and *Tiger.* National heroes, cities, states, and railroad executives were also often honored.

Many railroads, especially those in New England, used 4–4–0 locomotives both for passenger and freight service. A few companies used a different type of engine with all the wheels serving as drivers and no front "bogie" truck, for their freight service. The Baltimore & Ohio, for example, in the early 1850 used the 4–4–0 engines for most of their passenger service, but used Ross Winan's camel-back engines (0–8–0) for much of their freight service. These eight-wheeled engines with their smaller drivers were far from speedy, but they could easily pull fairly heavy loads up the stiff grades found in western Maryland and Virginia.

By 1850 the cowcatcher, headlight, whistle, and bell were standard equipment on all motive power—quite necessary on American railways, since the routes so frequently were built through wide open spaces without benefit of fencing. When the early locomotives of the 1830s collided with farm livestock, the engine frequently landed in the ditch or in the company shops, but after Isaac Dripps, the top mechanic on the Camden and Amboy, perfected his cowcatcher, the railroad generally had to pay for the cow. By midcentury, when the locomotive builder delivered an engine without a pilot up front, it was because the railway preferred to build and mount their own style of cowcatcher. Nighttime operations were common by the early 1850s, and most locomotives came equipped with large, square headlights, burning kerosene in front of a reflector, and with the side panels of the lamp often showing gay colors or other oranmentation.

Engine crews, especially in northern states, found riding on open engine platforms in winter more and more difficult as train speeds increased. By midcentury most manufacturers were adding wooden cabs as standard equipment to their locomotives. At this time there were about forty different firms building locomotives in the nation, most of them concentrated in the mid-Atlantic states. The three largest were run by Mathias W. Baldwin, Thomas Rogers, and the Norris brothers, Richard, Septimus, and William. Baldwin, a watchmaker-machinist in Philadelphia, had in 1830 built a crowd-pleasing miniature locomotive for the local museum run by his good friend Franklin Peale. In 1832 he built the full-sized *Old Ironisdes* for the Philadelphia, Germantown and Norristown Railroad. When the officials complained that the new engine was both too slow and too heavy and even tried to cut down the agreed-upon price of $4,000, Baldwin swore he would never build another engine. In fact, he never did anything else: by the eve of the Civil War the Baldwin Locomotive Works had built a thousand engines.

The general style and arrangement of passenger and freight cars in 1850 was not too different from the railroad equipment of the early twentieth century. By midcentury four-wheeled trucks, two on each car, were standard on practically all freight and passenger cars. The first stagecoach-style passenger cars of the early 1830s had long since given way to the longer corridor-type of car that the English actress Fanny Kemble called "a long greenhouse upon wheels." As Charles Dickens had noted on a trip to America, the American trains, unlike the English, had no first- or second-class carriages, but rather had gentlemen's and ladies' cars. Passenger equipment had a coal or wood stove at one end of the car, but hungry passengers did not have the luxury of dining on the train. Some few railroads had experimented with crude sleeping cars as early as the late 1830s, but none at midcentury had anything comparable to the sleeping facilities later to be made available by George M. Pullman.

The freight cars of the early 1850s were much smaller than those used in the mid-twentieth century. Cars were not much more than 30 feet in length with a top carrying capacity of about ten tons. Eight-wheeled (two trucks) boxcars on the Philadelphia and Columbia Railroad weighed about eight tons unloaded and were permitted to carry loads of nine tons.[19] The average load per car for all freight service was normally well under half of the rated maximum load. Many railroads in 1850 listed only two types of freight cars in their rosters of equipment: boxcars and platform or flatcars. The boxcars were used for merchandise, lumber, grain, livestock, and miscellaneous freight. The flatcars, once sideboards were attached, could also carry a variety of shipments. The B. & O. by 1850 had a number of short, ten-ton, iron-pot hopper cars in use. In the early 1850s small refrigerated shipments were occasionally sent in an ordinary boxcar, but the refrigerator car, with built-in ice compartments, was common only after the Civil War. The first cylindrical tank car also first appeared in the late 1860s, but in the early 1850s liquid freight was sometimes shipped in "tank cars" consisting of two or three tublike tanks fastened to platform cars.

The railroads of the nation in 1850 lacked many of the features and characteristics that later were to provide America with an efficient railway system. No one had yet thought of using the telegraph to dispatch or control train movements. The gauge—the distance between the rails, measured from inside to inside—varied in different regions; the English 4 ft. 8½ in. guage had not yet become standard for the industry. Few rivers of any size were spanned by railway bridges in 1850: no railroad bridge yet spanned the lower or middle Ohio, the Niagara, the middle and lower Hudson, or the Potomac in the vicinity of the nation's captal.

Because of breaks in gauge and the absence of bridges over major streams, the transshipment of freight at many cities and rivers was a commonplace occurrence. Nor were there many "union" depots or stations in the large cities of that day. The local interests, strong in the merchant-oriented society of midcentury America, were quite content with the fragmented rail system. Omnibus drivers, draymen, ferryboat operators, and proprietors of innumerable hotels were all happy that both freight and travelers had to stop and be transferred across dozens of cities and rivers.

There were other shortcomings and faults in those early railroads. The link-and-pin coupler found on both passenger and freight cars made all rail service slow and hazardous. The couplers were so arranged that brakemen generally had to stand between the cars in order to steer the link into the socket and drop the pin. This job so frequently caused accidents that brakemen often were recognized by a crippled hand or missing fingers. Locomotives of that day had no brakes, and the hand brakes on passenger and freight cars were barely adequate. The manual braking of a freight train, especially in an icy blizzard at night, was no easy task, even for brakemen with years of experience.

Some of these problems were to be partially solved in the 1850s, but most of the solutions would come only in the seventies and eighties. The prewar years were to be remembered more for vast extension in railroad routes and mileage than for safety improvements. Between 1850 and 1860 more than 21,000 miles of new railroad were projected and built in the United States. The year-by-year growth of American railroads is shown in Table 1.4.[20]

In all but two of the years in the decade, at least 1,800 miles of new line were completed; in four of the years more than 2,400 miles were laid, and in the top year, 1856, an average construction of nearly ten miles a day was achieved. With 21,000 miles of new construction, the network had more than tripled in mileage between 1850 and 1860. In each of the next five decades more new mileage was constructed than during the fifties, but the decade's percentage growth was exceeded only in the 1830s, when the rail network expanded from 23 to 2,808 miles.

Every state with railroads in 1850 added substantial new mileage in the next ten years, and half a dozen states constructed their first mileage during the decade. The distances

TABLE 1.4
RAILWAY MILEAGE IN THE UNITED STATES, 1850–60

Year	Miles of Line in Operation	Annual Increase
1850	9,021	—
1851	10,982	1,961
1852	12,908	1,926
1853	15,360	2,452
1854	16,720	1,360
1855	18,374	1,654
1856	22,016	3,642
1857	24,503	2,487
1858	26,968	2,465
1859	28,789	1,821
1860	30,626	1,837

built varied from California's 23 miles to the more than 2,600 miles built in Illinois. In 1860, on the eve of the Civil War, each of the thirty-three states in the Union except Minnesota and Oregon had some rail mileage in operation. The westward fingers of the expanding iron network had reached LaCrosse in Wisconsin, Cedar Rapids in Iowa, and Saint Joseph in Missouri. West of the Mississippi other short pieces of railway served parts of Arkanasas, Louisiana, and Texas. Thus by 1860 the rail network had practically reached the nation's western frontier line.

The rates at which the three regions built additional railroads in the 1850s varied. The eleven New England and mid-Atlantic states added only about 75 percent to their 1850 network for an 1860 total of more than 10,000 miles. The twelve southern states more than tripled their rail system to about 9,500 miles of line. The most rapid expansion was in the West, especially in the Old Northwest. The ten western states increased their rail system more than eightfold and had a network of more than 11,000 miles in 1860. As the nation faced war in 1860, the expanded iron network fairly well covered and served all the states east of the Mississippi River.

CHAPTER TWO

Yankee Railroads

TWICE DURING the spring and summer of 1851 President Millard Fillmore left Washington to help northeastern states celebrate the completion and opening of major new railroad routes. In May, Fillmore, along with Daniel Webster, his secretary of state, three other cabinet members, assorted senators, governors, mayors, railway officials, and a reported half-dozen presidential candidates, joined in a festive excurison opening the Erie Railroad between Piermont, New York, and Dunkirk on Lake Erie. Four months later the president journeyed to Boston to help that city in its three-day Great Railroad Jubilee, celebrating the completion of through rail service between Boston and Montreal.

The railroads of New England and New York, and their promoters, had much to celebrate at midcentury. But the Yankee railroads also had their problems. The Erie Railroad was to be noted far more for its uneven financial management than for its dividend record. The rail mileage in the Empire State would nearly double during the 1850s, but the rate of increase was to be well below that of any southern or western state. In New England there was a rather general belief by the early fifties that the region was almost overbuilt with railroads. In the early years of the decade Massachusetts' rail lines served every town of 5,000 population or more except for the offshore town of Nantucket. In the same period, well before the Panic of 1857, the securities of several New England railways were dropping in value.

However, the interest in railroads was strong enough to

overcome such faults and shortcomings. From 1850 to 1860 the rail network in the eleven New England and mid-Atlantic states increased by more than 4,000 miles. The details of this growth are shown in Table 2.1.[1]

TABLE 2.1
RAILROAD CONSTRUCTION IN THE NEW ENGLAND AND
MID-ATLANTIC STATES DURING THE 1850

State	Mileage in 1850	Mileage in 1860	Increase in Decade	Percentage of Increase	Investment per Mile in 1860
Maine	245	472	227	93%	$35,118
New Hampshire	467	661	194	42	35,470
Vermont	290	554	264	91	41,971
Massachusetts	1,035	1,264	229	22	46,291
Rhode Island	68	108	40	59	40,355
Connecticut	402	601	199	49	36,458
Total New England states	2,507	3,660	1,153	46%	$40,710
New York	1,361	2,682	1,321	97	48,619
New Jersey	206	560	354	172	52,767
Pennsylvania	1,240	2,598	1,358	109	56,440
Delaware	39	127	88	220	31,993
Maryland	259	386	127	49	56,282
Total Mid-Atlantic states	3,105	6,353	3,248	105%	$52,131
Total for 11 states	5,612	10,013	4,401	78%	$47,823

As the figures reveal, New England already had an abundance of railroad service by midcentury; thus its rate of increase in the decade was less than other regions. Not even Maine or Vermont, both relative latecomers in the railroad field, managed to double their mileage in the decade, and the average increase for the six-state region was well under 50 percent. The 22 percent increase in Massachusetts was far lower than for any other state in the nation. By 1860 her 1,264 miles of line amounted to about three-fifths of her top mileage figure, which would be reached in 1900. By 1855 Massachusetts could claim a mile of railway for each 6.5

square miles of area. In the same year other states well
endowed with rail mileage included Ohio, with a mile of
track for every 17 square miles; Pennsylvania, with one for
29 square miles; and Georgia, with one for 58 square miles.

To the south and west the five mid-Atlantic states, as a
region, more than doubled their mileage in the decade, and
built nearly three times the railroad that was constructed in
New England. The eleven-state area in general lagged far
behind the southern and western states in railroad building
during the 1850s. In cost per mile and quality of construction, Yankee roads were well out in front: as of 1860, the
cost per mile of road ranged from a low of $32,000 in Dela-
ware to a high of $56,000 for Pennsylvania. The regional
average, of nearly $48,000 a mile, was nearly twice the cost
of construction in southern states, and almost a third higher
than the investment per mile of line in the western states.
The heavier traffic anticipated, the denser population to be
served, and the resulting greater equipment required all
tended to explain this higher investment per mile of line in
the Yankee railroads.

Even though the northeastern lines had been expensive
to construct, many of them had made money for their
owners. A study of twenty-five roads with a total of about
2,000 miles of line in the New England and the mid-Atlantic
states reveals that just over half of the lines were paying dividends during the 1840s. The portion paying dividends
increased during the decade and by the late 1840s two-thirds
of the lines were rewarding their owners. Five roads paid not
a single dividend during the decade, while seven railroads
managed a dividend each year of the ten. Four of the
seven—the Boston & Lowell, the Boston & Providence, the
Boston & Worcester, and the Hartford & New Haven—were
New England roads, while the other three—the Utica &
Schenectady, the Camden & Amboy, and the New Jersey—
were mid-Atlantic lines. The dividend rate paid during the
decade averaged just under 7 percent.[2]

The payment of at least some dividends continued in the
1850s. In 1855 half of New Jersey railroads were paying divi-

Engine crew of the 1850s. Having one's picture taken at mid-century was a serious business for engineer Shay and fireman Foster. (COURTESY, SMITHSONIAN INSTITUTION.)

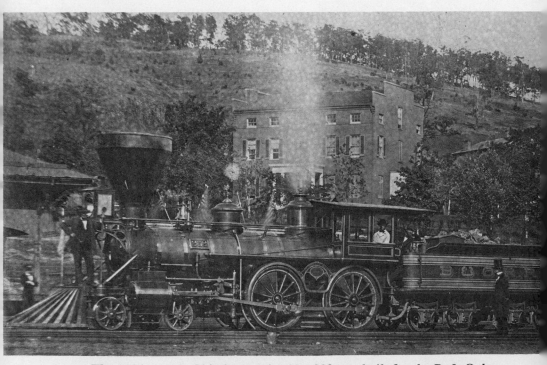

The Baltimore & Ohio locomotive No. 232 was built for the B. & O. by William Mason in 1857, and was one of several engines of similar style and type he made for the line. The large stack, although not conducive to streamlining, was a requirement for the wood-burners of the day. (COURTESY, SMITHSONIAN INSTITUTION.)

dends, ranging from 2.5 to 12 percent. Nineteen of the 46
New York railroads paid dividends for 1859, ranging from
4.5 to 12 percent. In Massachusetts twenty-three out of
nearly fifty lines paid dividends for 1858, with the rate ranging between 2.5 and 8 percent. However, there is little doubt
that on many lines the rate of dividend payment during the
1850s was excessive, well above what a later, more prudent
fiscal management would approve and justify. In those early
years many railroad managers were chiefly concerned with
completing the line and paying some return to the owners
and promoters of the project. They often forgot, or at least
badly underestimated, the ubiquitous costs of repairs, maintenance, depreciation, and obsolescence. The passage of time
forced many a railroad president and treasurer to reassess
earlier rosy predictions of the large profits that could result
from railroad operations.[3]

Northeastern railroads had been relatively expensive to
build, but they tended to be modest in length, particularly in
New England where the states were small and the towns
quite closely spaced. In 1860 more than half of the roads in
Massachusetts were no more than 20 miles long. The average
length of all Massachusetts lines was only 27 miles and the
average for all the New England states was no more than 37
miles. Only 10 percent of New England roads were 80 miles
long, and the longest was less than 150 miles long (see Table
2.2).[4] Railroad lines were longer in New York and Pennsylvania; the average length of the roads in the five mid-Atlantic states was 46 miles. For the eleven-state region, the
average length of the 235 lines in 1860 was 43 miles. In
southern states, on the other hand, the average road was
about 85 miles in length, and in the west it was almost 100
miles.

These ten major (those of more than 80 miles in length)
lines in New England together made up less than 1,100 miles
of road, less than a third of the total mileage for the six
states. Seven of these ten railroads were destined in later
years to become important portions of three large New
England systems—the Boston and Albany, the New Haven,

TABLE 2.2
MAJOR RAILROADS OF NEW ENGLAND IN 1860

Railroad	State	Length in 1850 (miles)	Length in 1860 80–99 miles	over 100 miles	Later Name
Atlantic & St. Lawrence	Maine	48		149	Grand Trunk
Boston, Concord & Montreal	N.H.	51	93		Boston & Maine
Northern	N.H.	82	82		Boston & Maine
Connecticut & Pas- sumpsic Rivers	Vt.	40	90		Boston & Maine
Rutland & Burlington	Vt.	119		119	Rutland
Vermont Central	Vt.	120		120	Central Vermont
Boston & Maine	Mass.	83	83		Boston & Maine
Old Colony & Fall River	Mass.	87	87		New Haven
Western	Mass.	117		117	Boston & Albany
Hartford, Providence & Fishkill	Conn.	50		122	New Haven

and the Boston and Maine. Two of the ten, both in Vermont, would continue for some time as relatively short independent railroads, while the Atlantic & St. Lawrence would eventually be controlled by the Grand Trunk Railway of Canada.

The Western Railroad, one of the earlier roads chartered in Massachusetts, by 1850 controlled enough subordinate and tributory mileage to be listed as a 150-mile railroad, several miles longer than the 117-mile main line running westward from Worcester via Springfield and Pittsfield to the New York state line. Back in the early 1830s, Nathan Hale— nephew of the Revolutionary War patriot—who was editor of the *Boston Daily Advertiser* and president of the Boston and Worcester, had urged that his railroad be pushed on west through the Berkshires to the Hudson River. In 1833 the Western Railroad was chartered, with Abbott Lawrence, manufacturer of cotton and woolen goods, Edward Everett, Unitarian clergyman and congressman, and Amasa Walker, Bos-

ton merchant, all supporting Hale. The road reached
Springfield by 1839 and headed into the rugged Berkshire
mountains. By this time George W. Whistler, husband of the
good lady portrayed as "Whistler's Mother," and later a
builder of railroads in Russia, was superintendent and chief
engineer of the road. Freight trains on the newly built mountain line often required one or two "helper" engines, more
because of the steep grades than the heavy traffic.

The Western Railroad and the Boston and Worcester
Railroad, connecting lines mutually dependent upon each
other, did have their differences. The shorter eastern line
was a private financial venture, while the longer western line,
built through the difficult terrain of the sparsely settled western counties, had required and obtained so much assistance
from Massachusetts that the state held a third of the company's stock. And the 44-mile B. & W. favored local passenger and freight service and the commuter traffic, while the
Western saw its prosperity largely coming from long-haul
through freight traffic. The B. & W. officials generally
wanted to keep fares and rates high, while the longer Western sought to reduce the rates. As a consequence relations
between the two lines at midcentury were often bitter and
acrimonious.

During the 1850s total revenue on the Western Railroad
ranged between $1.35 and $2 million a year with about 40
percent of the business coming from passengers. Roughly a
tenth of the passengers were through passengers, and perhaps a fifth of the freight tonnage was between the two terminal cities of Boston and Albany. Freight revenue came
largely from general merchandise, flour, and other farm produce such as dairy products, livestock and grain. At the end
of the decade the traffic of the Western was carried by an
equipment roster consisting of seventy-two locomotives, 59
passenger train cars and 1,183 freight cars. Throughout the
ten years the railroad paid yearly dividends, ranging from
6.5 to 8 percent.[5]

Two men dominated the affairs of the Western: William
H. Swift, president from 1851 to 1854, and Chester W. Cha-

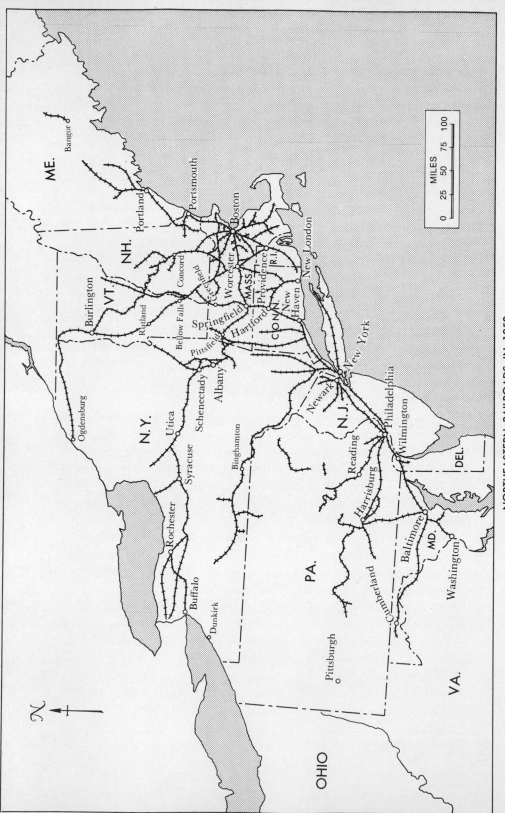

NORTHEASTERN RAILROADS IN 1850

ME.

Bangor

NH.

VT.

Portland

Portsmouth

Boston

Concord

Burlington

Rutland

Greenfield

Worcester

MASS.

Providence

R.I.

New London

Below Falls

Springfield

Hartford

New Haven

CONN.

Pittsfield

Albany

New York

Schenectady

Ogdensburg

N.Y.

Utica

Syracuse

Binghamton

Newark

N.J.

Philadelphia

Reading

Wilmington

DEL.

Rochester

Harrisburg

Baltimore

MD.

Buffalo

Dunkirk

PA.

Cumberland

Washington

Pittsburgh

VA.

OHIO

MILES

0 25 50 75 100

N

pin, who succeeded him in 1854. Swift was a 51-year-old West Pointer with considerable canal and railroad engineering experience. During his three years he was faced with increased operating expenses, a necessary cut in dividends, and a threat from a new line in the northwestern corner of the state, the Troy & Greenfield, which hoped to cut through the Berkshires with the Hoosac Tunnel. This project was being pushed by Alvah Crocker, Fitchburg paper manufacturer, politician, and promoter of railroads in the northern part of the state.

In 1854 Swift was succeeded by Chester W. Chapin, a large stockholder in the Western and one of the wealthier residents of Springfield with large investments in banking and insurance. As a young man Chapin had successively been interested in local drayage, stage lines, and steamboat service on the Connecticut River before shifting to railroads. Like Swift before him, Chapin felt a continuing threat from the Troy and Greenfield and the Hoosac Tunnel project. Alvah Crocker and Elias Hasket Derby, a railroad lawyer who had learned his law in the office of Daniel Webster, continued to push the Hoosac Tunnel as they mounted an offensive against the service provided by the Western. Luckily for the Western, the Hoosac Mountain resisted even the valiant construction efforts of Herman Haupt and the pneumatic drill he developed in 1858. Nathan Hale had retired from the presidency of the B. & W. in 1849, but his successors, Thomas Hopkinson (1849–57) and Ginery Twichell (1857–67), were equally good at making trouble. Twichell, who early in life had been a post rider and stage driver, was opposed to increased cooperation with the Western, feeling that any merger would lead to a domination by the larger road. Eventually the two lines were merged in 1867 into the Boston & Albany Railroad, with Chapin as president. At the time of its creation the new railroad company was reported to be the wealthiest corporation in the state.

Two of the longer New England roads in 1860, the Old Colony & Fall River and the Hartford, Providence & Fishkill, would eventually form important segments of a later major

New England system, the New Haven. Chartered in 1844, the Old Colony connected South Boston and Plymouth and was projected to serve the shoe towns, iron manufacturers, and cordage works along the 38-mile route. By the time the road was finished in 1845, a second road, the Fall River Railroad, was building from Fall River toward Boston and a connection with the Old Colony. Two years later, in May 1847, the two roads inaugurated the Boat Train from Boston to Fall River where connections were made with the Fall River Line of steamboats giving overnight service via Long Island Sound to New York City. This famous train was destined to remain in service for ninety years. At midcentury passenger traffic was very important for the Old Colony, normally producing about two-thirds of the total gross receipts.[6] Though the freight traffic was light, the railroad was innovative. As early as 1853 the Old Colony had three special flatcars, each of which could carry seven small boxlike containers that could be fastened securely to the car floor.

During the early 1850s the Old Colony and the Fall River had difficulties much like those experienced by the Western and the Boston and Worcester lines. President Elias Haskett Derby and his successor, F. B. Crowninshield, of the Old Colony were just as crotchety as Nathaniel B. Borden, president of the Fall River, but eventually in 1854 the two roads worked out an equitable merger and formed the Old Colony and Fall River Railroad, with a capital of $3 million. Many other short lines were added during and after the Civil War, and before it became part of the New Haven system the Old Colony was operating more than 500 miles of line in southeastern New England.

The Hartford, Providence & Fishkill, another line that would eventually be taken over by the New Haven, was projected by Rhode Island and Connecticut capitalists in the mid-1840s to provide rail service from Providence to Hartford and on to Fishkill Landing on the Hudson River. Private financing was difficult, and in the early 1850s the cities of Providence and Hartford both provided substantial aid. By 1854 the line was completed between the two cities and

The *General*, made by the Rogers Locomotive Works in 1855 for the state-owned Western & Atlantic Railroad, was built to the 5-ft. gauge, has 60-in. drivers, and weighed twenty-five tons. In April 1862, Union soldiers captured the *General* in the colorful but totally ineffective "Andrews Raid." (COURTESY, NASHVILLE, CHATTANOOGA & ST. LOUIS RAILROAD.)

The Harnden Express Company, chiefly serving the triangular area bounded by Boston, New York City, and Albany, was one of many express companies active in the 1850s. Before starting his express service, William F. Harnden had been a conductor and ticket agent on the Boston & Worcester. (COURTESY, RAILWAY EXPRESS AGENCY.)

three months later pushed on to Waterbury, Connecticut. William Sprague, a Rhode Island merchant and former congressman and U.S. senator, became president of the 122-mile road but soon was taking money out of his own pocket to keep the road afloat. Sprague died in 1856, and after the Panic of 1857 his heirs brought suit against the railroad, which resulted in the operation of the line by the trustees of the road's large bonded debt. After the Civil War the line became a portion of the New York & New England and still later of the New Haven.

A shorter line, the 62-mile New York and New Haven Railroad, chartered in 1844 and completed in 1848, might be considered the parent company of the New Haven System. From the outset passenger receipts on the New Haven road were three or four times as large as those from freight.[7] The early prosperity of the road was cut short with the terrible train wreck on May 6, 1853, when an eastbound early morning express train ran through an open drawbridge at South Norwalk, Connecticut. The death toll of forty-six, including five doctors returning from a medical convention, made it by far the worst accident in the generation-long history of American railroading. Connecticut lawmakers soon were calling it a "bloody massacre" instead of an accident, and the New Haven eventually paid out nearly half a million dollars in damages.[8]

A year later a major scandal hit the New Haven; it was discovered that Robert Schuyler, a nephew of Alexander Hamilton and president of the line from the beginning, had, by keeping three separate sets of books, illegally issued and sold company stock with a face value of $2 million. The New Haven required a major financial reorganization, but the basic earning power of the line permitted its early recovery. In the years after the Civil War dozens of short lines were to be added to form a 2,000-mile railroad system that dominated the transportation of southern New England.

Four other New England lines—the Boston & Maine; the Boston, Concord & Montreal; the Northern; and the Connecticut & Passumpsic Rivers—each under 100 miles in length in 1860, would ultimately be included in a major rail system in northern New England, the Boston & Maine. The first Boston & Maine was conceived in the mid 1830s as an 8-mile extension of the Boston & Lowell, running from Wilmington to Andover, Massachusetts. Its first president, Thomas West, an aggressive businessman from Haverhill, Massachusetts, successfully auctioned off a new issue of stock and extended the line further north. Exeter, New Hampshire, was reached in 1840 and South Berwick, Maine, in 1843. Unhappy with its use of the Boston & Lowell tracks, the B. & M. built its own line into Boston by 1845. While this 83-mile line up to southern Maine was not extended during the 1850s, the B. & M. was one of the best-constructed roads in New England. It was also a prosperous road and in 1860 had paid continuous dividends for more than twenty years. Since it faced the competition of cheap coastal water transport, a majority of its revenue came from passenger rather than freight traffic.[9]

The remaining three roads that would eventually join with the B. & M. were located several miles to the west, two in New Hampshire and the third in Vermont. The two roads in New Hampshire—the Northern, and the Boston, Concord & Montreal—were rival lines, both seeking to serve the central part of the state. Both companies were chartered in 1844 to run from Concord, the state capital and long famous for the stagecoach of the same name, northwestward to the Connecticut River. The Northern had heavy grades to contend with, but strong financial support from Boston pushed the road on north to Grafton by late summer 1847, an event that Daniel Webster helped to celebrate. The line was completed to White River Junction on the Connecticut River by 1849. The Boston, Concord & Montreal was slower to get started; only 20 miles were in operation by 1848. The road was built with frugality except for the high-grade English rails, which cost $70 a ton. Finally in 1853 the 93-mile line was finished to Wells River, 40 miles farther up the Connecticut. Both the New Hampshire roads had much more freight than passenger traffic. Only the Northern Railroad managed to declare occasional dividends during the 1850s.[10]

The Vermont road that eventually would come under

Boston & Maine control was the Connecticut & Passumpsic Rivers Railroad, which followed the west bank of the Connecticut from White River Junction northward toward Canada. The line, chartered in 1843, was like all early Vermont roads slow to be constructed. The Connecticut & Passumpsic was being pushed by Addison Gilmore, president of the Western in the late 1840s, and Erastus Fairbanks, Vermont Whig politician and temperance reformer. Late in 1850 the line reached Saint Johnsbury, where Fairbanks and his brothers were manufacturing the popular new platform scales. By 1858 the road, which connected with both the Northern and the Boston, Concord & Montreal lines, was completed to Barton in northern Vermont.

The two other major lines in Vermont, the Vermont Central and the Rutland & Burlington, had exciting and intermingled histories during the 1850s. The two roads were nearly equal in length, served the same general area between the Connecticut River and Burlington, and were both completed in the late forties. The Vermont Central had the easier grades over the Green Mountains, but the Rutland route up to Burlington was several miles shorter. The two companies were bitter rivals during the decade.

The Vermont Central, chartered on October 12, 1843, was organized two years later with hopes of being a portion of a new trunk line running from Boston via northern New York to Chicago. Charles Paine, Harvard graduate, manager of his father's woolen mills at Northfield, Vermont, and Whig governor of Vermont in 1841–42, was president of the new line. With substantial money from Boston, the road was completed late in 1849 from Windsor, Vermont, via White River Junction to Burlington. The railroad served Montpelier, the state capital, only with a 2-mile branch line, but had been routed through Northfield, the hilltop hometown of the president. Charles Paine was taking care of himself in other ways. He had the company's repair shops located in Northfield, on land he had profitably sold to his own company. During his seven-year tenure as president, Paine received a yearly salary of $5,000, far more than fellow rail executives in the state.

By the time Paine's road had reached Burlington, the 47-mile Vermont & Canada was being built north from Essex Junction (a few miles east of Burlington) via Saint Albans to Rouse's Point on upper Lake Champlain. Paine was a director on this new line, but the real power was in the hands of John Smith and his son, John Gregory Smith, two able lawyers living in Saint Albans. The two Smiths were more than a match for Paine. In 1849–50 the Vermont Central had taken a fifty-year lease on the Vermont & Canada providing an 8 percent rental based on the original cost of the Vermont & Canada. A unique clause provided that if the Vermont Central ever failed to pay the rent, the Vermont & Canada had the right to take over the parent company. The Vermont & Central failed to meet the payment due late in 1854, and the Smith line proceeded to take it over. Paine had been ousted from control the year before. Neither road was really prosperous during the 1850s. After John Smith died in 1858, John Gregory Smith took over the Vermont Central and in the next twenty years greatly extended the road.[11]

The Rutland & Burlington, like the Vermont Central, received its charter in the fall of 1843. The president of the road was Judge Timothy Follett, a Burlington businessman also interested in the steamboat carrying trade on Lake Champlain. Even though Follett and his fellow officials were less successful than Charles Paine in obtaining financial support from Boston, construction was rapid. By 1850 the 119-mile road was completed all the way from Bellow Falls on the Connecticut River to Rutland and on to Burlington. Follett's line endeavored to compete on even terms with the rival Vermont Central for the freight and passenger traffic moving in and out of Burlington. This was difficult for any traffic moving north into Canada, for Paine had cleverly located the connection between his line and the Vermont & Canada at Essex Junction, several miles east of Burlington, a place noted for its bleak station and inconvenient connecting schedules. Follett was also thwarted in his efforts to make substantial purchases of the capital stock of the Vermont & Canada line. Follett's line, like the Vermont Central, did not prosper during the 1850s. Both Follett and Paine had saddled their roads with bonded and floating debts too huge to permit the payment of any dividends.[12]

The last and longest of the ten major New England roads, the 149-mile Atlantic & St. Lawrence, connected Portland, Maine, with Montreal. This international railroad was the dream of such civic-minded Portland residents as John A. Poor, older brother of the editor of the *American Railroad Journal*. In the mid-1840s Boston and Portland were rivals for the honor of being Montreal's winter port. Early in February 1845, just as the Maine legislature was about to approve a charter for the Atlantic & St. Lawrence, a report reached Poor that Boston emissaries were about to close an agreement with the city fathers of Montreal favoring Boston over Portland. Braving a blizzard and temperatures as low as 18° below zero, Poor traveled by sleigh to reach Montreal in five days and prevent the commitment to Boston. (The decision favoring Portland may in fact have been due more to that city's half-day sailing-time advantage over Boston than to Poor's ardor and persistence.) The Canadian portion of the line, from Vermont to Montreal, was named the St. Lawrence & Atlantic.

On July 4, 1846 (Independence Day was a favorite date for the commencing of important internal improvements), the president of the A. & St. L., William P. Preble, jurist and diplomat, used a silver-plated shovel to move the first earth in the line's construction, and the governor of the state wheeled away a barrow filled with dirt. Largely upon the insistence of the St. Lawrence & Atlantic, the gauge of the international line was to be 5 feet 6 inches rather than the standard gauge common in the other New England states. With both the citizens and the city of Portland financially supporting construction costs, the road was built 50 miles to Danville by the end of 1851. The 52 miles in New Hampshire and the 18 miles in Vermont up to the Canadian border were finished by February 1853. Within a few months the Canadian portion was also completed, and the entire 292-mile line (149 in the United States, 143 in Canada) from Portland to Montreal was opened on July 18, 1853. Three

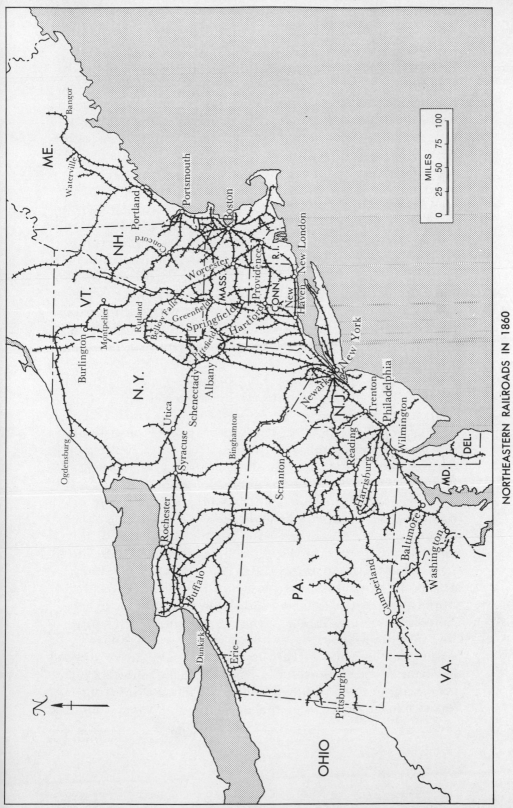

NORTHEASTERN RAILROADS IN 1860

weeks later a new Canadian corporation, the Grand Trunk Railway, leased both roads for 999 years, promising to assume all A. & St. L. debts plus paying 6 percent dividends on the stock. The A. & St. L. had cost more than $6 million to build, roughly twice the original estimate. Earnings on the road in the half-dozen years after 1853 certainly did not justify the earlier dreams of John A. Poor and his friends in Portland.[13]

These ten "major" New England railways which led some New Englanders to complain that their region was overbuilt with railroads, resulted in New England's becoming the mother of many railroad leaders during the ante- and postbellum decades. Twelve railroad men, all born in New England between 1794 and 1831, had careers far more involved with western or southern lines than with the railways of New England. More than a dozen railroads, stretching from Ohio to California and from Michigan to Louisiana, were projected, built, or operated by these Yankees in the middle and late decades of the nineteenth century.

One of the oldest was Asa Whitney (1797–1872), Connecticut merchant, who vigorously presented his dream of a railroad to the Pacific to aid the China trade for half a dozen years both to the public and the U.S. Congress. Whitney was ahead of his time, but more successful were Dr. Thomas C. Durant (1820–1885) and Grenville M. Dodge (1831–1916), both from Massachusetts. Durant, who had earlier been interested in several midwestern lines out of Chicago, was better known for his stock manipulation than his practice of medicine. He was the principal manager of the Union Pacific from 1863 to 1869. Dodge, Civil War general and surveyor of rail lines in Illinois and Iowa during the 1850s, was chief engineer of the U.P. from 1866 to 1870, and after the Golden Spike helped build several other lines in the Southwest. Still more important was Collis P. Huntington (1821–1900), a thrifty, hard-working Connecticut Yankee who ruthlessly dominated the Central Pacific and Southern Pacific lines in the last third of the century. Further north, the Northern Pacific after the Panic of 1873 was reorganized

and rejuvenated by the Vermonter Frederick Billings
(1823–1890).

Several New Englanders were important in the railroads
of the Midwest. John Murray Forbes (1813–1898), Boston
merchant, and James F. Joy (1810–1890), who moved to
Michigan to practice law, brought patient and shrewd financial management to such western roads as the Michigan Central, the Chicago, Burlington & Quincy, and the Hannibal &
St. Joseph. Amasa Stone (1818–1883), originally a carpenter
and builder of railroad bridges, built or managed a number
of railroads in Ohio and Michigan before and after the Civil
War. Several lines in Indiana were promoted and built by
Chauncey Rose (1794–1877), a New Englander who moved
west to the Hoosier state. William Osborn (1820–1894), after
several successful years in the East India trade, moved west
to become president of the Illinois Central, 1855–65, and
president of the Chicago, St. Louis & New Orleans, 1877–83.
Henry Bradley Plant (1819–1899), before the Civil War
superintendent of the Adams Express Company in the
South, after the war created the Plant System, consisting of
14 railroads in Alabama, Florida, and Georgia. Charles
Morgan (1795–1878), farm boy and grocer from Connecticut
and at midcentury a steamboat rival of Cornelius Vanderbilt
in the Caribbean, was after the Civil War deeply involved
with railroads in Louisiana and Texas. These dozen Yankees
are but representative of many other New Englanders whose
railroad careers were centered in areas far from their native
states.[14]

The railways in the mid-Atlantic states were much longer
than those of New England. The major lines (those of more
than 80 miles in length) in the five mid-Atlantic states are
listed in Table 2.3.[15]

These twenty major railroads, with an aggregate of
about 3,500 miles in 1860, constituted well over half of the
total mileage in the five-state region. As a group the major
roads in the mid-Atlantic states were quite different than the
New England lines. Aside from being longer, they were more

TABLE 2.3
MAJOR RAILROADS OF THE MID-ATLANTIC STATES IN
1860

Railroad	State	Length in 1850 (miles)	Length in 1860			Later Name
			80–99 miles	100–199 miles	over 200 miles	
Buffalo, New York & Erie	N.Y.	—		142		Erie
Hudson River	N.Y.	74		143		N.Y. Central
Long Island	N.Y.	86	86			Penn.
New York Central	N.Y.	447			555	N.Y. Central
New York & Erie	N.Y.	337			465	Erie
New York & Harlem	N.Y.	80		132		N.Y. Central
Niagara Bridge & Canandaigua	N.Y.	—		100		N.Y. Central
Ogdensburg (Northern)	N.Y.	58		119		Rutland
Syracuse, Binghamton & N.Y.	N.Y.	—	80			Lackawanna
Watertown & Rome	N.Y.	24	96			N.Y. Central
Camden & Amboy	N.J.	92	92			Penn.
Delaware, Lackawanna & Western	Pa.	—		113		Lackawanna
Lackawanna & Bloomsburg	Pa.	—	80			Lackawanna
Pennsylvania	Pa.	218			359	Penn.
Philadelphia & Erie	Pa.	—		148		Penn.
Philadelphia & Reading	Pa.	95		154		Reading
Philadelphia, Wilmington & Baltimore	Pa.	98	98			Penn.
Delaware	Del.	—	84			Penn.
Baltimore & Ohio	Md.	178			386	B. & O.
Northern Central	Md.	67		142		Penn.

recently constructed. Only four New England roads had built any additional mileage during the 1850s, whereas in the mid-Atlantic states 17 of the 20 railroads had built additional trackage during the decade. Seven of the mid-Atlantic lines had not even been started in 1850.

Nearly all of the 20 separate lines in existence in the 1850s were destined to merge with one of the major east–west trunk lines. By the end of the century seven of the lines were with the Pennsylvania system, five were with the New York Central, three with the Lackawanna, and two with the Erie. The remaining three independent lines were the Baltimore & Ohio, the Reading, and the Rutland.

In 1850 rail service from Albany and Troy west to Buffalo and Niagara Falls was provided by ten little railroads strung along the Mohawk Valley and the Erie Canal. Known as the Central Line well before the 1853 creation of the New York Central, the several connecting roads back in the early 1840s had agreed to follow a unified policy relative to fares, schedules, and the handling of immigrant travel. The representatives of the several lines also had a common concern—the competition with both the New York & Erie Railroad and the Erie Canal. Many of the roads' charters included more or less restrictive clauses concerning their freedom to carry freight, since the legislators in Albany had been zealous in protecting the rights of the state-owned Erie Canal.

A prime mover in the creation and direction of the Central Line was the iron merchant, banker, land speculator, and Democratic political leader in Albany, Erastus Corning. Crippled as an infant, Corning was soon befriended by an uncle in the hardware business, and by the age of 19 had saved $500 from his wages and varied mercantile pursuits. As a young iron merchant in Albany, Corning was an early investor in the Mohawk & Hudson, but soon gave greater attention to the connecting 78-mile Utica & Schenectady. As the first and only president of that line, Corning for twenty years (1833–53) received no salary, being content with an arrangement whereby his own firm supplied most of the rails, hardware, and assorted iron products needed by the Utica & Schenectady. The road paid handsome dividends from 1837 until the formation of the New York Central in 1853, but Corning made far more because of his position as a favored supplier of railroad iron.[16]

At midcentury, because of the state limitations on their hauling of freight, the Central Line railroads obtained most of their revenue from passenger traffic. The ten short connecting lines, arranged from city to city like so many beads on a string, advertised a fourteen-hour express passenger service between Albany and Buffalo, but frequently imperfect connections might add several hours to the 290-mile trip. Freight traffic on all of the connecting lines greatly expanded when the restrictions favoring the Erie Canal were removed by legislation in the summer of 1851.[17] The euphoria brought on by the new freight business quickly declined as the several railroad presidents became aware of a growing rail competition to the south. The Erie opened its line to Dunkirk in May 1851, the Pennsylvania was pushed through to Pittsburgh late in 1852, and shortly thereafter the tracks of the B. & O. were completed to the Ohio at Wheeling. The several roads included in the Central Line were ready for a formal consolidation.

In the move toward a formal merger of the several connecting railroads, Erastus Corning of the Utica & Schenectady played the dominant role. The railroads applied in 1851 to the state legislature for a law permitting the merger, and Corning asked for help from his old friend Thurlow Weed, newspaper editor and a leader of the Whigs then in power in Albany. The New York Central Consolidation Bill was enacted early in April 1853, and in the next two months the eight operating lines plus two projected (but unbuilt) roads completed the formal proceedings of merger. At the stockholders' meeting on July 6, 1853, Corning held enough proxies to have himself elected president. Dean Richmond, like Corning a native of New England and a businessman interested in two Buffalo railroads, was selected vice-president. Stockholders exchanged their original stock for shares in the New York Central, with the stronger companies receiving a premium payable in thirty-year, 6 percent bonds of the new railroad. Corning received a fair share of these new bonds, and he also profited from his holdings in one of the two projected but unbuilt lines, the Mohawk Valley.

The New York Central in 1853, with a total capital of about $23 million was reported to be one of the largest corporations in America. For a short time Corning managed to have the same cozy procurement arrangement that had been so profitable on the Utica line. These extra profits were slowed somewhat after a mildly critical report by a stockholders' committee was released in the mid-1850s. The 555-mile road prospered with each year, showing marked increases in freight traffic. By 1857 the yearly revenues were more than $8 million, twice the total of the separate roads back in 1852. In 1856 the equipment roster of Corning's line included 209 locomotives, 321 assorted passenger cars, and 2,621 freight cars. Up and down the line were 76 passenger depots, 72 freight houses, 25 engine houses with stalls for 196 engines, and 9 blacksmith shops. Dividends were paid at a normal rate of 8 percent per year until 1860, when they were reduced to 6 percent.[18] It is not surprising that so profitable a property as the New York Central soon caught the acquisitive eye of Cornelius Vanderbilt.

At Albany the New York Central connected with two roads, the New York & Harlem Railroad and the Hudson River Railroad, both of which ran down the east side of the Hudson River to New York City. The New York & Harlem was chartered in 1831 and for several years was little more than a short line serving the city of New York. In the 1840s it started to build northward well east of the Hudson, and by early 1852 had reached Chatham, southeast of Albany, where it used the tracks of the Western Railroad to enter the state capital. In the early 1850s the Harlem line was under the leadership of Robert Schuyler who a few years later would be involved in scandal as head of the New Haven. The Hudson River Railroad was chartered in 1846 to provide rail service down to New York City for such east bank river towns as Peekskill, Poughkeepsie, and Hudson. These towns during most of the year were well served by the river steamers owned by such men as Cornelius Vanderbilt and Daniel Drew, but often the townfolk desired more dependable transport than river craft could provide in the frozen and icy winter months. The famed railroad engineer John B. Jervis directed the early construction of the new rail line. Over 70 miles were completed by 1850, and the entire 143-mile road was finished into Albany by October 1851.[19]

The Harlem and the Hudson River lines were very competitive during the decade. Their inclination to reduce fares and rates, plus the continuing competition from riverboats, kept them from paying dividends. At this time Erastus Corning of the New York Central preferred to route his freight between Albany and New York by riverboat rather than rail, except when winter weather stopped all river traffic. Thus he had little interest in controlling the two roads, although either could have been obtained without too large an investment. Commodore Vanderbilt was more discerning. He made his first investment in the Harlem in the spring of 1857, and by 1862 was president of the line. He also controlled the Hudson River Railroad by 1865. With both rail lines south of Albany in his grip, Vanderbilt was able to move against the New York Central. In January 1867, when the Hudson was thick with ice, the Commodore refused to accept any further New York Central freight destined for New York City. Henry Keep, then the New York Central president, did not have Corning's iron will and quickly capitulated. Before the end of the year Vanderbilt was in full control of the New York Central.[20] Two years later Vanderbilt merged the New York Central and the Hudson River into the New York Central and Hudson River Railroad. The New York & Harlem was acquired through a long-term lease on April 1, 1872.[21]

Two shorter lines in New York also were added to the New York Central. The Watertown & Rome was chartered in 1832, but construction was delayed until 1849. The 72 miles north from Rome to Watertown were completed by 1851, and a year later the line was extended on to Cape Vincent on the Saint Lawrence River. The 96-mile road had been built economically, was fairly prosperous, and paid frequent dividends during the 1850s. After the Civil War it expanded its operation with indifferent success, and as the Rome, Watertown & Ogdensburg was leased in 1891 to the New York Central & Hudson River system. The other road was the Niagara Bridge & Canandaigua, chartered in 1851 and opened in April 1854, a year before the completion of John A. Roebling's 825-foot suspension bridge across the Niagara River. This 100-mile railroad unsuccessfully competed for traffic with the western third of Corning's New York Central. The Niagara Bridge & Canandaigua was leased to the New

York Central in 1858 at 6 percent on $1 million capital stock.

The New York & Erie Railroad, generally known as the Erie, was the other major line crossing New York State to Lake Erie. The Erie was chartered on April 24, 1832 as a projected line from the Hudson River through the Southern Tier of counties in New York State to Lake Erie. Early sponsors of the line were William C. Redfield, a Connecticut-born saddle maker who was interested both in railroads and meteorology, and Eleazar Lord, also from Connecticut, who was shifting from the church and missionary work to fire insurance and railroads. Lord was president of the road three different times, 1833–35, 1839–41, and 1844–45. President Lord had some unique ideas as to how to build a first-class railroad. He wanted to build the road on piling to make the line impervious to flood, frost, and deep snow, and he insisted on a broad 6-ft. gauge to keep connecting railroads from stealing any trade from New York City. The pile-driving scheme was soon abandoned, but Erie stuck to its offbeat broad gauge until 1878. Hard times slowed construction, and the Erie had only 53 miles in operation when Lord was succeeded in 1845 by Benjamin Loder, a hard-headed and wealthy dry-goods merchant from New York City.

During the next half-dozen years Loder pushed his contractors, and their thousands of rowdy immigrant workers, to build more and more line. More than 200 miles were laid by 1849, and another 200 miles were added by 1851. When the 460-mile road from Piermont-on-Hudson to Dunkirk on Lake Erie was completed in the spring of 1851, it was reported to be the longest railway in the world. Its cost of more than $23 million was admittedly several times the original estimates, but the pride of New Yorkers in the road was such that the New York City aldermen saluted the completed road as "the Work of the Age."

President Loder insisted upon a celebration as grand as the completed Erie. On May 14 and 15, 1851, two special excursion trains made the trip from Piermont to Dunkirk crowded with nearly three hundred assorted governmental, civic, and railroad dignitaries. Included among the top brass were President Millard Fillmore, several members of his cabinet, and such presidential hopefuls as former Governor William H. Seward, Senator Stephen A. Douglas, and Secretary of State Daniel Webster. The aging Webster insisted on a seat where he would miss none of the scenery. Obliging Erie officials placed him in a rocking chair securely fastened on a flatcar at the end of the second train. Protected by a steamer rug, Daniel had a bottle of good Medford rum for company between frequent stops for speechmaking. The excursion party stopped to view the Starrucca Viaduct with its many graceful stone arches, was greeted by sixteen whistling locomotives at Susquehanna, and eventually made an overnight stop at Elmira where a seven-hour banquet, with toasts included, left the assemblage exhausted and a bit groggy. Still another feast and barbecue awaited the guests when they reached Dunkirk at four the next afternoon.

Loder continued as Erie president until 1853, and for a while his road seemed to be making money. Both passenger and freight traffic increased, and for several years in the line even paid some dividends.[22] Loder was blessed in the early 1850s with an excellent general superintendent, the portly and efficient Charles Minot, recently lured away from the Boston & Maine. Minot was a gruff and simple man, popular with his men, and so democratic in spirit that he refused to use the private business car provided for him. Minot's successor, Daniel C. McCallum, was not so well-liked: he was responsible for a long and ugly strike by locomotive engineers that was costly to the Erie both in revenue and reputation.

More trouble came to the Erie in the late 1850s. The three presidents between 1853 and 1861 did not begin to measure up to Ben Loder. The tough competition from the newly unified New York Central was hard to withstand. And finally the Erie had been poorly financed and was suffering under a total funded and floating debt that stood at nearly $26 million in 1855.[23] Both Cornelius Vanderbilt and Daniel Drew loaned money to the Erie in the mid-1850s. Drew, who looked like a rustic deacon and was remembered both for his "lost weekends" and his gifts to a school of religion, was soon on the board of directors and then treasurer of the company. The road was in bankruptcy by 1859, but the really tough years for the Erie came in the sixties, when Drew, as president, was aided in the management of the road by a pair of Yankee rascals: Jay Gould, a quiet introvert from Connecticut, and the brassy Jim Fisk from Vermont.

Several lines connecting with the Erie in southern New York were also built in the 6-ft. gauge. In 1860 the longest of these was the 142-mile Buffalo, New York & Erie, which connected with the Erie at Corning, running northwestward to Buffalo. The road was organized in 1857 and leased six years later to the Erie at an annual rental of $238,100.[24]

The Pennsylvania Railroad was the third of the northeastern trunk lines completed in the 1850s. During the 1840s the population growth of Philadelphia had been lagging behind her rivals to the north and south, New York City and Baltimore. As the Mexican War started, freight was still crossing Pennsylvania on a combination of short railways, inclined planes, and canals, all of which were slow and expensive. The whole system was so bad that Pittsburgh merchants sometimes sent their goods to New York City by Ohio and Mississippi riverboats down to New Orleans. The public was demanding an all-rail route over the Alleghenies, especially after the B. & O., serving the rival city of Baltimore, sought to build a branch line up to Pittsburgh. In April 1846, several Philadelphia businessmen incorporated the Pennsylvania Railroad to build a 248-mile road from Harrisburg to Pittsburgh. Samuel V. Merrick, a Yankee from Maine and a manufacturer of fire engines and heavy marine machinery, was elected president of the new line in the spring of 1847.

Merrick at once selected J. Edgar Thomson, who had extensive experience on the Camden & Amboy and on the Georgia Railroad, as chief engineer to supervise the construction of the Harrisburg-Pittsburgh line. Thomson, a quiet man who could be rude and abrupt on occasion, was a good railroader. Even though experts had said a rail passage over the Alleghenies was impossible, he soon had surveyed a route over the mountains. Sixty-one miles of line west of Harrisburg were opened in September 1849, and a year later the road was finished on to a connection with the Allegheny Portage Railroad, which used inclined planes to get over the mountains. The line from Pittsburgh east to the mountains was also soon completed, and on December 10, 1852 service between Philadelphia and Pittsburgh was possible over a railroad and inclined-plane route. East of Harrisburg trains ran over the tracks of the Harrisburg, Portsmouth, Mt. Joy & Lancaster Railroad, and the Philadelphia & Columbia Railroad. The Pennsylvania leased the first of these lines in 1849 and later purchased the Philadelphia & Columbia. During 1852 to 1854 Thomson built practical grades, tunnels, and the famous Horseshoe Curve through and over the mountains, and by 1855 the entire 355-mile trip from Philadelphia to Pittsburgh was being made with locomotive-drawn trains. The inclined planes over the Alleghenies were then retired from use.[25]

By 1849 Thomson was made general superintendent, and in 1852 was elected president, a position he held until 1874. One of Thomson's assistants in his first years on the road was Herman Haupt, the engineer who later would tackle the Hoosac Tunnel in Massachusetts. It was Haupt who hired Thomas A. Scott in 1850 as station agent at Hollidaysburg. Scott stayed with the Pennsylvania, rose rapidly, and became president after Thomson's death in 1874.

Even though the completed and fully equipped road had cost more than $18 million as of 1855, the Pennsylvania was fairly prosperous. Between 1848 and 1855 it paid interest on all paid-in stock subscriptions at the rate of 6 percent a year. Between 1856 and 1860 it paid annual cash dividends averaging 6 percent a year. In 1857 Thomson purchased for $7.5 million the state's Main Line of Public Works, including canals, the Portage Railroads, and the Philadelphia & Columbia Railroad. Even before this purchase Thomson was actively pushing a program of financial aid for lines in Ohio and Indiana which would provide connections toward Chicago and the Mississippi River. By the late 1850s the Pennsylvania had annual gross earnings averaging more than $5 million a year, with most of the revenue coming from freight rather than passenger traffic. In 1857 the equipment roster of the line consisted of 133 locomotives, 67 passenger cars, and 2,016 freight cars.[26]

Six major lines in the mid-Atlantic states were destined after 1860 to come under the control of the Pennsylvania. Two of the six, the Long Island Railroad and the Camden & Amboy, were east of Philadelphia, both of them serving New York City. The Long Island, incorporated in 1834 and projected as a line from Brooklyn to Greenport on Long Island Sound, was intended to give faster service between Boston and New York City than would be possible via the difficult terrain of Connecticut. Because of the economy of freight movement on the Sound, the passenger traffic on this road was always greater than the freight business. The line prospered until a rival road along the Connecticut shoreline was opened in the late 1840s. By 1900 the Pennsylvania had acquired control of the Long Island through a purchase of a majority of the capital stock. Travel to New York City from the South was early furnished by the Camden & Amboy Railroad, which was chartered in 1830, and put in operation a few years later under the leadership of Robert L. Stevens. The Camden & Amboy was a prosperous road and paid good dividends during the 1850s.[27] Control by the Pennsylvania was formalized by a long-term lease completed by 1871.

Two other lines, both in Pennsylvania, were to be controlled by the Pennsylvania Railroad by the 1860s. The Philadelphia & Erie, originally known as the Sunbury & Erie, was chartered in 1837, but construction commenced only in 1852. The line was to run from Sunbury on the Susquehanna River where it connected with the Northern Central, northwestward to Erie on Lake Erie. By 1860, when just over half of the projected 287-mile road had been completed, the promoters ran out of money. In 1862 the Pennsylvania advanced the necessary money to complete the road and leased it for 999 years. The second road was the Philadelphia, Wilmington & Baltimore, a 98-mile line formed in 1838 out of four short connecting railroads running from Philadelphia southwestward to Baltimore. Once the Pennsylvania was operating its trains through to Philadelphia, it was important to have favorable connections to the south. The Philadelphia, Wilmington & Baltimore was also an attractive property because of its low debt, its favorable operating ratio, and its good dividend record.[28] When the Baltimore & Ohio nearly obtained control over the P. W. & B., the Pennsylvania quickly started to purchase the stock of this vital connecting road to the south. By the summer of 1881 a majority of the stock had been acquired by the Pennsylvania.

The last two lines destined for control by the Pennsylvania were the Northern Central Railroad, running north from Baltimore, and the Delaware Railroad, which ran the length of the state of Delaware. The Northern Central was an 1854 consolidation of several connecting roads built or projected northward from Baltimore to Sunbury, Pennsylvania, where it connected with the Philadelphia & Erie. Near Harrisburg the Northern Central also intersected the main line of the Pennsylvania. During the 1850s Simon Cameron, the wealthy political boss in Pennsylvania, and Zenus Barnum, Baltimore hotel proprietor and telegraph company executive, were both financially interested in the Northern Central. The line to Sunbury was finished by 1858 and shortly thereafter the Baltimore & Ohio acquired control. Following the election of Abraham Lincoln in November 1860, John W. Garrett, the B. & O. president, and others threw their Northern Central stock on the market. Thomson of the Pennsylvania purchased the stock, and soon his road had a working control of the Northern Central. The other line, the Delaware Railroad, chartered in 1836, was not built until the 1850s. The 84-mile line, running from near New Castle to the southern state line, was finished in 1860. In 1855, even before completion, the road was leased to the Philadelphia, Wilmington & Baltimore. As noted above the P., W. & B. was to come under the control of the Pennsylvania during 1881.

The oldest of the four trans-Allegheny roads was the Baltimore & Ohio, whose ground-breaking had occurred on July 4, 1828, with the venerable 90-year-old Charles Carroll, sole surviving signer of the Declaration of Independence, doing the honors. Progress on the projected line to Wheeling had not been rapid, and twenty years later Abe Lincoln had only been able to ride the B. & O. as far as Cumberland, Maryland. President Louis McLane, former U.S. Senator, minister to England, and cabinet member under Andrew Jackson, had found the mountains too steep, the opposition from Maryland and Pennsylvania too great, and construction financing too difficult. McLane's successor, the energetic Thomas Swann, was more successful during his five years (1848–53) in the presidency.

With a force of 5,000 men and 1,250 horses, and a monthly payroll that sometimes exceeded $200,000, Swann pushed the iron track of the B. & O. through and over the mountains toward Wheeling on the Ohio River. Eleven tunnels and numerous bridges, fills, and cuts smoothed the iron road over the final hills, and on Christmas Eve, 1852, the last spike was driven at Roseby's Rock, some eighteen miles southeast of Wheeling. The 200-mile extension from Cumberland to the Ohio River had cost more than $6.6 million.[29]

Traffic and revenue naturally increased with the completion of the route over the mountains to the Ohio. In the late 1840s revenues had averaged only $1.2 million a year. By 1854 and 1855 total revenue had climbed to more than $3.6 million a year. On the Main Stem (Baltimore to Wheeling) freight revenue was five times the passenger revenue in the mid-1850s. But on the 40-mile branch line from Baltimore to Washington the reverse was true: passenger revenue was three times as large as freight.[30] Early in 1853 President Swann reported that a number of new coal mines were being opened in the Cumberland area, and that receipts from the coal traffic had reached $35,000 a month. Coal cars made up a major share of the freight equipment of the B. & O. Late in the decade the equipment roster listed 3,548 freight cars (including 1,290 coal cars), 126 passenger cars, and 235 locomotives.[31] During the fifties service west of Wheeling greatly increased as numerous roads were completed in Ohio. By 1857 eleven-hour service over the Cincinnati to Wheeling route (246 miles) was available, while the 379-mile trip from Wheeling to Baltimore took an additional seventeen hours.

Even before the B. & O. had reached Wheeling, the top officials of the company, with the full support of the merchants of Baltimore, were planning a second rail head on the Ohio River—at Parkersburg, a full ninety miles downstream from Wheeling. On February 14, 1851, Baltimore & Ohio interests incorporated the Northwestern Virginia Railroad to build a 104-mile road from Grafton, Virginia (halfway between Cumberland and Wheeling), west to Parkersburg. Such a line would provide a far more direct route to Cincinnati and Saint Louis. The road was pushed over and through the western Virginia mountains with the help of many bridges and trestles and twenty-three tunnels. Built at a cost of $5.4 million, the line was opened on May 1, 1857. Thus on the eve of the Civil War the B. & O. in reality was a much longer road than officially shown by the 1860 Census figures. In 1860 the Baltimore & Ohio was operating a 513-mile system, including the main line to Wheeling, the branch south to Washington, and the recently completed road to Parkersburg.

As of 1860 the B. & O. had issued more than $13 million of common and preferred stock and had a funded debt of $10,781,000. Both the city of Baltimore and the state of Maryland each held a bit more than a quarter of the stock, while individuals held stock worth nearly $5.5 million. Between 1848 and 1852 annual dividends of from 3.25 to 7 percent were paid in stock. Between 1853 and 1859 regular cash dividends of 3 percent were paid during four of the seven years.[32] John W. Garrett, Baltimore financier, was elected president of the B. & O. in 1858, at an annual salary of $4,000. He was an impressive man, both in stature and qualities of leadership. The B. & O. would need such leadership in the difficult war years that lay ahead.

Not all the railroads in the mid-Atlantic states crossed the Alleghenies as did the Baltimore & Ohio, the Pennsylvania, the Erie, and the New York Central. Several of the lines of more modest length had the important function of transporting coal to the major urban centers in Pennsylvania and New York State. Among them were the Philadelphia & Reading, and the Delaware, Lackawanna & Western.

The Delaware, Lackawanna & Western was an 1853 consolidation of two railroads, the Lackawanna & Western and the Delaware & Cobb's Gap. By 1856 the D. L. & W. consisted of an 113-mile main line running from Delaware, on the New Jersey line, via Scranton to Great Bend, on the New York line some fourteen miles southeast of Binghamton. The same interests that owned the railroad also had extensive holdings of anthracite coal along the line of the road and naturally used the D. L. & W. to get the coal to market. During the late 1850s the railroad revenue from the coal traffic was typically three to four times that of all other freight, and ten times the passenger revenue.[33] Much of the coal went on south to Philadelphia; some traveled east across the Hudson to New York City. In 1857 control was obtained over the Syracuse, Binghamton and New York Railway, an 80-mile line running north from Binghamton to Syracuse, New York, through the purchase of a major part of its common stock. Connecting service between Binghamton and Great Bend was provided by the Erie Railroad. After the Civil War, in 1873, the D. L. & W. was consolidated with the Lackawanna and Bloomsburg, an 80-mile line running westward from Scranton to North Cumberland on the Susquehanna River.[34]

The Philadelphia & Reading was another early important carrier of anthracite. Chartered in 1833, it had completed its main line from Philadelphia northwestward to Reading and on to Pottsville by 1842. Year after year three-quarters or more of its total revenues came from the haulage of coal. Most of the coal was moved to Philadelphia, either for local use or water shipment on to more distant markets. In the late 1840s and early 1850s the railroad paid several

good dividends, either in stock or in cash.[35] In 1858 the
Lebanon Valley Railroad, a 54-mile line from Reading westward to Harrisburg, was merged into the main line. Much
additional mileage in eastern Pennsylvania was to be added
to the Reading in the years after the Civil War.

The last of the longer lines in the mid-Atlantic region
was the Ogdensburg Railroad in New York State. Chartered
in 1845 as the Northern Railroad, the entire 119-mile road
from Ogdensburg to Rouse's Point was in operation by 1851.
At Ogdensburg it connected by a ferry over the Saint
Lawrence with a Canadian line giving service to Ottawa, and
at Rouse's Point it connected with the Vermont Central. The
line, never too prosperous, was reorganized in 1857 as the
Ogdensburg Railroad. In the mid 1880s it came under the
control of the Central Vermont Railroad, and still later it
became a portion of the Rutland Railroad.[36]

The Yankee railroads of the mid-Atlantic states and New
England in the decade before the Civil War included some of
the longest railroads in the world. While the South and the
West were both to lay down more new iron during the fifties,
the Northeast railroads were of better construction, had cost
more per mile to construct, and possessed much larger rosters of motive power, passenger cars, and freight equipment.
Furthermore, the four major trunk lines completed westward
from eastern seaports to Lake Erie or the Ohio River in the
early 1850s would trigger and accelerate further construction
into Ohio and other states further west. A major portion of
both the western and southern construction completed during the 1850s was dependent upon the states of the Northeast in still another way: men and money from New England,
New York, Pennsylvania, and Maryland were of prime
importance in many of the new lines projected and built west
of Pittsburgh and south of the Potomac. Both management
and financial backing available only in Boston, New York
City, Philadelphia, or Baltimore were to make possible much
of the new construction in the South and the West.

CHAPTER THREE

The Railroads of Dixie

ATLANTA WAS a railroad town. It had originally
been named Terminus as the designated southern terminal
of the Western & Atlantic, the state-owned line projected in
the late 1830s and built in the 1840s. In 1843 it was renamed
Marthasville, in honor of a daughter of Wilson Lumpkin,
former governor and U.S. senator and an early advocate of
internal improvements. In 1845 it became Atlanta; it was
probably named by J. Edgar Thomson, chief engineer of the
Georgia Railroad, which reached the small settlement in September of that year. As the 137-mile Western & Atlantic was
being completed in 1850, Atlanta was already the junction
point for three lines: the W. & A. to Chattanooga, the
Georgia Railroad to Augusta, and the Macon & Western,
which provided connecting rail service into Savannah.
Atlanta grew with the railroads, from a handful of houses in
the mid-1840s to perhaps a hundred or two by 1848 and
finally to a city of 10,000 by 1860. On the eve of the Civil
War three of the five major "trunk" routres serving the
southern states passed through Atlanta. A newspaper in the
rival Georgia city of Athens in the summer of 1860 noted the
success of Atlanta: "The remarkable growth of this place
shows what railroads will do towards building a town." The
growth of Atlanta certainly reflected the new southern interest in railroads during the 1850s.[1]

During the decade the southern states increased their
rail mileage faster than the rest of the nation. The twelve
states south of the Potomac and Ohio rivers and the state of

Missouri more than quadrupled their iron network while the northern states only tripled their mileage. On the eve of the Civil War the twelve states (the Confederacy plus Kentucky) had considerably less mileage than the northern states on a bases of area, but in proportion to population the two regions were about equally supplied with railroads.

Most southerners promoted their new railways with enthusiasm and vigor. No proposed new rail line was too difficult to the long-winded promoters as they sold their wares at railroad conventions in Memphis or New Orleans. The dreamers seemed obsessed with two ideas: construction of any new railroad would support southern success in its race with the North; and any new line, regardless of its location or length, would certainly become an important link in a great new route handling a vast cross-country traffic. Men of commerce in the city were generally not too hard to convince, but often the back-country folk would not buy the high-flown schemes of the railroad promoter, as James DeBow found in 1851 during a trip into Tennessee and Mississippi. He wrote: ". . . the sturdy farmers of the interior, who clustered together to hear us talk about them [the proposed railroads], evinced by their looks the incredulity of the King of Siam, when assured by the missionaries that in their country water would sometime become hard enough to walk upon."[2]

During the 1850s every southern state built railroads: more than 7,400 miles of new line were completed in the twelve states. The details of this expansion are shown in Table 3.1.[3]

Only Georgia could claim more than 500 miles of line in 1850, but a decade later Virginia, Georgia, and Tennessee each had more than 1,000 miles of track. Virginia, including the counties that during the Civil War would become West Virginia, added trackage far faster than Georgia, and by 1860 was easily the first state in mileage in the region. At midcentury four-fifths (or 1,717 miles) of all southern mileage was found in the five coastal states, Virginia to Florida, while the seven Gulf and interior states had only 416 miles of

TABLE 3.1
RAILROAD CONSTRUCTION IN THE SOUTH DURING THE
1850S

State	Mileage in 1850	Mileage in 1860	Increase in Decade	Percentage of Increase	Investment per Mile in 1860
Virginia	481	1,731	1,250	260%	$36,679
North Carolina	283	937	654	231	18,796
South Carolina	289	973	684	230	22,675
Georgia	643	1,420	777	121	20,696
Florida	21	402	381	1,814	21,356
Kentucky	78	534	456	585	33,511
Tennessee	—	1,253	1,253	—	24,677
Alabama	183	743	560	306	25,022
Mississippi	75	862	787	1,049	27,982
Louisiana	80	335	255	319	35,988
Arkansas	—	38	38	—	30,394
Texas	—	307	307	—	36,706
Total for 12 states	2,133	9,535	7,402	347%	$26,947

line. Thanks largely to rapid construction in Tennessee and
Mississippi, the seven states nearly matched (3,656 miles to
3,746 miles), the rate of rail construction of the five coastal
states during the 1850s. The coastal states only tripled their
trackage, while the seven states from Kentucky to Texas
increased theirs nearly tenfold. On the eve of the war the
coastal states had 5,463 miles of line; the seven states to the
west had 4,072 miles.

During the 1850s the South built 7,402 miles of railroad
to 4,401 miles in the mid-Atlantic and New England states.
The rate of increase in the South, 347 percent, was more
than four times the 78 percent increase in the Northeast.
Virginia and Tennessee both built more railroads in the
decade than the entire six-state region of New England. Of
the eleven northern states only three, New Jersey, Pennsylvania, and Delaware, doubled their mileage during the
decade, whereas each southern state more than doubled its
rail network during the same years.

The investment in southern railroads as of 1860 ranged from a low of $18,796 per mile in North Carolina to a high of $36,706 in Texas, with an average of $26,947 for the twelve states. Such figures were far below those in the northeastern states, where the average investment per mile of line in stood at $47,823. In the South five states had railroads valued at less than $25,000 per mile, and only three were above the figure of $35,000. Of the eleven northeastern states only one, Delaware, had railroads valued at under $35,000 per mile.

The railroads of the South were longer than those of the North, probably because of the larger states and the greater distance between cities. Census figures for 1860 reveal that the twelve southern states had only 115 different railroads, less than half the 235 lines found in the eleven-state northern region from Delaware to Maine.[4] Massachusetts and Pennsylvania combined had nearly as many separate railroads as were found in the entire South. On the eve of the Civil War only 30 lines of 80 miles or more were found in the eleven northern states; there were 48 in the South. The average length of all southern lines was 83 miles; in the northeastern states the average length was only 43 miles.

Southern lines generally were not as prosperous as those farther north. Operating revenues on most southern roads were low because the freight traffic largely consisted of the seasonal movement of staple crops. Moreover, passenger travel by rail was not too extensive in the South. As a result, many southern lines found it difficult to pay dividends to their stockholders. During 1852, 1853, and 1854 a small third of southern roads were paying dividends while nearly half of New England and mid-Atlantic lines were doing so.[5] Railroads in Georgia were more likely to be able to pay dividends than other southern lines: during the early 1850s nearly 40 percent of all southern dividend-paying railroads were located in Georgia. The railroads of Georgia rather consistently had a much larger portion of their total capital represented by stock than bonds, which probably contributed to their better financial position.[6]

In the twelve southern states in 1860 there were thirty-five major railroads over 100 miles in length. On the eve of the Civil War the South had few of the nation's longest railroads, but they had their full share of those having between 100 and 250 miles of line. The twenty-two major lines located in the southern Atlantic states, Virginia to Florida, are listed in Table 3.2.[7]

These major southern lines in the five southern Atlantic states constituted a larger portion of the total rail network in the region than was true in the states to the north. In the New England and mid-Atlantic states less than half of the total mileage was in major lines of 80 miles or more in length. In the five states from Virginia to Florida about two-thirds of the total regional mileage was found in the twenty-two major lines of a 100 miles or more in length. As in the northern states the major lines in the five southern states in later years tended to be merged into larger systems. By the end of the century nearly two-thirds of the twenty-two roads were found in one of the three recently created new rail systems, the Southern, the Atlantic Coast Line, and the Seaboard Air Line.

Virginia, the southern state with the greatest mileage on the eve of the Civil War, had five of the longer lines. In addition, it could claim about 340 miles of the Baltimore & Ohio system, earlier reviewed as a Maryland line. Among the southern states, Virginia had one of the most generous policies concerning purchase of the capital stock of individual railroads. When the remainder of the stock of a Virginia line had been privately taken, the state was willing to subscribe up to three-fifths of the original stock issue. Thus, in 1855, Virginia held about 36 percent of the nearly 30 millions of railroad capital stock.[8]

Many of the nineteen lines operating in Virginia on the eve of the Civil War, including three of the five major lines in the state, ran parallel to the mountains or in a northeast–southwest direction. The Orange & Alexandria Railroad was an important line running from the Potomac southwestward to Lynchburg where a connecting road continued on to Bris-

TABLE 3.2
MAJOR RAILROADS IN THE SOUTHERN ATLANTIC STATES IN
1860

Railroad	State	Length in 1850	Length in 1860		Later Name
			100–199 miles	over 200 miles	
Orange & Alexandria	Va.	—	157		Southern
Richmond & Danville	Va.	27	143		Southern
South Side	Va.	10	132		Norfolk & Western
Virginia Central	Va.	70	189		C. & O.
Virginia & Tennessee	Va.	—		214	Norfolk & Western
North Carolina	N.C.	—		223	Southern
Wilmington, Charlotte & Rutherfordton	N.C.	—	110		Seaboard Airline
Wilmington & Manchester	N.C.	—	161		Atlantic Coast Line
Wilmington & Weldon	N.C.	161	176		Atlantic Coast Line
Charleston & Savannah	S.C.	—	103		Atlantic Coast Line
Charlotte & South Carolina	S.C.	—	109		Southern
Greenville & Columbia	S.C.	47	164		Southern
Northeastern	S.C.	—	102		Atlantic Coast Line
South Carolina	S.C.	242		242	Southern
Central of Georgia	Ga.	191	191		Central of Ga.
Georgia	Ga.	213		232	Georgia
Macon & Western	Ga.	102	102		Central of Ga.
Atlantic & Gulf	Ga.	—	109		Atlantic Coast Line
Southwestern	Ga.	—		209	Central of Ga.
Western & Atlantic	Ga.	138	138		L. & N.
Florida	Fla.	—	154		Seaboard Air Line
Pensacola & Georgia	Fla.	—	116		Seaboard Air Line

tol and Tennessee. Chartered on March 22, 1848, the Orange & Alexandria included 88.5 miles of road between Alexandria and Gordonsville by 1854. The 60 miles between Charlottesville and Lynchburg were finished by 1859. Trackage rights were obtained from the Virginia Central for service between Gordonsville and Charlottesville. John S. Barbour, Jr., a Virginia gentleman farmer and Jeffersonian Democrat who later served in both houses of Congress, was president of the Orange & Alexandria from 1852 until well after the Civil War. As a portion of the principal line to Tennessee and the West, the O. & A. claimed some of the fastest passenger service in Virginia. Even so, the 170-mile trip from Alexandria to Lynchburg took eight hours on the eve of the Civil War. In 1860 the equipment roster of the road comprised 13 locomotives, 26 passenger, mail, and baggage cars, and 140 freight cars. On the eve of the war the road was not paying dividends but had quite good earnings, based more on passenger than freight traffic.[9]

Two other lines, the Virginia & Tennessee and the Richmond and Danville, also ran parallel to the mountains. Chartered in 1849, the Virginia & Tennessee was built between 1852 and 1857 as a continuation of the Orange & Alexandria route. The Lynchburg to Bristol road was the longest in the state, other than the B. & O., and had the reputation for being a progressive carrier. It charged some of the lowest passenger fares in Virginia and had an equipment and motive power roster exceeded only by the B. & O. Nearly as important was the Richmond & Danville. This 143-mile route, connecting two important trading centers, was chartered in 1847, and the stock subscription books were soon filled with support from the state, the city of Richmond, and private citizens. Under the able leadership of the road's president, W. P. Tunstall, the line was completed by spring 1856. It prospered and was paying modest dividends on the eve of the Civil War.[10] Both the R. & D. and the Virginia & Tennessee had many hired black slaves in their work gangs.

The two remaining major lines in Virginia were the Virginia Central and the South Side. The Virginia Central was formed in 1850 from the earlier Louisa Railroad, a short line north of Richmond. As the 189-mile line was completed during the early 1850s, it extended from Richmond via Hanover Junction on to Gordonsville and Charlottesville, where it served the two portions of the Orange & Alexandria. West of Charlottesville the Virginia Central ran toward the mountains via Staunton to the end of the track at Jackson's River. A prosperous Virginia planter, Edmund Fontaine, was president of the road until after the Civil War. The 132-mile South Side, chartered in 1846 and completed by 1854, ran from Petersburg via Burkeville on the Richmond & Danville on west to Lynchburg. Like the Richmond & Danville and the Virginia & Tennessee west of Lynchburg, the South Side was built in the 5-ft. gauge, common in most of the South.

On the eve of the Civil War North Carolina had eight different railroads, none a short line; four were major roads of at least 100 miles in length. Like Virginia, North Carolina was generous with state aid in railroad construction and subscribed to stock, which gave a measure of control, rather than lending money to new rail projects. Nearly all the mileage in North Carolina was built to standard gauge, 4 feet 8½ inches. This was not surprising since the connecting railroads in eastern Virginia, running northward through Richmond on up to the Potomac, were also standard gauge. North Carolina was a poor state before the Civil War and had to be economical in her railroad building. The average investment per mile of line in 1860 was under $19,000, about $8,000 per mile less than the average for the South, and little more than half the cost of the lines in Virginia.

The North Carolina Railroad, the longest line in the state on the eve of the Civil War, was chartered January 27, 1849 and was quickly organized with former governor John M. Morehead as president. The new line had a capital of $3 million, $2 million of which were furnished by the state. President Morehead, a visionary but practical man, was the dominant figure in the sale of stock, the survey of the route, and the construction of the line. When completed early in 1856, the 223-mile road ran in a flat horseshoe curve from

Roundhouse and yards of the Orange & Alexandria, a major Virginia line running from Alexandria to Lynchburg. (COURTESY, SOUTHERN RAILWAY.)

Baltimore & Ohio station in Washington, D.C. Built of Connecticut brown stone in 1852, the depot served the B. & O. in the nation's capital until the Union Station was completed in 1907. (COURTESY, BALTIMORE & OHIO RAILROAD.)

Goldsboro via Raleigh, Greensboro, and Salisbury to Charlotte. As the first railway into the North Carolina Piedmont, it greatly lowered wagon freight rates and brought some prosperity to farmers and townfolk alike. The line's revenue was roughly divided between passenger and freight traffic, but none of the trains was speedy. On the eve of the Civil War the westbound mail required nearly fifteen hours to travel from Goldsboro to Charlotte. With more than twenty stops, the average speed was about 15 miles per hour. The North Carolina on the eve of the war was paying no dividends.[11]

The other three major North Carolina roads all served Wilmington, the leading seaport and railroad terminus, and in 1860 the largest city in the state, with a population of nearly 10,000. The oldest and most important of the three lines was the Wilmington & Weldon, originally chartered in 1835 as the Wilmington & Raleigh. Edward B. Dudley of Wilmington, later governor of the state, was the line's first president. When Raleigh failed to subscribe to stock, the northern terminal of the line was shifted to Weldon on the Roanoke River where a connection could be made with a Virginia railroad. With private capital still scarce, state aid in the late 1830s came to the assistance of the line. The road from Wilmington via Goldsboro to Weldon was completed in 1840, and for a time the 161-mile line was the longest railroad in the world. The name was changed to the Wilmington & Weldon in 1855. As the major north–south line across the state, the Wilmington & Weldon in the 1850s normally had a passenger revenue easily as great as that from freight traffic. Unlike most roads in the state, the line was paying dividends on the eve of the Civil War.[12]

The two other roads serving Wilmington were the Wilmington & Manchester and the Wilmington, Charlotte & Rutherfordton. The Wilmington & Manchester was chartered in 1846 and completed its 161-mile line from Wilmington to Wateree, South Carolina, by 1854. At Wateree it connected with the South Carolina Railroad which gave service to Columbia, Charleston, and Augusta. North Carolina gave financial support only to that portion of the road within the borders of the state. Like the Wilmington & Weldon, a majority of the line's revenue came from passengers rather than freight.[13] The other line, the Wilmington, Charlotte & Rutherfordton, was projected in the mid-1850s to run from Wilmington westward to Charlotte, but by the end of the decade the completed 110 miles reached little more than halfway to that city.

Five of the ten South Carolina railroads on the eve of the Civil War were major lines; together they made up about three-quarters of the total mileage in the state. South Carolina also aided her projected rail lines, but the assistance was less generous than Virginia's, and the overall planning present in North Carolina was lacking. At the time of the Civil War the state investment in rail securities was little more than a tenth of their total cost.[14] All South Carolina roads were built in the 5-ft. gauge.

The South Carolina Railroad was one of the oldest in the nation, and on the eve of the Civil War it was also the longest southern road east of the Appalachians. Chartered as the Charleston & Hamburg in 1827 as the child of Charleston money, the main line was completed to Hamburg in 1833 under the direction of Horatio Allen. A separate branch line north to Columbia was completed in 1840, and a second one to Camden in 1848. In 1844 the three roads were consolidated as the South Carolina Railroad.[15] James Gadsden, former U.S. army officer, sponsor of several southern railroad conventions, and the minister to Mexico who arranged the Gadsden Purchase in 1853, was president during the 1840s.

No new mileage was added in the 1850s, but the South Carolina remained very prosperous. During the presidencies of H. W. Conner (1850–53) and John Caldwell (1853–62), gross revenues increased from $1 million to $1.5 million a year. Freight revenue, much of it from cotton, year after year was twice that produced by passenger traffic. The operating expenses were sufficiently low so that the operating ratio was seldom higher than 50 percent. This favorable ratio

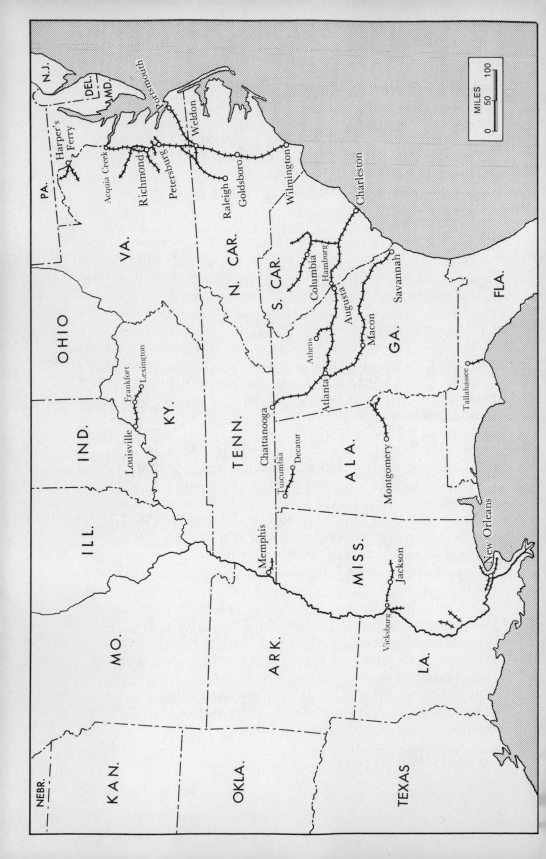

allowed annual dividends throughout the 1850s, ranging from 6 to 10 percent, and averaging just under 8 percent for the decade. The increase in traffic naturally created a need for more equipment. In 1850 the equipment roster listed 37 locomotives and 455 cars of assorted types: by 1859 the line was operating 62 locomotives and 849 cars. On the eve of the Civil War the locomotive roster, which included engines named for presidents Gadsden, Conner, and Caldwell, was reported to be the largest collection of motive power below the Potomac.[16]

Two of the remaining four major lines in the state—the Charleston & Savannah and the Northeastern—were tributary to Charleston and were largely financed by that city. The Northeastern was chartered in 1851 to provide service between Charleston and Florence, where it connected with the Wilmington & Manchester. The 102-mile line was opened in November 1856. Light local traffic, competition from river transport, and a yellow-fever epidemic in Charleston combined to keep the road from prospering in its first years of operation. Charleston and the state of South Carolina provided the major financial backing for the 103-mile Charleston & Savannah. Chartered in 1854, the line was opened for traffic in November 1860. The construction costs were so heavy that the line was forced to default upon its bond interest during its first year of operation.

The final two major roads in South Carolina in the fifties were in the northwestern part of the state. Both the Greenville and Columbia and the Charlotte & South Carolina connected with the South Carolina Railroad at Columbia, the state capital. The Greenville and Columbia, chartered in 1846, was built from Columbia to Newberry, 47 miles, by 1851. A circuitous route to Greenville, 144 miles northwest of Columbia, was opened late in 1853. Short branch lines to Abbeville and Anderson were also added during the fifties. The road was flimsily constructed, having a reported cost in 1855 of only $13,400 per mile of line. The Charlotte & South Carolina was chartered in 1846 and opened from Columbia to Charlotte, North Carolina, in 1852. The 109-

mile line connected at Charlotte with the North Carolina Railroad and thus was part of a through line from the north, an advantage not possessed by the Greenville & Columbia. The Charlotte & South Carolina was able to pay several 6 percent dividends in the late 1850s.[17]

Six of the major roads in the south Atlantic states were located in Georgia. Georgia had been an early leader in southern rail promotion, and thus the rate of construction in the 1850s was relatively slow. Four of the six major lines, in fact, had most or even all of their construction completed by 1850. This early construction had no doubt contributed to Georgia's having been able to build her network so economically. In 1860 among southern states only North Carolina had a lower rail investment per mile of line. As in South Carolina and Florida, Georgia had adopted the 5-ft. gauge for all her lines.

Georgia railroads prior to the Civil War were known for their ability to pay dividends and their safe operation as well as for their economical construction. At midcentury F. P. Holcombe, a railroad engineer, noted that in the past dozen years no single passenger had lost his life on the railroads of Georgia.[18] Georgia provided far less general state aid to railways than her sister states to the North. In the years before the Civil War she preferred to aid specific projects. Her major rail investment was the 138-mile road from Atlanta to Chattanooga, the Western & Atlantic, which was entirely constructed and owned by the state.[19]

The Georgia Railroad was one of the oldest southern lines, and on the eve of the Civil War the longest railroad in the state. The line was chartered in 1833 as a road intended to connect Athens and other towns in northeastern Georgia with Augusta, which was just across the Savannah River from the recently completed Charleston & Hamburg. In the early life of the railroad, the citizens of Athens were far more active in their financial support of the project than were the businessmen and merchants of Augusta. Legislation in 1835 gave banking privileges to the Georgia Railroad, but such activities always remained subordinate to the transportation function. During the fifteen years that J. Edgar Thomson was chief engineer of the Georgia Railroad, the road reached Atlanta and 213 miles of line were completed. Earlier in 1841 John P. King, lawyer, former U.S. senator, and Augusta cotton manufacturer, had succeeded to the presidency of the line, replacing William Dearing of Athens. King was to remain in the presidency until well after the Civil War. His election marked the shift in corporate control from Athens to Augusta.

By 1854 the Georgia Railroad had a total of 231 miles of line, with branches to Athens, Warrenton, and Washington in addition to the 171-mile main line between Augusta and Atlanta. Under John King's management, the operating revenue grew from $526,000 in 1849–50 to $1,159,000 in 1859–60. Normally the freight revenue was nearly two-thirds of the total, with cotton the largest single item. In seven of these ten years at least 150,000 bales of cotton were moved on the Georgia line, and in both 1859 and 1860 more than 219,000 bales were carried to market. President King managed to keep the "running expenses" low, and as a result the operating ratio was often below 60 percent and rarely as high as 70 percent. Because Thomson had built a solid line with low grades, because the road had good connections both at Atlanta and Augusta, and because the line had largely been built with capital stock rather than borrowed money, the road paid good dividends. Between 1836 and 1860 the company paid dividends annually except for four years in the early forties, and by the Civil War it had repaid in dividends its whole capital. For the years 1850 through 1860 the rate ranged from 3.5 to 8 percent, averaging 7 percent for the period.[20]

The general prosperity plus the growing traffic of the road naturally resulted in an increase of equipment. Between 1850 and 1857 the number of locomotives on the Georgia Railroad went from 29 to 52, freight cars from 258 to 692, and passenger cars from 19 to 24. There was also money available to invest in the stocks and bonds of connecting lines to the West which might create additional traffic for the

Georgia road. By the year 1859–60 more than a million dollars had been invested in the securities of such lines as the Nashville & Chattanooga, the Atlanta and LaGrange, the Rome, and the Augusta & Waynesboro.

Southeast of the Georgia Railroad some fifty miles was located the Central of Georgia Railroad, the other major line in the state. It was given a charter in 1833; banking privileges were added by admendment in 1835. Its first president was William Washington Gordon, West Point graduate, lawyer, and former mayor of Savannah. He died in 1842 and was succeeded by Richard R. Cuyler, an energetic businessman who lived on a lovely plantation just outside Savannah. Under Cuyler's leadership the line was finished from Savannah to Macon by October 1843. After seven years of labor, the 191-mile road had cost, not counting equipment, about $2.5 million or only about $13,000 per mile.

Under Cuyler's direction, the operating revenues of the Central of Georgia increased in the late 1840s and through the 1850s: $328,000 in 1845, $688,000 in 1850, $1,428,000 in 1855, and $1,715,000 in 1860. As in the case of the Georgia Railroad, most of the revenue was from freight. Expenses were kept low, and in most years the operating ratio ranged between 45 and 55 percent. As a result a very generous dividend policy was possible. Between 1847 and 1860 Cuyler's board of directors was able to vote regular semiannual dividends in June and December. During the fourteen years the yearly cash dividends ranged from 4 to 15 percent and averaged 8.5 percent, with the rate for the six years (1855–60) averaging 11 percent.[21] Its low original cost plus the possession of a seaport terminal, Savannah, probably explain the advantage in prosperity that the Central had over the Georgia Railroad.

Two other major lines in Georgia, the Macon & Western and the Southwestern, connected at Macon with the Central of Georgia. There can be no doubt that these two connecting lines greatly augmented the prosperity of the Central of Georgia. After the Civil War both lines came fully under the control of the Central—the Southwestern by lease in 1869,

This coal-burning "Camel" locomotive was one of several freight engines built for the Baltimore & Ohio by Ross Winans. Winans opposed the use of pony trucks and in the "Camel" designed an engine with all the weight on the drivers. (COURTESY, BALTIMORE & OHIO RAILROAD.)

and the Macon & Western by merger or consolidation in 1872.

The older and shorter of the two lines was sponsored by L. L. Griffin and other businessmen of Macon and received a charter in 1833 as the Monroe Railroad. President Griffin managed to construct the road from Macon to within 20 miles of Atlanta, but in the spring of 1845 the line was forced into bankruptcy. It was reorganized as the Macon & Western, with northern capitalists supplying the money, and Daniel Tyler, former army officer and Connecticut industrialist, as president. By 1846 Tyler had completed the 102-mile line into Atlanta. The northern businessmen were willing to let southern interests direct the road as long as they received a good return on their money. In the 1850s the Macon & Western had an increasing traffic, low expenses, and few bonds outstanding. During most of the decade dividends were 8 percent or higher, and in 1859 President Isaac Scott was able to pay a dividend of 11 percent. The Central of Georgia slowly increased its holdings of Macon & Western capital stock during the decade.

The second road out of Macon, the Southwestern, was chartered in 1845 to serve the region southwest of Macon toward Albany and Columbus. Local people along the projected route were slow to subscribe to the stock; the principal subscribers were the Central of Georgia and the city of Savannah. In 1851 the $250,000 subscribed by the Central was nearly half of the total invested in the company. By 1852, 53 miles of line was finished; in that year gross receipts amounted to $129,000. More than 90 miles were in operation by 1855, when President Cuyler of the Central also became president of the Southwestern upon the death of L. O. Reynolds. Cuyler continued to extend the road, and by 1860 the 209-mile Southwestern consisted of the 106-mile main line from Macon south to Albany plus western branches to Georgetown and Fort Gaines, towns on the Georgia-Alabama border. In 1860 the Southwestern had $3,318,000 of capital stock and a small bonded debt of $396,000. Gross receipts that year were up to $676,000, with cotton traffic supplying

most of the revenue. Regular dividends, normally 8 percent a
year, had been paid since 1852.[22]

The Western & Atlantic, fifth of the major lines in
Georgia, was one of the most important railroads in the state,
as the 138-mile route from Atlanta to Chattanooga was a vital
connecting rail link to the interior states to the northwest.
Unlike all of the other major railroads in the state, the W. &
A. was fully owned by the state of Georgia. Legislation sponsored by such men as former Governor Wilson Lumpkin,
President Gordon of the Central of Georgia, and Herschel V.
Johnson of the Georgia, was passed by the state legislature
on December 21, 1836; it provided for state funds to construct the road from Chattanooga on the Tennessee River to
some point on the Chattahoochee River in northwestern
Georgia. Construction was slow, but nearly $5 million of state
funds finally resulted in completion of the road to Atlanta by
1850.[23] At Atlanta the W. & A. connected with the Georgia
Railroad and the Macon & Western roads giving service to
the coast.

The road in 1850 included much flimsy construction,
long stretches of plate-rail, and a short roster of rolling stock.
Thus much of the early earnings were spent in improving
the property. Receipts from operations expanded greatly in
the fifties, increasing from $198,000 in 1849–50 to $836,000
in 1859–60. The freight arriving in Atlanta during the
decade consisted mainly of wheat, corn, oats, flour, bacon,
and livestock from interior states. Much of the increase in
traffic in the early 1850s, as well as the improvement of the
property, was the result of the hard work of Superintendent
William Wadley, a former blacksmith from New Hampshire
who in 1834 had migrated south, where he had served for
several years on the Central of Georgia. The equipment roster of the W. & A. grew rapidly, increasing from 13 locomotives, 6 passenger cars, and 10 freight cars in 1851 to 53 locomotives, 24 passenger cars, and 635 freight cars in 1857. One
of the new locomotives was the Rogers-built *General,* a 25-ton
woodburner that half a dozen years later would make its
mark in the Civil War. The growth in revenue, which was

heavily from freight rather than passenger traffic, had been sufficient by the mid-1850s to basically complete the program of improvements and betterments. With yearly revenue up to nearly $700,000 by 1854–55, it was possible to start making payments back to the state treasury. During 1854–55 the railroad repaid $100,000 to the state, followed by additional payments in each of the following six years. By 1861 more than $1.7 million had been paid into the Georgia state treasury.[24]

The Atlantic & Gulf was the least important of the six major lines in Georgia, the last to be built, and the only railroad of the entire group that was not paying regular dividends on the eve of the Civil War. The Atlantic & Gulf was chartered in 1856 as a westward extension of the Savannah, Albany, & Gulf, a road slowly being built down the coast from Savannah. A Georgia state subscription of $500,000 to the stock of the Atlantic & Gulf finally helped build the road from Screven down toward the Florida state line. The 109-mile line was finished by 1860 but had no time to prosper before the outbreak of the Civil War.

The two major lines in Florida—the Florida Railroad and the Pensacola & Georgia—were probably the least important of the 22 major lines located in the five southern Atlantic states. Even though Florida offered to support the bond issues of some of its projected rail lines during the 1850s, it definitely sought to confine the trade of the state to Florida ports. Thus on the eve of the Civil War no line in Florida had a connection with the railroads of Georgia. The 154-mile Florida Railroad ran diagonally across upper Florida from Fernandina on the Atlantic to Cedar Keys on the Gulf. Construction had started in 1855, and a road of sorts was completed by 1861 with David L. Yulee, lawyer and U.S. senator, as president. The second road, the 116-mile Pensacola & Georgia, was chartered in 1852 and constructed from Lake City to Tallahassee between 1856 and 1860. Since Florida was a thinly populated and poor state, it is not surprising that its railroads on the eve of the Civil War were noted for their flimsy construction, lack of equipment, small operating revenues, no dividends, and few remaining company fiscal records.[25]

More than a third of the major southern railroads, those over 100 miles in length, were located in the Gulf and interior states. The thirteen major lines located in these seven states, Kentucky, south to the Gulf states, are listed in Table 3.3.[26]

As compared with the five southern Atlantic states to the east, there were far fewer major lines in the seven Gulf and interior Southern states. The thirteen major lines were all located in the five states east of the Mississippi; neither

TABLE 3.3
MAJOR RAILROADS IN THE GULF AND INTERIOR SOUTHERN STATES IN 1860

| | | | Length in 1860 | | |
| | | | 100–199 | over 200 | |
Railroad	State	Length in 1850	miles	miles	Later Name
Alabama & Florida	Ala.	—	115		L. & N.
Alabama & Tennessee River	Ala.	—	110		Southern
Mobile & Ohio	Ala.	—		483	Mobile & Ohio
Montgomery & West Point	Ala.	88	117		Western Ry. of Ala.
New Orleans, Jackson & Great Northern	La.	—		206	Ill. Central
Mississippi Central	Miss.	—		236	Ill. Central
Southern (of Miss.)	Miss.	60	143		Ill. Central
East Tennessee & Georgia	Tenn.	—	111		Southern
East Tennessee & Virginia	Tenn.	—	130		Southern
Memphis & Charleston	Tenn.	—		291	Southern
Memphis & Ohio	Tenn.	—	130		L. & N.
Nashville & Chattanooga	Tenn.	—	159		L. & N.
Louisville & Nashville	Ky.	—		253	L. & N.

THE RAILROADS OF DIXIE   79

Arkansas nor Texas had any railroads as long as 100 miles. There were fewer major southern lines west of the mountains, but they tended to be longer: the twenty-two coastal lines averaged 167 miles, the thirteen western lines averaged 191 miles. Quite naturally the thirteen major lines also tended to be newer roads, since only two of the thirteen roads had any mileage in existence in 1850. Nearly half of the twenty-two major lines east of the mountains had been well established by midcentury. The western Gulf and interior lines did have one thing in common with the coastal lines: most of them later were to be merged into larger systems. By the early twentieth century, all but two of the thirteen lines were firmly under the control of one or another of three major systems: the Southern, the Illinois Central, and the Louisville & Nashville.

Four of the major roads were located in Alabama, a state somewhat less generous with financial aid than the coastal states to the east. Two of the four, the Alabama & Florida and the Montgomery & West Point, connected the state capital, Montgomery, with railroads in Florida and Georgia. A third road, the Alabama and Tennessee River, ran from Selma toward northeastern Alabama, while the fourth road, the Mobile & Ohio, by the eve of the Civil War was the longest railroad in the South.

The Mobile & Ohio was part of a north-south transregional railroad proposed to connect Chicago and the Great Lakes with the Gulf of Mexico. Senator Stephen A. Douglas of Illinois was seeking a federal land grant for the Illinois Central Railroad, the northern half of this route, while Senator William R. King of Alabama sought a comparable grant for the Mobile & Ohio in the states of Alabama and Mississippi. The Mobile & Ohio had been chartered in 1848 when business interests in Mobile became increasingly worried about a decline of commerce in that city. The land-grant bill passed both houses of Congress, and President Fillmore signed the act on September 20, 1850; the Mobile & Ohio was thus scheduled to receive six sections of federal land for each of more than 300 miles of line to be built en route to Tennessee and Kentucky. The U.S. Census classified the line as an Alabama railroad, and much of the financial support came from Mobile and Alabama, but in reality only a small portion of the 483-mile Mobile & Ohio—63 miles—was located in the state. More than 250 miles were located in Mississippi just to the west. Tennessee granted aid to the Mobile & Ohio; Mississippi loaned the road $200,000; Alabama loaned $400,000, and the city of Mobile helped with a five-year tax levy on all city real estate. However, in 1853–54, Sidney Smith, president of the M. & O., was not successful in selling bonds, backed by the land grant, in the London money market.

Even though the early financing was slow, progress was made in building the Mobile & Ohio. By 1853, 33 miles had been built, and on July 4, 1856, the road reached Macon, Mississippi, 198 miles north of Mobile. In that same year the Mobile & Ohio elected a new president, Milton Brown of Jackson, Tennessee, lawyer, former Whig congressman, and a representative of interests favoring the northern division of the line. The 87-mile portion of the M.& O. from Jackson, Tennessee, to Columbus, Kentucky, was completed by 1859, and the entire 483-mile road was finished on April 22, 1861. River traffic on the 20-mile steamboat connection from Columbus to the Illinois Central up at Cairo was to be quickly snuffed out by the Civil War. In the late fifties gross yearly revenues on the M. & O. were approaching $1 million. However, most of the net revenue was needed to pay the interest charges on a large bonded debt, and company officials were finding it difficult to sell many of the federal land-grant acres. The Mobile & Ohio never came close to declaring any dividends in the antebellum years.[27]

The remaining three major roads in Alabama were all less important than the Mobile & Ohio, but each was located entirely with the state. Oldest was the Montgomery & West Point, the only standard gauge line in Alabama, which was chartered in 1834, opened in part in 1854, and completed a couple of years later. This 117-mile road, which ran from Montgomery eastward to West Point and Columbus, both on the Georgia line, made more from passenger than freight traffic and was prosperous enough to pay occasional dividends late in the decade.[28] South of Montgomery, the 115-mile Alabama & Florida ran from the capital city down to Pollard, near the state line, where a connecting road ran on into Pensacola. This road had received a federal land grant in 1856, but it had been completed just before the Civil War and was of light construction and very short on equipment. The last of the Alabama lines was the Alabama & Tennessee River Railroad, chartered in 1848 to build from Selma toward the northeastern corner of the state. Construction started in 1850 but was slow, and by the end of the decade the line had only reached Talladego, 110 miles northeast of Selma. Revenues were never sufficient to pay any dividends during the 1850s.[29]

Just over 100 miles west of Mobile was its commercial rival, New Orleans, the major seaport on the Gulf. On the eve of the Civil War Louisiana had nine different railroads, but its only major line was the New Orleans, Jackson & Great Northern. Because of her long domination of the lower Mississippi River traffic, New Orleans, and consequently the state of Louisiana, had not been very aggressive in promoting railroads.

However, James DeBow in 1850 was noting in the pages of his *Review* real or at least relative declines in the export and wholesale trade of the Crescent City. A year later an editorial in the *American Railroad Journal* stated that in New Orleans, "The public mind . . . is getting pretty thoroughly aroused upon the subject of railroad connections with the interior. . . ."[30] Soon such men as the two law partners Judah P. Benjamin and John Slidell and the Whig banker-businessman James Robb were joining DeBow in sponsoring railroad conventions in New Orleans. Robb, who had come to New Orleans from the North at the age of 24, was also using his political influence to push a state legislative program that would permit extensive state and local financial support for railroads. Louisiana in 1853 passed a law setting up a system

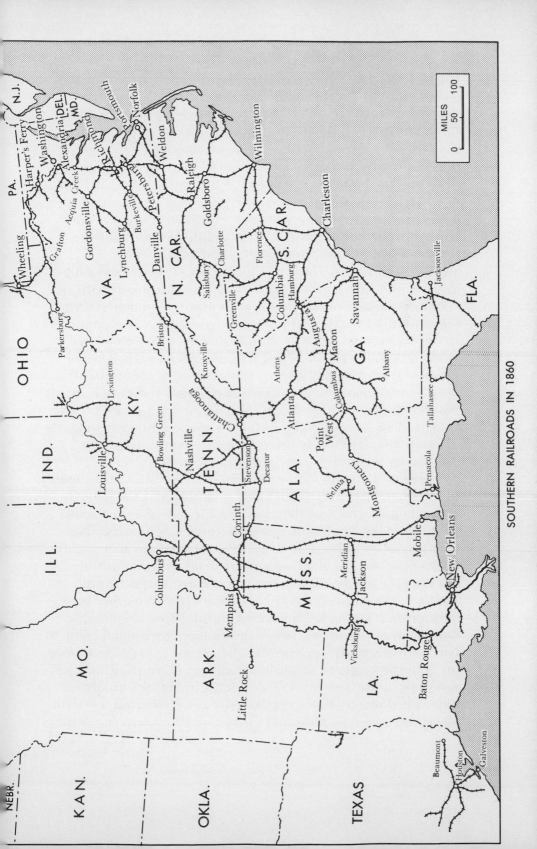

SOUTHERN RAILROADS IN 1860

in which the state could purchase up to a fifth of the capital stock of any new rail project.

A year earlier, in 1852, the New Orleans, Jackson & Great Northern had been chartered both in Louisiana and Mississippi. The new, 206-mile line was projected as a rival route to the Mobile & Ohio, and was to run north from New Orleans to Canton, Mississippi, with 88 miles of line in Louisiana and 118 miles in Mississippi. At first James Robb, the president, was no more successful in borrowing money in London than Sidney Smith of the Mobile & Ohio had been. Later bonds were sold in England, and substantial local financial support was obtained from New Orleans and Louisiana. With iron and credit from England, locomotives from Philadelphia, and coaches built in Madison, Indiana, the road began to build northward toward Mississippi. In the summer of 1854 a small wooden depot was erected in New Orleans and rail passenger service was started to Bayou La Branche, 20 miles north of the Crescent City.

Construction in Mississippi was pushed, and the entire 206-mile line to Canton was completed by spring 1858. Early in the morning of March 31, 1858, a special train carrying company officials and assorted VIPs left New Orleans for Canton. In front of the woodburning locomotive was a flatcar carrying a small cannon that periodically fired off salutes. North 150 miles, near Hazelhurst, Mississippi, the train stopped. John Calhoun of Louisiana, president of the road since 1855, resplendent in a tall beaver hat, drove the final spike in the completed line. Canton was finally reached at 11:00 P.M., and the good citizens of that city, despite the late hour, celebrated the event with a huge barbecue and banquet. Thus was completed the first leg of a second through route from the Gulf to the Ohio River.

North of Louisiana, Mississippi was quite well supplied with railroads on the eve of the Civil War. Among the Gulf and interior southern states in 1860, only Tennessee had more rail mileage or had constructed it more quickly. A major part of the Mississippi mileage was controlled by outside companies; the Mobile & Ohio along her eastern border,

the New Orleans, Jackson & Great Northern from Louisiana
up to Canton, and the Memphis & Charleston cutting
through the northeastern corner of the state. Only two Mis-
sissippi-based railroads could claim more than 100 miles of
line in 1860: the Southern Railroad of Mississippi and the
Mississippi Central.

The Mississippi Central was chartered in 1852 to build
from Canton north to the Tennessee border. Judge Harvey
W. Walter and Walter Goodman of Holly Springs, Mississippi, were the major promoters of the road. Goodman, the
president of the line, managed to obtain a few cash subscriptions, traded some stock for labor, bridge timbers, and cross-
ties, and peddled another $38,000 of stock at the ground-
breaking ceremonies late in 1853. He had enough cash and
credit to order English iron and to purchase two brass-
trimmed locomotives which arrived by flatboat from Massachusetts in May 1855.

Slave labor was used to build the first 102 miles of the
road, but in 1858 there still remained unfinished the "Big
Gap" of 86 miles south of Water Valley. Goodman's request
for financial help, made to president William H. Osborn of
the Illinois Central, was turned down, but later he did receive
new support from George Peabody, an American banker living in London. The "Big Gap" was finished with English
money, and the Mississippi portion of the line was completed
by January 1860. Earlier, in 1859, the Mississippi Central
had taken over a 48-mile road from the state line up to Jackson, Tennessee. From 1860 on the 236-mile Mississippi Central and 206-mile New Orleans, Jackson, & Great Northern
were operated as a single unit. North of Jackson, Tennessee,
the combined line used the tracks of the Mobile & Ohio up
to Columbus, Kentucky. The editor of the *American Railroad
Journal,* commenting on the first New York City to New
Orleans rail service, said that the state of Mississippi should
be proud of their new line, a road largely financed by the
cotton planters of the state.[31]

In the central part of the state an important east-west
road, the Southern Railroad of Mississippi, was also com-

pleted just before the Civil War. In the early 1830s a short road was built east of Vicksburg, and as the Vicksburg & Jackson it was extended to Jackson, the capital of the state by 1841. Extending the line east from Jackson to Meridian on the Mobile & Ohio was slower work. The Southern Railroad of Mississippi, organized in 1846, took fifteen years to finish the line from Jackson to Meridian. Earlier in 1856 it had taken over the Vicksburg & Jackson, and thus when through service from Vicksburg to Meridian was in full operation in 1861, the Southern Railroad was running a 143-mile line. For some strange reason the Vicksburg to Meridian line was built in the offbeat gauge of 4 feet 10 inches. One of the principal backers of the Southern, and later president, was Dr. Morris Emanuel, a doctor who doubled as an apothecary in Vicksburg. After the war, in 1867, the Southern was reorganized as the Vicksburg & Meridian.[32]

Five of the major railroads were located in Tennessee, which had by far the greatest mileage of the seven Gulf and interior states. The rapid building in the state during the 1850s was accelerated by the generous Tennessee assistance of $10,000 granted for each mile of completed track. By the time of the Civil War, nearly all the fourteen roads in the state had shared in this largesse, and the total aid was over $13 million.[33]

The 291-mile Memphis & Charleston was the most important east-west line in the Gulf and interior states, and the second longest road in the South, exceeded only by the Mobile & Ohio, which it crossed at Cornith, Mississippi. Originally chartered in 1846, and receiving the good wishes of John C. Calhoun of South Carolina, plus additional financial support from the cities of Charleston, New Orleans, and Philadelphia, the Memphis & Charleston was completed from Memphis to Stevenson, Alabama, by 1857. Nearly two-thirds of the route was located in northern Mississippi and Alabama, and east of Stevenson, the tracks of the Nashville & Chattanooga were used to reach Chattanooga. Samuel Tate, a railroader whose reputation equaled that of William Wadley, was president of the road in the late 1850s and during the Civil War. Unlike most southern roads, Tate's line had more revenue from passenger than freight traffic. Gross annual revenues were over a million dollars by this time, but the line had fairly large bond-interest requirements and declared no dividends for its stockholders. The strategic location of the Memphis & Charleston made it a vital line in the war effort of the Confederacy.[34]

Two other major Tennessee roads, the Nashville & Chattanooga and the Memphis & Ohio, served central and western portions of the state. The Nashville & Chattanooga was chartered late in 1845 and organized in 1848 with Vernon K. Stevenson of Nashville as president. Basically following a route earlier selected by Thomson of the Georgia Railroad, the Nashville & Chattanooga was built between the two cities from 1848 to 1854. By 1851 service was started over a line 61 miles out of Nashville, and three years later the road was completed to Chattanooga. Like all other lines in the state, the Nashville & Chattanooga was built in 5-ft. gauge. By 1856 its equipment roster included 37 locomotives, 23 passenger cars, and 317 freight cars, and annual gross revenues were above $550,000. Dividends of 6 percent were being paid on the eve of the Civil War.[35] The 130-mile Memphis & Ohio was chartered in 1852 and built between 1854 and early 1861 from Memphis to Paris, Tennessee, where it connected with a road that gave service into Kentucky and the Louisville & Nashville. After the Civil War both the Memphis & Ohio and the Nashville & Chattanooga would come under the control of the L. & N.

The remaining two Tennessee lines, the East Tennessee & Georgia and the East Tennessee & Virginia, provided vital service through eastern Tennessee up to Bristol on the Tennessee-Virginia line. Both roads received the normal Tennessee financial aid at the rate of $10,000 per mile of completed road. The East Tennessee & Georgia was chartered in 1848 and opened its main line from Chattanooga up to Knoxville in 1856. A short branch line also ran from Cleveland south to Dalton, Georgia, on the Western & Atlantic. The East Tennessee & Virginia was chartered in 1849 and completed its 130-mile road from Knoxville to Bristol in 1855. At Bristol it connected with the Virginia & Tennessee and the entire rail network of Virginia. The traffic on the Chattanooga-Knoxville-Bristol route was important, but the net revenue in the late 1850s was never sufficient to allow either line to pay any dividends. The route, a major lifeline for the Confederacy, was subject to many raids by Union forces. The two lines were merged in 1869 into the East Tennessee, Virginia & Georgia.[36]

In Kentucky the state government gave little aid to her railroads. City and county governments were often generous with financial assistance, but the state had fewer than 550 miles of road in operation on the eve of the Civil War. The Louisiana & Nashville, with 253 miles of line, was the only major railroad in Kentucky.

When the states of Tennessee (February 9, 1850) and Kentucky (March 5, 1850) chartered the Louisville & Nashville Railroad, they were approving a different kind of project. Unlike most other southern lines, the L. & N. had the express purpose of diverting trade to the north through the river town of Louisville. The railroad's first president, Levin L. Shreve, a prominent Louisville businessman, faced the twin problems of route location and finance. The city of Louisville between 1851 and 1855 subscribed $2 million in city bonds, and Tennessee offered the normal $10,000 per mile for the route located in that state. Private stock subscriptions also were taken, but the sale of bonds on the London market was next to impossible for several years. President Shreve found it hard to push construction, and former governor John L. Helm, who succeeded Shreve in 1854, was not much more successful. By fall 1856 only 30 miles of line were fully in operation.

Activity on the L. & N. increased after 1857, when two men, James Guthrie and Albert Fink, entered the employ of the road. The lame, uncouth, but highly respected Guthrie became vice-president of the L. & N. after serving four years, 1853–57, as secretary of the treasury under Franklin Pierce. The German-born Albert Fink was a giant of a man, standing six foot seven, and when he came to the L. & N. he was already acclaimed as a bridge designer and engineer. Guthrie and Fink pushed ahead with construction, and the entire 185-mile main line to Nashville was put in operation in November 1859. Before the war a branch line was also built to Lebanon, and a second line southwest from Bowling Green was headed toward Memphis. The completed road had growing revenues and a favorable operating ratio but did not pay any dividends until the early sixties. James Guthrie became president in 1860, succeeding Helm. As the war clouds shaped up in the early months of 1861, Guthrie's road strove to carry the huge traffic moving south—goods ordered in the North by the Confederacy. This prosperous trade continued until September 1861, when Guthrie rather reluctantly decided that he was a Union man. For the next few months he controlled only the northern portion of the L. & N.[37]

There were no major lines of more than 100 miles in length in Arkansas and Texas, the two southern states west of the Mississippi. In Arkansas the single road, the Memphis & Little Rock, was far from finished; in 1860 it was only 38 miles long. On the eve of the Civil War, Texas had over 300 miles of railroad, but the longest of the six roads was only 90 miles. Most of the Texas lines were in the vicinity of Houston, more than 100 miles west of the closest rails in Louisiana.

Major or minor lines, the railroads of the twelve southern states did not compare with those north of the Potomac and Ohio rivers. The railroads of Dixie in 1860 represented an investment of less than $27,000 per mile of road, well under the nearly $48,000 average for the northeastern states, and also much below the figures for the the midwestern lines north of the Ohio River. Many of the southern lines were newly built, and most still lacked the physical and financial maturity typical of northern railways. Serving a sparse population with few urban centers, southern lines typically had a traffic more local than interstate in character. Thus it was the rare southern railroad that was declaring or paying out dividends in the 1850s.

Southern lines were generally inferior in construction, rail, motive power, and rolling stock. They tended to have steeper grades, sharper curves, less ballast, and more weakly constructed bridges than those in northern states. While most of the track was laid with wrought-iron T rail, some lines still had portions laid with the earlier U or even strap-iron rail. Nearly all southern lines were extremely short of passing sidings or secondary track. It was unusual to find a road in the South that could claim siding mileage equaling 10 percent of its main line trackage. In the North many roads had secondary or siding trackage equal to a fifth or a third of their main line mileage.[38]

The South was much inferior in motive power on the eve of the Civil War. Far fewer locomotives were on the typical southern line than were found on the average railroad in the North. The five lines of more than 100 miles in length in New England (two in Vermont and one each in Maine, Massachusetts, and Connecticut) had a total length of 627 miles, and in 1859–60 had an aggregate roster of 197 locomotives. In the same year Virginia's five major roads had a total length of 835 miles but had only 113 engines. The Richmond & Danville (143 miles) in Virginia had only 22 locomotives while the Northern Central (142 miles) in Maryland and Pennsylvania was operating 42 locomotives. On the eve of the war the Mobile & Ohio (483 miles) had but 25 engines while north of the Ohio the longer Illinois Central (738 miles) had more than four times the motive power, 113 locomotives. The oldest railroad in the South, the South Carolina (242 miles), with 62 locomotives, had the largest power roster in Dixie. One of the oldest northern railroads, the B. & O. (386 miles), probably had the record for northern lines, with 235 locomotives. In fact the four major trunk lines of the North (B. & O., Pennsylvania, Erie, and New York Central) together had 876 locomotives in 1859–60—not far short of the entire southern motive power roster.[39]

Since most southern motive power was built in northern

shops, northern and southern locomotives had the same brass, bright paint, baloon stacks, and large headlights. Both passenger and freight engines were generally of the American (4–4–0) type, a bogie truck in front and four connected drivers. Most southern engines weighed from fifteen to twenty-five tons, cost from $8,000 to $10,000 new, and, because of inferior track, rarely exceeded a speed of 25 miles per hour. The large stacks poured out clouds of pine smoke since southern engines invariably were woodburners. Only in the North were serious efforts being made to convert to coal.

The railroads of the South were as short of passenger and freight cars as they were of locomotives. Again the North had an advantage of about two to one. The five longest New England roads on the eve of the war had a total of 130 passenger and 3,188 freight cars, while the five roads in Virginia had but 78 passenger and 1,392 freight cars. The Richmond & Danville had 20 passenger and 410 freight cars while 38 passenger and 1,455 freight cars were in use on the Northern Central. The Mobile & Ohio had 18 passenger and 361 freight cars, while the longer Illinois Central in 1860 was operating 96 passenger and 2,305 freight cars. The B. & O. had 124 passenger and 3,272 freight cars to only 59 passenger and 720 freight cars for the South Carolina.[40]

The southern rail system was not fully integrated with the rest of the nation, or even with itself. In 1860–61 no railroad bridge crossed the entire length of the Ohio River, and the B. & O., not a southern line, only crossed the Potomac at Harper's Ferry. Connecting rail bridges were not present at Cairo, Louisville, Cincinnati, or Washington, D.C. Many southern railroad centers did not have a physical rail connection between converging lines. The several lines and depots serving Richmond were all separated by several city blocks. Comparable problems existed in such cities as Petersburg, Wilmington, Charleston, Savannah, and Montgomery.

Variations in gauge further compounded the problem of rail integration in the South. In Virginia the trackage was rather equally divided between the 4 ft. 8½ in. standard gauge of the North, and the 5-ft. gauge popular in the

South. North Carolina, with but two minor exceptions, used standard gauge, connecting with that laid from Alexandria and Acquia Creek south through Richmond to the North Carolina line. South Carolina, Georgia, Florida, and Tennessee exclusively used the 5-ft. gauge, which was also predominant in Kentucky, Mississippi, and Alabama. Louisiana followed a mixed pattern, and southern states west of the Mississippi River much preferred lines built to a 5 ft. 6 in. width.[41]

In every respect except actual length of line, the average southern railroad was a smaller organization than its northern counterpart. With less traffic, the typical southern road had fewer employees: although nearly a third of the total mileage in 1860 was located in the South, that region employed only a fifth of the total railroad workers in the nation. The South was unique in its heavy use of black slave labor, especially for manual and heavier work. Some lines, especially those in Virginia, hired the labor of slaves belonging to others. But many companies owned a fairly large number of slaves to be used exclusively on the line of the railroad. In 1854 the 88-mile Montgomery & West Point owned 66 slaves valued at $36,850. A few years later, in 1859, the longer South Carolina Railroad listed in its annual report the ownership of 88 slaves valued at $ 78,000.[42]

The traditional southern dislike for mechanical pursuits left much of the more complex railroad operation in the hands of northern men. Men like William Wadley or Albert Fink had come into the region to help run the railroads. Some of the Yankees returned north with the outbreak of war, but others more interested in railroading than political issues stayed in the South. Some of those who remained on the job were viewed with suspicion during the war, but most were loyal to the southern cause.

Southern dependence upon the North for much of its equipment and track material was more vital than its need for northern management. The states north of the Potomac had a dozen locomotive plants for every one in the South. While Virginia, South Carolina, and Tennessee produced some railroad cars, Pennsylvania alone could supply annually twice the southern output. A few of the company shops, such as those of the Central of Georgia, claimed they could manufacture both cars and engines, but soon the Confederate officials were pressing these establishments into ordnance production. When war came, track maintenance soon became a serious problem. Much of the iron on southern roadbeds had come from England, partly because of heavy British investment in southern railroad bonds, but also because many southern rail officials believed that English iron was both superior and cheaper (even with the tariff) than the northern product. The South could produce some of its own rails, but its 1860 production of 26,000 tons was only a ninth of that of the North. When war in 1861 cut both outside sources of supply, railroad executives at once began to hoard iron and buy everything in sight.

The southern railroads had grown rapidly in mileage and service during the fifties. But their original light construction, their modest traffic and earnings, and their relative lack of equipment kept them from being equal to their northern counterparts. At the end of the 1850s, the railroads of Dixie were ill prepared to face the tasks that lay ahead.

CHAPTER FOUR

Uncle Sam and the Railroads

ON FRIDAY afternoon, September 20, 1850, the citizens of Chicago heard some welcome news over the telegraph: "President Fillmore has signed the Central Railroad Bill." The message meant that the federal government was offering the state of Illinois 2.5 million acres of land to help in the construction of a 700-mile railroad—a 365-mile main line from Chicago south to Cairo, with a branch line north to Dunleith in the northwestern corner of the state. Soon the dozen other Illinois towns served by telegraph heard the news. They all celebrated the success of the railroad project, which its sponsor, Stephen A. Douglas, had called, "one of the most gigantic enterprises of the age." The *Chicago Tribune* claimed it would place Illinois in the front rank of states, and an editor in Shawneetown welcomed a new commercial route that would not freeze over or dry up. Chicago, which had grown from a town of 4,500 to a city of 30,000 during the 1840s, was about to get its second railroad, Illinois was to have a railway running the length of the state—and Uncle Sam was going to help pay for it![1]

The Douglas railroad bill was the first federal land-grant legislation passed for the benefit of American railroads. In signing the historic measure, Fillmore was starting a program of federal aid to railways that would last for many years. Presidents Fillmore, Franklin Pierce, Abraham Lincoln, Andrew Johnson, and Ulysses S. Grant between 1850 and 1871 approved grants of more than 155 million acres of land for eighty-odd railroads. Nearly a sixth of these acres would later be forfeited by unfinished lines and returned to the government, but eventually the railroads of the nation were to receive full and final title to more than 131 million acres of federal land.

During the 1850s land grants in excess of 22 million acres were offered to eleven midwestern and southern states for purposes of railroad construction.[2] More than three-fifths of this total was given to the six midwestern states of Michigan, Wisconsin, Illinois, Minnesota, Iowa, and Missouri. Uncle Sam was also generous to the railroad industry during the fifties in other ways. In 1852 Congress provided that new railroads could have a free right-of-way from the public domain. Later money was to be provided, via an army appropriations bill, to pay for several survey parties seeking out the best route for a railroad to the Pacific. The Gadsden Purchase of 1853 was made to ensure a western rail route favored by southern interests. Much of the sectional political activity of the mid- and late 1850s was influenced by rival interests favoring their own particular route for a railway to the Pacific.

The interest of the federal government in railroads at midcentury is not surprising given the temper of America at that time. Americans were not in full agreement about the Mexican War, but they were proud of the growth of their country during the "Manifest Destiny" expansion under President Polk. In the six decades since the inauguration of George Washington and the first Census of 1790, the area of the nation had tripled, and the population had increased sixfold. And yet America was still a youthful nation, and many of her citizens were as old as the Republic. Senator William R. King, cosponsor of the Illinois Central land-grant bill; James Guthrie, builder of the L. & N.; and Eleazor Lord, three-time president of the Erie, had all been children when Washington was president. Americans at midcentury had a strong pride in the heritage of their nation. They applauded the 1843 completion of the Bunker Hill Monument, whose first construction had been aided by Gridley Bryant's railway, and five years later they were ready to start a monument to

George Washington in the nation's capital. Americans had already agreed that Washington's birthday and Independence Day were the two national holidays of first importance.

America was prosperous in 1850. The expanding internal improvements of the nation—canals, river steamboats, and railroads—were encouraging a growing division of labor among the three sections of the nation. The mid-Atlantic and New England states provided most of the manufacturing and commercial needs of the nation. The Midwest of the Ohio and upper Mississippi valleys supplied surplus food for the South and the urban areas of the Northeast. And southern states, with their massive yield of cotton, provided the bulk of American exports. Foreign trade was increasing, but domestic trade and commerce was growing even faster and by mid-century was several times the foreign trade in dollar volume. Even so, the expanding imports in the years after the Mexican War were paying tariff duties sufficient to finance fully the federal government. In each of the years from 1850 through 1857, federal income was larger than expenses, with annual surpluses running from $1 to $15 million, the yearly balances ranging from 1.5 to 20 percent of total annual expenditures.[3]

With such prosperity, it was not too difficult for government leaders to decide to help western railroads, especially since they were giving something that existed in great abundance—federal land. By the early 1850s most Americans agreed that railroads possessed several advantages over the turnpike, the canal, and the river steamer. Most Americans were farmers: 80 percent of the population was rural. When they were not located close to canals or navigable rivers, the farmers naturally were eager for a railroad. The growing enthusiasm for railways is revealed in the construction figures in the years after the Mexican War. In nearly every year between 1849 and 1853 there was more new building than in the previous year: 1,369 miles built in 1849, 1,656 in 1850, 1,961 in 1851, 1,926 in 1852, and 2,452 in 1853.[4] All Americans seemed to want more railroad mileage.

Artists crowd the pilot of the Tyson ten wheeler which pulled their 1858 B. & O. excursion train. Henry Tyson, master mechanic on the B. & O. from 1856 to 1859, designed his new 4-6-0 engine for both freight and passenger service. (COURTESY, SMITHSONIAN INSTITUTION.)

In the decades before the railroad land-grant act of 1850, several precedents were established for governmental support of internal improvements. When President Thomas Jefferson signed the National, or Cumberland, Road Bill on March 29, 1806, it was the beginning of federal aid for highway construction. Construction contracts were let in 1811, and the road was completed from Cumberland, Maryland, to Wheeling on the Ohio River by 1818. Because of the rugged terrain through the mountains, the completed 130-mile hard surfaced road had cost $1,718,000. Henry Clay and Andrew Jackson used the road to travel to and from the nation's capital. The new route was also crowded with Conestoga freighters, Yankee peddlers, circus wagons, and foreign travelers. As the road was extended through Ohio and Indiana in the 1820s and 1830s, more federal money was provided for construction and maintenance. A total of $6,824,000 had been spent by 1838. Using chiefly private money, the road was built on to Vandalia, Illinois, by 1852.

Federal aid for the National Road was in the form of money rather than land. The first land grant for the construction of wagon roads was an 1823 grant to Ohio for a road from Lake Erie to the western border of the Connecticut Western Reserve. A second Ohio wagon road grant in 1827 provided that "no toll shall at any time be collected of any mail coach, nor of any troops, or property of the United States." This same provision also applied to later land grants to canals and railroads. Also in 1827 a grant was made to Indiana for a road to be built from the Ohio River, via Indianapolis, to Lake Michigan. The grants to Ohio amounted to 80,773 acres, and the Indiana grant was for 170,580 acres. No other wagon road land grants were made before 1860.

Land grants made to states for canal construction started in 1824 when Indiana received land for a canal that became the Wabash and Erie. Subsequent grants to Indiana and Ohio had by 1848 provided a total of 1,723,000 acres of the public domain for this internal improvement. In these same years other grants aided canal projects in Ohio, Illinois, Michigan, and Wisconsin. Several of these grants inaugurated the program of granting only alternate sections of land, with the reserved acres to be sold by the government at a higher price of $2.50 an acre. Before the Civil War the total of these canal grants came to 3,724,000 acres.[5] Like the wagon grants, the canal grants stipulated freedom from tolls for government traffic.

Thus by midcentury there were strong precedents for extending federal land grants to another internal improvement—the railroad. A western frontier state, Illinois, was to be a prime mover in the railroad land-grant development. In 1837 an ambitious internal improvement program adopted by Illinois included plans for a north–south railroad running the length of the state, known as the Central Railroad. This proposed railway hardly proceeded past the planning stage, and received little national attention until U.S. Senator Sidney Breese made several unsuccessful efforts in the middle 1840s for a land grant for the project. Stephen A. Douglas, who moved from the House to the Senate in 1847, was to be more successful. In spring 1848 Douglas sponsored a bill to grant federal land to Illinois for the building of a north–south railway the length of the state. The Douglas bill was easily passed in the Senate but failed in the lower house, despite the best efforts of such Illinois congressmen as Abraham Lincoln of Springfield, John Wentworth of Chicago, and John A. McClernand of Shawneetown.

The second effort, made by Douglas during the Thirty-First Congress, was successful. Several factors help explain the passage of the 1850 land-grant act. The chances for success were strengthened in 1849 when his good friend, General James Shields, replaced Breese in the U.S. Senate. Douglas also gained more local support when the new bill provided that a branch of the rail route be built up to Chicago. He agreed with the suggestion of Senator George Wallace Jones of Iowa that the northwestern terminal of the road should be extended past Galena up to Dunleith, just across the Mississippi from Dubuque, Iowa. The bill was made more attractive to politicians from the South when an amendment was added providing a land grant in Alabama and Mississippi for a road running from Mobile up to the mouth of the Ohio River, where it would connect with the Illinois road. This amendment, proposed by the prim, spare William R. King of Alabama, was to benefit the Mobile & Ohio. Senator King, with twenty-five years of seniority, had many friends and great influence among top Democrats.

The Douglas land-grant measure was the subject of much debate in late April and early May 1850. Senator Andrew P. Butler of South Carolina opposed the bill, seeing it as a gift from the original states to frontier states, and compared it to gifts given by King Lear to his ungrateful children. Jefferson Davis of Mississippi gave the proposal his qualified support, and Senator William H. Seward was favorably inclined, noting similarities between the Gulf to Great Lakes railway and the earlier Erie Canal in his own state of New York. The Little Giant from Illinois added the cogent argument that Uncle Sam would really lose nothing, since the new road, once built through Illinois, would quickly make the remaining alternate sections worth the $2.50 asked per acre.

The Senate easily approved the Douglas land-grant measure on May 3, 1850 by a vote of 26 to 14. The great bulk of the support came from western or Gulf states, with most of the opposition from northeastern states. Daniel Webster was absent, but he favored the bill since he had long advocated a generous and liberal policy relative to public lands. He personally held substantial investments in the lands of central Illinois and the timberlands of Wisconsin. In the House, opposition to the measure was stiff. However, during the summer the combined efforts of senators Douglas, King, and Webster plus the stalwart work of the Illinois House delegation eventually won out. By a vote of 101 to 75 the House passed the measure on September 17, 1850. Three days later President Fillmore signed the measure, and the citizens of Illinois had something to celebrate.[6]

The 1850 act gave public land to Illinois, Mississippi, and Alabama through which the Great Lakes to Gulf railway would run. Kentucky and Tennessee were not included since neither state had any federal lands. The act provided for a

200-foot right-of-way through public lands, plus six alternate sections of land for each completed mile of the route. Illinois received 2,595,053 acres for the line north of the Ohio River, while Mississippi obtained 737,130 acres and Alabama 419,528 acres for the new rail route south of Cairo. The remaining alternate sections, retained by the government, were to be doubled in price from $1.25 to $2.50 an acre. Where the alternate railroad sections had earlier been sold by the government, substitute or "indemnity" sections could be selected within 15 miles of the rail line. Unless the projected railways were to be started within two years and completed within ten years, all the land was to return to the government. Also included was a provision providing freedom from tolls for federal government traffic.

Backers of additional rail projects were also requesting land grants in the summer of 1850. Two proposed roads in Missouri, running westward from the Mississippi, failed to obtain grants from the federal government.[7] However, in 1852 Congress passed legislation that provided that all railroads chartered within ten years and completed within fifteen years were to be granted a 100-foot right-of-way through the public domain. They also were to be allowed extra space as needed for depots or stations.

The passage of the Douglas land-grant bill in September 1850 did not immediately cause a rush of requests for additional federal aid. Little land-grant activity occurred during the second session of the Thirty-First Congress (1850–51). However, in the early weeks of the next session (1851–52), many states with public lands and embryo railroad projects were introducing such legislation. Early in 1852 the commissioner of the Land Office estimated seven different western and southern states had introduced bills asking for more than 13 million acres of federal land to build more than 3,000 miles of new road. By March 1852, the *American Railroad Journal* was reporting that twelve western and southern states were requesting grants for thirty-one different railroads with a proposed total construction of 9,000 miles of new line.[8]

Most of these requests made in the winter of 1851–52

were not granted. The Senate was much more sympathetic than was the House—fifteen railroad land-grant bills passed the Senate, but only one made it through the House. The only successful act was one signed by President Fillmore on June 10, 1852, granting land to Missouri for two railroads. The Pacific Railroad (southwestern branch) was to receive 1,161,204 acres and the Hannibal & St. Joseph was to be given 603,506 acres. These two grants, similar in detail to the earlier grants sponsored by Douglas and King, had failed to pass back in the summer of 1850.[9] Both lines were to build most of their projected routes before the Civil War.

President Fillmore approved a few more railroad bills during the short session of Congress in the winter of 1852–53. On February 9, 1853 grants were approved for two roads in Arkansas and a third line which was projected through Missouri and Arkansas. The three lines, which were given a total of more than 1,850,000 acres, completed very little of their projected mileage before the war. During his term Fillmore had approved railroad land grants amounting to a total of 7,372,883 acres.

After 1853 there was a definite lapse of railroad legislative activity. Only in the last year of Franklin Pierce's term was there a renewal of such land-grant legislation. Between May 1856 and March 1857 eight different states received land grants for more than 30 different projected roads. Iowa was the first state to obtain such aid. Earlier in the decade Iowans were undecided about such grants, but by 1856 they were eagerly supporting several lines projected westward across the state. Early in May 1856 the House had approved land grants for four railroad routes running across Iowa from the Mississippi to the Missouri. In the upper house Senator Jones of Iowa had some opposition from eastern senators, but eventually the bills were approved, and President Pierce signed the legislation on May 14, 1856.[10] The Iowa grants, amounting to 2,789,000 acres, went to lines that by 1860 were to build a third of the way across the state from the four river towns of Dubuque, Clinton, Davenport, and Burlington.

Once the Iowa grants were approved, others quickly followed. On May 17, 1856, grants totaling 1,760,000 acres were given to four projected Florida roads, and 394,000 acres were provided for a road in Alabama. Two weeks later, on June 3, 1856, acts were approved granting land to four states. Five roads in Alabama were granted 2,016,000 acres; two roads in Louisiana received 1,072,000 acres; five companies in Michigan were given 2,360,000 acres; and five lines in Wisconsin were provided with 1,904,000 acres. Later in the summer, on August 11,1856, Mississippi was given 198,000 acres for a road from Vicksburg to Meridian. In the short session of Congress (1856–57) Pierce approved one final railroad grant. On March 3, 1857, only a day before leaving office, he signed a measure providing 2,380,000 acres for five lines projected in Minnesota, a territory that would not even be admitted to statehood for another year.[11] All of the grants approved by President Pierce, which came to a total of just under 15 million acres, were granted to the states, which subsequently passed them on to individual railroads. The grants were very similar to those earlier given in 1850 for the Great Lakes to Gulf railway.

The eight states granted land during the Pierce administration had varied success with their projected lines in the few remaining prewar years. The roads of Iowa, Florida, and Mississippi had built most of their projected mileage before the Civil War. In Alabama, Louisiana, Michigan, and Wisconsin only a portion of the proposed mileage was completed before the war. Minnesota in 1860 had no operating rail mileage.

During the term of President James Buchanan (1857 to 1861) no further land grants were made to railroads. The Panic of 1857 not only slowed commercial activity in the nation but also retarded railroad building—by the late 1850s new construction had slumped to half the rate of 1855 to 1856. And the growing sectional controversy seemed to crowd the consideration of further railroad grants out of the political limelight. Each of Buchanan's three successors, Lincoln, Johnson, and Grant, approved many additional land

The Lackawanna Valley. When the twenty-nine-year-old George Inness painted this Scranton landscape in 1854 for the Delaware, Lackawanna & Western, the railroad president asked that three locomotives be included. For the $75 fee received Inness included only the locomotive in the foreground. (COURTESY, NATIONAL GALLERY OF ART.)

grants, however, especially Lincoln. With southern legislators no longer in the government, it was easy for Congress to select central and northern routes for railroads to the Pacific and to be very generous with federal land.

However, the less generous grants of land given in the Fillmore and Pierce years to projected western and southern lines were also important. The grants given to eleven states for more than three dozen projected roads served as a more than ample precedent for the subsequent grants authorized during and after the Civil War. And the total land provided in the grants—some 22 million acres—was quite generous. The more than 34,000 sections of land given by Uncle Sam in the decade was nearly equal to the area of Indiana and was four times the size of Massachusetts!

Eight of the eleven states receiving land grants bordered the Mississippi River: the five states just west of the river, Minnesota south to Louisiana, plus Wisconsin, Illinois, and Mississippi. Certainly the land hastened rail construction in the region, especially in Illinois, Iowa, and Missouri, areas sparse in population and short on ready capital, where the federal land furnished an early basis for credit so that construction could start. By 1860 the U.S. Census was showing the frontier line in most places had moved west of the Mississippi. A railroad map of the same year would show the westward-moving finger of the growing iron network not too far behind.

By the mid–nineteenth century, Americans and their government were dreaming about an iron road to the Pacific. As soon as the first Americans settled in the Oregon country, there were murmurings concerning the need for improved transportation to the far Pacific. A few visionaries during the 1830s even had the boldness to write or talk about railroads being built to the coast. Those few Americans who paid any attention to these fanciful ideas were certain that the government would have to help finance such a massive undertaking.

Asa Whitney was probably the first serious promoter of a railroad to the Pacific. Born a Connecticut Yankee, Whitney had no desire to spend his life tilling his father's stony acres; he chose instead a life of commerce in New York City. By the early 1840s Whitney had grown rich through the China trade. He had also gathered sufficient evidence to be convinced that a railroad to the Pacific Northwest was not only practical but would greatly increase Chinese-American commerce.

In a memorial to Congress, dated January 28, 1845, Whitney asked for a charter and a 60-mile-wide land grant running from Milwaukee on Lake Michigan over the Rockies to the mouth of the Columbia River. He planned to sell the land grant to finance construction and to build the road with cheap labor—the recent immigrants from Germany and Ireland. Many who heard of or read about Whitney's scheme viewed the man as an innocent, impractical visionary. But after months of travel and lobbying efforts Whitney had won the approval of seventeen state legislatures. He was less successful in Congress, which studied his bill in 1845, 1846, and 1847 but never approved the project. Part of Whitney's problem was the opposition of such men as Congressman Stephen A. Douglas and Senator Thomas Hart Benton. In fall 1845 Douglas wrote Whitney that Chicago would be a better eastern terminal than Milwaukee, and San Francisco Bay a better Pacific coast terminus than the mouth of the Columbia River.[12] Benton, the veteran Missouri senator, had long been a supporter of such essential western interests as railroads, but he was unyielding in his insistence that the road to the Pacific must start from Saint Louis rather than some port on the Great Lakes.

By the late 1840s other events were to complicate the Whitney proposal. The war with Mexico soon made California an American possession, and the discovery of gold made that portion of the Pacific coast most attractive. There had really been only one route to Oregon, but with the Mexican cession the Santa Fe Trail and other routes to the Pacific were becoming practical. Finally, other cities than Milwaukee, Chicago, and Saint Louis were soon to compete vigorously for the honor of being the eastern terminal for a railway built to the Pacific.

Half a dozen cities up and down the Mississippi Valley held conventions in support of railroads and internal improvements between 1845 and the early 1850s. Memphis in November 1845 held the first convention of any importance. Sixteen states sent delegations, and the venerable John C. Calhoun, recently in Tyler's cabinet and not yet returned to the Senate, was selected to preside over the sessions. The convention concentrated on railroad building in the South but also endorsed the notion of a rail line to the Pacific, naturally to follow some southern route. A year and a half later, in July 1847, a comparable convention was held in Chicago, originally as a protest against a recent veto of a River and Harbor Bill by President Polk. The meeting, attended by 2,300 people from eighteen states, was well covered by the press. Horace Greeley of the *New York Tribune* was present and stressed the need for closer commercial ties between mid-Atlantic and western states. After the formal sessions had ended Greeley himself took the chair, and resolutions were adopted in favor of a transcontinental railroad following a central route.

A third convention was held in Saint Louis in October 1849, specifically to review the ways and means of obtaining a railroad to the Pacific. Two of the largest delegations came from Missouri and Illinois. The two railroad-minded senators from these states, Douglas and Benton, were rivals for the chairmanship. Douglas won, but suspected that the "honor" had been given him in order to muzzle him. The final action of the convention was to favor a Pacific railroad from Saint Louis to San Francisco, with major branch lines also to be built to Chicago and Memphis. A few days later a second convention in Memphis convened. Such national figures as Asa Whitney and Senator Jefferson Davis were in attendance, but the sessions were dominated by southerners. Quite naturally the convention endorsed a southern route to the Pacific with the eastern terminus to be located at Memphis. In the next few years other conventions were held in Iowa City, New Orleans, and Little Rock. Almost without exception each meeting favored a railway that would serve its own geographic region. They could agree on one point—in some

Chicago skyline and the new Illinois Central station, completed in 1856.
Early visitors to the depot, who felt the station much too large, were soon
proven very wrong. (COURTESY, ILLINOIS CENTRAL RAILROAD.)

The new rail service
between Cincinnati and St.
Louis, available with the
1857 opening of the broad
gauge Ohio & Mississippi,
was a trip of only 340
miles, about half the riverboat distance via the Ohio
and Mississippi rivers.
(COURTESY, INDIANA HISTOR-
ICAL SOCIETY.)

fashion the federal government should help finance and support the iron road to the Pacific.[13]

Only visionaries thought it possible to build more than one railroad to the Pacific. Most promoters realized that the extraordinary costs of building a line over mountains and deserts, through Indian country, and ahead of the frontier would be so great that only one route could be selected—the question was which.

The federal government sought a solution to the problem when Congress, on March 3, 1853, appropriated $150,000 to the War Department for surveys of several routes for the Pacific railroad. The approach was a natural one, since many U.S. army officers had helped with numerous railroad surveys in the early years of construction during the 1830s. General plans for the surveys were made by two army colonels, John J. Abert and Stephen H. Long. Colonel Abert, who definitely favored a southern route, had long headed the Topographical Bureau. Colonel Long had had much experience with railroad surveying, especially for the early Baltimore & Ohio. The colonels recommended the survey of four routes to the Pacific, three under the direction of topographical engineers and one under Isaac I. Stevens, governor of Washington Territory and formerly an army engineer.

The surveys approved by the new secretary of war, Jefferson Davis, crossed the western plains and the Rocky Mountains along four rather parallel routes: a northern survey along the 47th parallel, a central survey along the 38th parallel, another near the 35th parallel, and the last along the 32d parallel.[14] Secretary Davis was not at all certain that $150,000 would be sufficient to complete all the proposed explorations, but he at once organized the several expeditions. Since Davis insisted that the military, commercial, and agricultural aspects of the various routes also be considered, the survey parties were instructed to collect data on the meteorology, geology, botany, and zoology of the West.

Governor Stevens was placed in charge of the northern route running west from Saint Paul, with assistance from

Captain George B. McClellan, who headed up a survey party to study a route through the passes of the Cascade range. The second party, which followed the 38th parallel west from Saint Louis across the plains of Kansas to the Great Salt Lake and northern California, was placed under Captain T. W. Gunnison. Lieutenant A. W. Whipple was directed to make the survey along the 35th parallel from Fort Smith, Arkansas, via Albuquerque on west to southern California. Finally, the most southern route along the 32nd parallel was placed in charge of Captain John Pope and Lieutenant John G. Parke.

Eventually the preliminary surveys of the several proposed routes were completed. The northernmost route (47th parallel) was estimated to be at least 1,800 miles in length and to have an approximate cost of perhaps $125 million. The central route, near the 38th parallel, was believed to have a length of between 2,300 and 2,500 miles and to cross mountains so rugged as to make the entire project "impracticable." The third route along the 35th parallel via Albuquerque to San Pedro (now Los Angeles) was estimated to be under 2,100 miles in length. Lieutenant Whipple at first made a staggering mathematical error running into tens of millions of dollars in his estimate, but the corrected figure was lowered to $99 million. Finally, the southern route along the 32d parallel from Texas to San Diego was estimated to have a length of less than 1,700 miles and a price tag of perhaps $72 million.[15]

As a southerner, Secretary Davis naturally favored this route from Texas to San Diego. Objectively the 32d parallel route had many advantages. Both in length and projected cost it had advantages over those further north. Being further south, and passing through lower elevations, the menace of winter snows was minimal. Finally, the southern route had the added advantage of being projected through a continuous sequence of organized states and territories, namely, Texas, New Mexico, and California. The proponents of the southern line were embarrassed, however, that the projected route at one place dipped well below the American-Mexican border.

Northerners of course feared that a southern railroad to the Pacific might tip California and much of the West into the prosouthern camp. At the same time Davis and his southern supporters felt that a central or northern route to the Pacific would hasten the admission of additional free states. Even before the final debates were held on this railroad issue, Davis was trying to help the transport problems in Texas. In his annual departmental report to President Pierce, on December 1, 1856, he discussed the importation of a cargo of thirty-two camels for use at army posts in the interior of Texas.[16]

Even before the survey had been fully completed, prosouthern interests in the Pierce administration were taking care of the disturbing problem that a portion of the southern route lay in Mexican territory. In May 1853 President Pierce had appointed James Gadsden, president of the South Carolina Railroad during the forties and perennial promoter of railroad conventions, as minister to Mexico. Gadsden had specific instructions to negotiate the purchase of an area south of the Gila River needed for the preferred southern route. By December Gadsden had signed a treaty for the purchase of a sandy triangle of land south of the Gila now comprising portions of southern New Mexico and Arizona. Pierce sent the treaty to the Senate early in 1854, but the necessary two-thirds favorable vote was hard to achieve, since Senator Thomas Hart Benton was bitterly opposed: he said the area was worthless and quoted Kit Carson's comment that a wolf could not make a living from it. Finally in June 1854 the necessary support was obtained; the nation spent $10 million for 29,640 square miles of desolate and sandy Mexican real estate south of the Gila River.

Senator Stephen A. Douglas was one of a handful of northwestern senators that had supported the Gadsden Treaty. But in the early months of 1854 he was more vitally concerned with the Kansas-Nebraska bill, which, as chairman of the Committee on Territories, he had introduced in January. Under this proposal two new territories—Nebraska, west of Iowa, and Kansas, west of Missouri—were to be organized, with the status of slavery in each territory to be settled by the respective territorial legislatures according to the principle of popular sovereignty. Eventually included in the proposal was a specific provision providing for the repeal of the Missouri Compromise. There was a rather general expectation among congressmen that Kansas would become a slave state, whereas Nebraska would be a free state. With help from Jefferson Davis and others Douglas obtained the support of President Pierce for his proposal. The Kansas-Nebraska Act was passed by the Senate on March 3, 1854 by a vote of 37 to 14, and on May 22, 1854 the House approved it by a vote of 113 to 100. Eight days later the president signed the legislation.

Certainly historians have never fully agreed as to why Douglas pushed the Kansas-Nebraska bill. Perhaps he only wanted to further the expansion and settlement of his own region. Others have claimed he was courting the South in order to further his own presidential ambitions. There can be no doubt that the proposal was intended to help the building of a Pacific railroad along a central route. Secretary Davis, in advancing his preference for a southern route, had pointed to the presence of territorial government in New Mexico and its absence in the region of the central route. Detractors of Douglas have of course pointed to the financial gain Douglas could have expected if a Pacific railroad had Chicago as its eastern terminal. The senator had substantial land holdings in Chicago and northern Illinois.

The passage of the Kansas-Nebraska Act created far more violent reactions and results than Douglas had expected. Not only did it repeal the Missouri Compromise but it helped to destroy the Compromise of 1850. It drastically reshaped American politics: a split appeared within the Democratic party, the Whig party started to disappear, and the new Republican party was born. Most importantly, the fires of the slavery and sectional controversies burned more intensely than they had for many years. This heated sectional struggle rather quickly diverted attention away from any further serious consideration of a Pacific railway.

Douglas did manage to revive the Pacific railway issue

briefly during the short session (1854–55) of the Thirty-Third Congress. Earlier, during the first months of 1854, Douglas had been one of nine members appointed to a select committee of the Senate created to consider specific proposals for a rail line to the Pacific. This committee tended to favor a Douglas proposal that *three* railroads—following northern, central, and southern routes—be built to the coast. When the Pacific railway issue was reviewed during the short session, the Douglas three-route proposal was given priority by select committees from both houses. In mid-January 1855 Douglas was quite hopeful that the bill would be approved. The three-route proposal passed the Senate by a close vote on February 19, but the lower house failed to act, and the measure died with the adjournment of the session.[17]

Eventually in 1860 the final reports of the 1853 U.S. army surveys were published in 13 volumes. The lengthy reports fully covered Indian life, weather, geology, and the fauna and flora of the West—but it was far too late to help break the stalemate over the establishment of a single rail route to the Pacific. For several years past the hostility between North and South had made such a decision impossible. The Panic of 1857 rendered an agreement over a railroad to the Pacific coast even more difficult. During the hard times of the late 1850s several voices in the nation were declaring that the country already had too many railroads. Certainly the Buchanan administration had many problems more urgent than the issue of a railroad to the Pacific. Such decisions were to be postponed until the Lincoln presidency.

CHAPTER FIVE

Iron Roads in the West

ON April 22, 1856, the citizens of Rock Island, Illinois, and Davenport, Iowa, cheered vigorously as they watched three puffing engines pull eight passenger cars safely across the newly finished Chicago & Rock Island Railroad bridge over the Mississippi. The five fixed spans and longer "swing" or draw span had a total length of nearly a third of a mile and had taken three years to complete. The six spans of this first railroad bridge over the mighty river had been constructed out of a million feet of timber and more than 600,000 pounds of wrought and cast iron. A few people on the river banks—the ferry boatmen, the stage drivers, and the friends of the river steamers—scoffed at the achievement, but most onlookers were enthusiastic about the new rail service from Iowa to the eastern seaboard.[1] Now the people of eastern Iowa could reach New York City by rail in no more than forty-two hours.

Perhaps the proudest man on the river bank that spring day was 52-year-old Henry Farnam, supervisor of the construction of the bridge and, since 1854, president of the Rock Island. This self-taught surveyor from New York and Connecticut had had extensive experience with eastern canals and Michigan railroads before coming to Chicago. With his partner, Joseph E. Sheffield, Farnam had finished the construction of the Chicago & Rock Island ahead of schedule. When formally opened in June 1854, the 181-mile road from Chicago had cost less than $4 million, and included 28 locomotives, 28 passenger cars, and 350 freight cars. A few months later Farnam was elected president of the road, upon the retirement of John B. Jervis.

In the 1850s the western states planned and built dozens of railroads like the Chicago & Rock Island. The enthusiasm started early. An editorial by Henry V. Poor in the *American Railroad Journal* in fall 1850 noted this widespread desire for railroads:

> The public feeling in the West, upon the subject of railroads, is excited to an extraordinary degree. The people of every town and county in the great valley, are now putting forth all their means to secure to themselves the advantages of railroads. This feeling has received a great impulse from the action of the leading cities there, and the recent grant of land to the State of Illinois for her great line. Cincinnati has just voted to subscribe $1,000,000 to the four projected roads leading from that city. St. Louis has subscribed $500,000 for her great line westward. . . . The West is now the great theatre of railroading in this country. It will always continue to be so, from its extent, from the necessity there exists there for these works, in enabling its population to forward the products of their soil to market.[2]

During the decade the West built nearly 10,000 miles of railroad, far more than either the South or the Northeast. (The western states here included are the five states of the Old Northwest, the three trans-Mississippi states of Minnesota, Iowa, and Missouri, and the two Pacific coast states of Oregon and California.) Eight of the ten states had railroads in operation by 1860. The other two states, Oregon and Minnesota, each had some rail line in operation by the spring of 1862. The details of railroad development and expansion in the West are shown in Table 5.1.[3]

In 1850 only one western state, Ohio, had more than 500 miles of railroad. Ten years later all but one of the western states with operating railroads had well above 500 miles in operation, and three of these states had more than 2,000 miles of line. In 1850 the 1,276 miles of line in the West was less than a quarter of the mileage operating in the eleven northeastern states, and only about three-fifths of the trackage in the southern states. By 1860 the more than 11,000

TABLE 5.1
RAILROAD CONSTRUCTION IN THE WEST DURING THE
1850S

	Mileage in 1850	Mileage in 1860	Increase in Decade	Percentage of Increase	Investment per Mile in 1860
Ohio	575	2,946	2,371	412%	$37,311
Indiana	228	2,163	1,935	848	33,080
Illinois	111	2,790	2,679	2,413	36,603
Michigan	342	779	437	127	38,813
Wisconsin	20	905	885	4,425	36,393
Minnesota	—	—	—	—	
Iowa	—	655	655	—	28,709
Missouri	—	817	817	—	50,826
Oregon	—	—	—	—	
California	—	23	23	—	51,428
Total	1,276	11,078	9,802	768%	$36,548
	(5 states)	(8 states)			

miles in the West was well above the mileage in the other two
regions. In 1850 New York, Pennsylvania, and Massachusetts
ranked first, second, and third in railroad mileage. On the
eve of the Civil War the same three states were only third,
fourth, and eighth in rail mileage. The West was indeed the
"great theatre of railroading in the country."

Much of the leadership earlier enjoyed by the mid-Atlantic and New England states was lost to the Old Northwest
during the 1850s, when the region added thousands and
thousands of miles of new line. Ohio, which had ranked only
fifth in 1850, by 1860 was claiming 2,946 miles of line and
was first among all the states. Illinois in 1850, with only two
short lines running west of Chicago and west of Springfield,
had only 111 miles of railroad and ranked eighteenth in
mileage in the nation. Ten years later her 2,790 miles of line
placed her second in mileage, just behind Ohio. The five-
state area had over 9,500 miles of road in 1860. Behind Ohio
and Illinois, Indiana (2,163 miles) ranked fifth, while Wisconsin ranked twelfth and Michigan fifteenth in the nation. By
the eve of the Civil War the iron network between western
Pennsylvania and the Mississippi River seemed quite com-

plete, with most of the new lines running east and west. In 1860 six different lines crossed into Ohio from Pennsylvania and Virginia, eight roads crossed the Ohio-Indiana border, and seven railroads ran from Indiana into Illinois. In western Illinois eight different westward-running roads had reached the Mississippi River by 1860.

Naturally the western states had a percentage rate of increase far above the rest of the nation. During the 1850s New England increased its iron network by only 46 percent, the mid-Atlantic states little more than doubled their rail mileage, and the southern states increased their system by a healthy 347 percent. In the western states the increase was a staggering 768 percent between 1850 and 1860. The new construction in Ohio, 2,371 miles, was twice the total for the six New England states, while Indiana and Illinois together, with 4,613 new miles of line, built more than was added in the five mid-Atlantic states during the decade. The four states directly west of Pennsylvania—Ohio, Indiana, Illinois, and Iowa—together constructed 7,640 miles of road, more than was constructed in the entire South during the 1850s. The states just west of the Mississippi by themselves constructed substantial mileage. The 1,472 miles built in Iowa and Missouri was 25 percent greater than the total new construction in New England. Only two states among the eleven northeastern states—Pennsylvania and New York—added more mileage in the 1850s than Iowa or Missouri.

Money as well as mileage was involved in the rapid railroad development in the West. The 11,000 miles of western mileage in 1860 represented an average investment of $36,548 per mile, not much below the national average of $37,487. Each of the five states in the Old Northwest had per mile cost figures very close to the average for the entire area. Variations were found only west of the Mississippi, with Iowa on the low side and Missouri and California on the high. In the East the average investment was $47,823 per mile for the eleven New England and mid-Atlantic states, while the twelve southern states, with their more lightly built lines, had an average per mile of only $26,947.

Certainly there was more new money invested in western

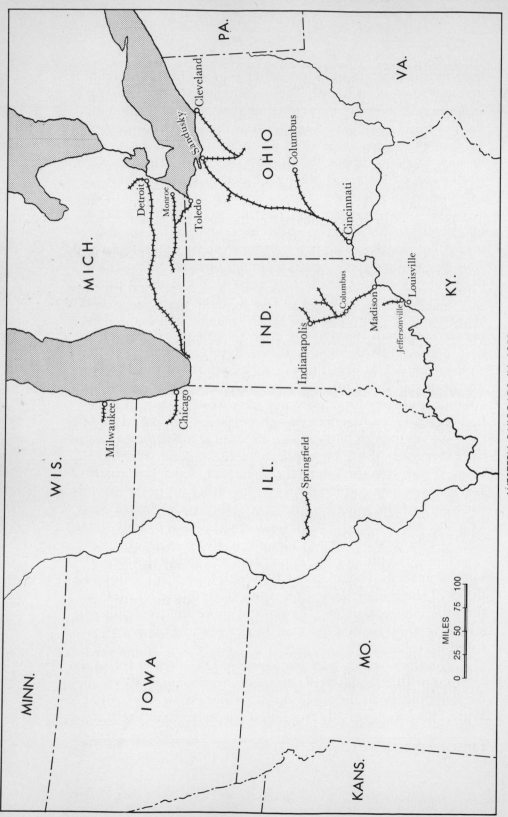

WESTERN RAILROADS IN 1850

MINN.

WIS.

IOWA

MICH.

Milwaukee

Detroit

Monroe

Chicago

ILL.

Springfield

IND.

Indianapolis

Columbus

Madison

Jeffersonville

KANS.

MO.

KY.

Louisville

Cincinnati

Columbus

OHIO

Toledo

Sandusky

Cleveland

PA.

VA.

MILES
0   25   50   75   100

lines in the 1850s than in any other region. The $390 million invested in western lines in the decade before the Civil War represented about 45 percent of all new railroad capital in the period. The money spent on new lines in Ohio—just over $100 million—was twice the investment for rail construction in New England during the decade. The two trans-Mississippi states of Iowa and Missouri together outspent New England for new construction. The three states west of Pennsylvania—Ohio, Indiana, and Illinois—together had a larger investment for new construction than the total for the five mid-Atlantic states. The two leading western states, Ohio and Illinois, together spent nearly as much on new railroads as the total new investment in the twelve states of the South.[4]

The western states had the most rail mileage of the three regions, and smallest number of individual companies. The western railroads listed in the 1860 Census represented less than a quarter of the national total. The 113 roads in the western states compared to 115 different lines in the twelve southern states and the 235 separate roads in the eleven mid-Atlantic and New England states. As a result, western lines had a greater average length—98 miles—as compared to 83 miles for the South and only 43 miles in the Northeast. Naturally there was also a preponderance of longer roads in the western states on the eve of the Civil War. Forty-one roads of 100 miles or more in length were operating in the West; only thirty-five of the same length were found in the South. New England and the mid-Atlantic states had a total of only thirty roads of 80 miles or more in length in the year 1860.

The great bulk of the longer western railroads were located in Ohio, Indiana, and Illinois. These three states had thirty of the longer lines, while only eleven were located in the other western states. The lines of more than 100 miles in length in 1860 located in Ohio, Indiana, and Illinois are listed in Table 5.2.[5]

The thirty major lines (fourteen in Ohio, six in Indiana, and ten in Illinois) listed above made up the vast bulk of all the rail mileage in the three states on the eve of the Civil War. These major roads accounted for more than three-

TABLE 5.2
MAJOR RAILROADS IN OHIO, INDIANA, AND ILLINOIS IN 1860

Railroad	State	Length in 1850	Length in 1860 100–199 miles	Length in 1860 over 200 miles	Later Name
Bellefontaine & Indiana	Ohio	—	118		New York Central
Central Ohio	Ohio	—	137		B. & O.
Cincinnati, Wilmington & Zanesville	Ohio	—	132		Pennsylvania
Cleveland, Columbus & Cincinnati	Ohio	135	141		New York Central
Cleveland & Pittsburgh	Ohio	—		203	Pennsylvania
Cleveland & Toledo	Ohio	—	188		New York Central
Columbus, Piqua & Indiana	Ohio	—	103		Pennsylvania
Dayton & Michigan	Ohio	—	144		B. & O.
Marietta & Cincinnati	Ohio	—		204	B. & O.
Pittsburgh, Ft. Wayne & Chicago	Ohio	—		467	Pennsylvania
Sandusky, Dayton & Cincinnati	Ohio	173	173		New York Central
Sandusky, Mansfield & Newark	Ohio	116	126		B. & O.
Steubenville & Indiana	Ohio	—	125		Pennsylvania
Toledo, Wabash & Western	Ohio	—		243	Wabash
Cincinnati & Chicago	Ind.	—	108		Pennsylvania
Evansville & Crawfordsville	Ind.	—	132		Chgo. & Eastern Ill.
Indianapolis & Cincinnati	Ind.	—	109		New York Central
Louisville, New Albany & Chicago	Ind.	35		288	Monon
Madison & Indianapolis	Ind.	86	135		Pennsylvania
Ohio & Mississippi	Ind.	—		340	B. & O.

(*Table 5.2 Cont'd*)

Chicago, Alton & St. Louis	Ill.	—	220	Alton
Chicago, Burlington & Quincy	Ill.	13	138	Burlington
Chicago & Northwestern	Ill.	—	213	Chgo. & N.W.
Chicago & Rock Island	Ill.	—	181	Chgo. & R.I.
Galena & Chicago Union	Ill.	42	261	Chgo. & N.W.
Great Western	Ill.	55	182	Wabash
Illinois Central	Ill.	—	738	Ill. Central
Logansport, Peoria & Burlington	Ill.	—	171	Pennsylvania
Quincy & Chicago	Ill.	—	100	Burlington
Terre Haute, Alton & St. Louis	Ill.	—	208	New York Central

quarters of the total rail lines in the area. The six roads in Indiana made up over half of that state's mileage, but the major lines amounted to four-fifths of the total in both Ohio and Illinois. In all three states most of the 1860 mileage had been built during the 1850s. Only eight of the lines had any mileage in 1850, and in only three instances were the lines basically completed by that date.

As in the South and the Northeast, many of these major western lines were to be merged into larger systems in later years. Within a generation after the Civil War nearly two-thirds of the total group of railroads (nineteen out of thirty) were to come under the control of three large eastern systems: the Pennsylvania (eight lines), the New York Central (six lines), and the Baltimore & Ohio (five lines). The domination by these eastern systems was most evident in Ohio and Indiana. In those two states seventeen out of the twenty railroads would ultimately be controlled by one of the three giant rail systems. The three remaining roads would eventually be included in smaller midwestern lines—the Wabash, the Chicago & Eastern Illinois, and the Monon.

The picture was different in Illinois, where only two of the ten major roads in 1860 were later to merge with big eastern railroads. The growing rail center of Chicago was the home base for eight of the major roads in the Prairie State. Such lines as the Illinois Central, the Burlington, the Chicago & Northwestern, and the Chicago & Rock Island were far more immediately concerned with midwestern traffic directed toward Chicago than with traffic or rail connections oriented toward eastern states.

Ohio at midcentury already had several operating railroads, and in 1850 ranked fifth in mileage among the states. As the state increased its mileage fivefold during the fifties, all but three of the fourteen major lines rapidly constructed new mileage. Thirteen of the fourteen lines would ultimately come under the control of the Pennsylvania (five lines), the New York Central (four lines), or the Baltimore & Ohio (four lines). Several of the roads were actually planned and constructed as western extensions of the larger eastern roads.

Five major roads in Ohio—the Pittsburgh, Fort Wayne & Chicago, the Cleveland & Pittsburgh, the Columbus, Piqua & Indiana, the Steubenville & Indiana, and the Cincinnati, Wilmington and Zanesville—were either planned by the Pennsylvania Railroad or were destined to be rather quickly merged into that major eastern rail system. These five roads, forming a total network of more than 1,000 miles, served directly or indirectly most of the major cities in Ohio. They were connected in the east with Pittsburgh, the western terminal of the Pennsylvania Railroad.

The 467-mile Pittsburgh, Fort Wayne & Chicago was by far the most important of the five roads. The first segment of this westward-looking line was the Ohio & Pennsylvania Railroad, chartered in both states early in 1848 to run from the Ohio River at Pittsburgh into northern central Ohio. Ground was broken in July 1849, and by the end of 1851 some 83 miles of road had been built from Allegheny City (just across the Ohio from Pittsburgh) to Alliance, Ohio. During 1852 and 1853 General William Robinson, president of the Ohio & Pennsylvania, succeeded in getting the Pennsylvania Railroad to subscribe to $300,000 of stock in the

This wood-burner of the mid-1850s is stopping for fuel at an Illinois woodlot. Stops for fuel were fairly frequent, since the average engine consumed one to two cords of wood each day. (COURTESY, CHICAGO & EASTERN ILLINOIS RAILROAD.)

smaller western line. Robinson, the first mayor of Allegheny City, had long been interested in the iron mills and transportation of western Pennsylvania. The Ohio and Pennsylvania opened its entire 187-mile line, from Allegheny City to Crestline, Ohio, on April 11, 1853. By 1855–56 the line represented a total investment of more than $6 million and owned 51 locomotives, 53 passenger and baggage cars, and 608 freight cars. Its revenues were about a million dollars yearly, three-fifths from passenger traffic. The line was prosperous enough to be planning the construction of a bridge over the Allegheny River at Pittsburgh, and it was giving financial support to a western connecting road into Chicago.[6]

West of Crestline a connecting road, the Ohio & Indiana, was to give service on to Fort Wayne, Indiana. The line was chartered in Ohio and Indiana in 1850 and 1851, and work began in the spring of 1852. Construction was slow until Thomson and his Pennsylvania Railroad agreed to subscribe to $300,000 of the company's capital stock. The 131-mile line was completed and opened for traffic to Fort Wayne in November 1854. Costing about $3 million to build, the Ohio & Indiana by 1855 had annual revenues of $247,000. As on the connecting road to Pittsburgh, the Ohio & Pennsylvania, passenger revenues on the Ohio & Indiana were larger than those from freight.[7]

The last westward portion of the Pittsburgh to Chicago line was the Fort Wayne & Chicago Railroad, chartered in Indiana and Illinois in 1852 and 1853. Construction was delayed on this road, and by 1855 the line had been built only to Columbia, 20 miles west of Fort Wayne. Even worse, the credit of the new line was exhausted and the company was burdened with a substantial unfunded debt. In the early months of 1856, the other two lines east of Fort Wayne also faced financial problems. As a result, the consolidation of the three roads into the Pittsburgh, Fort Wayne & Chicago was completed by August 1, 1856.

The president of the newly organized Pittsburgh, Fort Wayne & Chicago was George Washington Cass, nephew of the active Democratic political leader Lewis Cass, and

recently elected president of the Ohio and Pennsylvania.
Cass, a long-time leader in steamboat and stage-line transportation in western Pennsylvania, was also active in the Adams Express Company, a major express line in the northeastern states. Another leading director in the new Pittsburgh to Chicago railroad was Thomson of the Pennsylvania. New credit from the Pennsylvania permitted Cass's line to be extended westward 45 miles to Plymouth, Indiana, and also aided in the 1857 completion of the new railroad bridge across the Allegheny into Pittsburgh. The new money also financed the upgrading and ballasting of much track in Ohio and the purchase of 25 new engines and more than 300 passenger and freight cars.[8]

In January 1858 Thomson was elected chief engineer of the company with full powers to complete the Pittsburgh, Fort Wayne, and Chicago line into Chicago. With the same vigor he had earlier shown in Pennsylvania and Georgia, Thomson quickly started the project. Using old rail taken up from the Portage Railroad in central Pennsylvania, plus financial support from the Pennsylvania Railroad, he completed the 85 miles of line into the Windy City by January 1, 1859. By March 1858, the completion of the bridge over the Allegheny made possible a physical connection at Pittsburgh between the Pennsylvania Railroad and its subordinate line to the west. The new through route soon had a 20 percent increase in traffic, and its 177 locomotives, 159 passenger cars, and 1,293 freight cars during 1859 produced total revenues of $1,966,000. However, expenses and debt charges were also up, and the bondholders forced the Pittsburgh, Fort Wayne & Chicago into receivership late in 1859. William B. Ogden, a veteran rail executive from Chicago, was appointed receiver for the road. The company was successfully reorganized, and a decade later was leased in perpetuity to the Pennsylvania Railroad.[9]

The other four Ohio lines that would later be controlled by the Pennsylvania were less important than the road to Chicago. Oldest was the Cleveland & Pittsburgh, chartered in Ohio in 1836 and in Pennsylvania in 1850. In 1851 and 1852 the road was constructed 101 miles from Cleveland to Wellsville on the Ohio River. Later in 1856 it was extended 23 miles up the river valley to Rochester, Pennsylvania, where it connected with the Ohio & Pennsylvania (Pittsburgh, Fort Wayne & Chicago). By the mid-1850s the road had cost about $5 million, had annual revenues of more than $500,000, and paid occasional dividends. By 1860 branch lines built in eastern Ohio pushed the total route to 203 miles. In that same year the Cleveland & Pittsburgh was leased to the Pennsylvania Railroad.

A third line, the Steubenville & Indiana, was chartered in 1854 to build a railroad from Steubenville on the upper Ohio River across Ohio to the Indiana state line. At Steubenville this road had a connection with a branch of the Cleveland & Pittsburgh, which provided an indirect route up the Ohio Valley to Pittsburgh. In 1854 half a million dollars' worth of the line's bonds were guaranteed by the Pennsylvania. During 1854 and 1855 the road was built westward from Steubenville 125 miles to Newark, Ohio, where the connecting line, the Central Ohio, gave service into Columbus. Within a few years the Steubenville & Indiana was merged with other connecting lines to form the Pittsburgh, Cincinnati & St. Louis, which was controlled by the Pennsylvania.

The last two Ohio lines later to be under Pennsylvania control were the Columbus, Piqua & Indiana and the Cincinnati, Wilmington & Zanesville. Both roads were located in southern Ohio and were rather limited in mileage. The Columbus, Piqua and Indiana line, built between 1853 and 1859, ran 103 miles west from Columbus to Union City on the Ohio-Indiana border. The Cincinnati, Wilmington, & Zanesville was incorporated in 1851 and built between 1853 and 1855 from Zanesville, on the Ohio Central, to Morrow, where it had trackage rights on the Little Miami into Cincinnati. Lacking major terminals of its own, the 132-mile road never prospered and was in receivership by 1857.[10] Both this line and the Columbus, Piqua & Indiana road were controlled by the Pennsylvania within a few years after the Civil War.

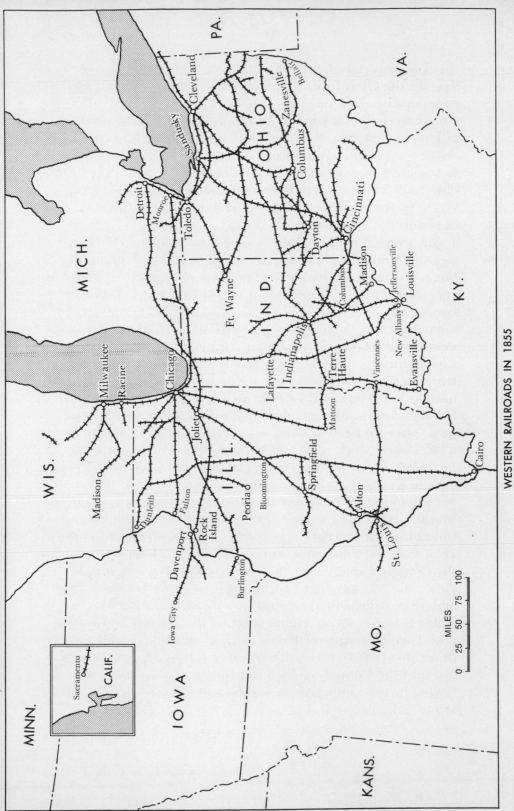

WESTERN RAILROADS IN 1855

MINN.

WIS.

MICH.

PA.

VA.

OHIO

Cleveland
Sandusky
Zanesville
Bellaire
Columbus
Toledo
Dayton
Cincinnati
Detroit
Monroe

IND.

Ft. Wayne
Indianapolis
Columbus
Madison
Jeffersonville
Louisville
New Albany
Evansville
Vincennes
Terre Haute
Lafayette
Mattoon

KY.

IOWA

Iowa City
Burlington
Davenport
Rock Island
Dunleith
Fulton
Peoria
Bloomington
Madison
Milwaukee
Racine
Chicago
Joliet

ILL.

Springfield
Alton
St. Louis
Cairo

MO.

KANS.

CALIF.
Sacramento

MILES
0   25   50   75   100

Four major railroads in Ohio—the Cleveland and Toledo, the Cleveland, Columbus, and Cincinnati, the Sandusky, Dayton & Cincinnati, and the Bellefontaine & Indiana—would all later be included in the New York Central system. Two of these lines were basically finished by mid-century; two were constructed during the fifties. None of the four on the eve of the Civil War dominated the region as had the Pittsburgh, Fort Wayne & Chicago.

The Cleveland & Toledo, plus a shorter line, the 96-mile Cleveland, Painesville & Ashtabula, eventually were to be major portions of the Lake Shore Line, the principal route of the New York Central across Ohio.[11] During the 1840s Cleveland had not been active in the promotion of railroads, since she had the Ohio Canal and a fine location on Lake Erie. But overland transport was still important. Published reports at the end of the decade estimated that in 1849 some 75,000 hogs and 20,000 head of cattle had been driven eastward along the lake shore toward Buffalo. In that same year the Cleveland, Painesville & Ashtabula was granted a charter to build a line from Cleveland, a city of perhaps 15,000, up the lake shore to the Pennsylvania state line. Alfred Kelley, long a sponsor of canals in Ohio, was offered the presidency but declined, since he was already deeply involved with the direction of two other roads in Ohio, the Columbus & Xenia and the Cleveland, Columbus & Cincinnati.

During 1851 and 1852 the new line was constructed up the lake shore to Conneaut, 68 miles east of Cleveland, and near the border of Pennsylvania. One of the contractors for this first construction was Amasa Stone of Connecticut, long president of the railroad. During the early construction in 1851 Alfred Kelley had left the presidency of the Cleveland, Columbus & Cincinnati to become president of the Cleveland, Painesville & Ashtabula. Kelley, in poor health because of his earlier strenuous life as a canal builder, was the man of whom Henry Clay had said, "He had too much cast-iron in his composition to be popular." Popular or not, Kelley still possessed the strong leadership needed to meet the opposition of Erie, Pennsylvania, as the C.P.& A. sought to cross the 40-mile strip of Pennsylvania lake shore on its way to connect with the Erie and New York Central lines in western New York State.

As the line east of Cleveland was projected and built toward Pennsylvania and Erie, the residents of that city, the state of Pennsylvania, and the managers of the Pennsylvania Railroad all became aroused. They did not wish to see the western commerce and trade of Ohio diverted to the railroads of New York. The commercial interests in Pennsylvania and Philadelphia were quite jealous of the growing trade of the Empire State and New York City. Earlier, in 1848, the Pennsylvania state legislature had actually passed a law which for a brief time prohibited the construction of any "Ohio gauge" line within the borders of the state! The C.P.& A., like most lines in Ohio, was built in the gauge of 4 feet 10 inches introduced into Ohio when the *Sandusky,* the first locomotive in the state, happened to be built in that unusual gauge. The city fathers of Erie became so excited that they managed to get a state law passed in 1851 to the effect that all lines built east of Erie must be either in the broad 6-ft. gauge or the standard gauge of 4 feet 8½ inches. The city officials figured that if the rascals from Ohio succeeded in reaching their town, at least the break in gauge at Erie would work to their benefit.

In the meantime Alfred Kelley and friends of the Cleveland, Painesville & Ashtabula had acquired control of a Pennsylvania Corporation, the Franklin Canal Company. Earlier, in 1849, this company had acquired a change in its charter that permitted it to build a railroad along its towpath. Suddenly the Franklin Canal became more of a railroad than a canal, and by November 1852, track of the Ohio gauge was built into Erie, with several miles of the line being some distance from any towpath. Influence of some kind, possibly monetary, was brought to bear upon the state legislature in Harrisburg, and in the spring of 1853 the Pennsylvania lawmakers repealed the 1851 law that had prohibited the "Ohio gauge" to be built east of Erie. Open violence now reigned in the vicinity of Erie for some weeks, with track being torn up and relaid with regularity. Eventually Kelley and his C.P.& A. won out, and by the mid-1850s peace prevailed in the area. The two lines between Erie and Buffalo, both under the influence of the New York Central and both constructed in the Ohio gauge, connected at Erie with the C.P.& A., which now operated 96 miles of 4 ft. 10 in. track running westward to Cleveland. In the late 1850s Amasa Stone became president of the line, remaining in that position until after its merger into the Lake Shore Railway Line in 1869.[12]

The construction of a line from Cleveland westward to Toledo was less difficult. Two different lines, the Junction Railroad and the Toledo, Norwalk & Cleveland, were chartered by 1850. During 1853 the Junction built 63 miles of line from Cleveland west to Sandusky. During the same year the Toledo, Norwalk & Cleveland constructed an 88-mile line from Toledo to Grafton, where it connected with the Cleveland, Columbus & Cincinnati for service into Cleveland. The two rival roads were merged in September 1853 into the Cleveland & Toledo Railroad. Two years later a 40-mile line from Sandusky was built to Millbury, just outside of Toledo, but the track was so hard to maintain that it later was torn up. In 1857 the Cleveland & Toledo represented a total investment of more than $6 million, and included an equipment roster of 32 locomotives, 73 passenger cars, and 417 freight cars. Passenger traffic made up nearly two-thirds of the million-dollar annual revenue. Even though the Cleveland & Toledo was built in standard gauge, instead of the 4 ft. 10 in. gauge more common in the state, it had close working connections with the Cleveland, Painesville & Ashtabula. A decade later the two roads were merged to form the Lake Shore Line under the control of the New York Central.[13]

Railroad service south of Cleveland was provided by the Cleveland, Columbus & Cincinnati, chartered in 1845. Stock subscriptions were hard to find in Ohio, and eastern capitalists were equally uninterested. Finally one of the road's major sponsors, Henry B. Payne, a Cleveland attorney and Democratic political leader, convinced Alfred Kelley to become a director, and later president, of the unbuilt line. Under Kelley's leadership contracts were let to a firm headed by Amasa Stone, who would be superintendent and still later president of the road. The road from Cleveland to Columbus was largely built in 1850 and opened early in 1851. By 1853 three trains a day were running over the 135-mile line.

Since connecting roads had earlier been built between Columbus and Cincinnati, no further construction efforts were made by the C. C. & C. When Kelley left the line for the challenges facing the Cleveland, Painesville & Ashtabula, his place was taken by Payne, who had earlier recruited Kelley. The 1850s were prosperous years for Payne and the C. C. & C., and the line paid regular dividends throughout the decade, mainly because the road's cost of about $4 million was nearly all in capital stock with a very small bonded indebtedness. The prosperity of the road even permitted it to provide financial aid to other roads being built in the state. In the years after the Civil War the C. C. & C. merged with other midwestern lines to form what eventually became the Cleveland, Cincinnati, Chicago & St. Louis ("Big Four"), a road controlled by the New York Central.[14]

Two other major lines in Ohio were ultimately to become New York Central property. The older of the two roads, the Mad River & Lake Erie, was chartered in 1832, when the people of Sandusky discovered they were not included in the canal-building program of the state. As hopes and aspirations for the rail project were in greater supply than hard cash, construction was very slow. However, by 1848 the road was completed from Sandusky to Bellefontaine, a distance of 102 miles. Between 1848 and 1851 the line was extended through Springfield to Dayton, where there was connecting rail service to Cincinnati. During the mid- 1850s the 173-mile railroad paid modest dividends. Later, in 1858, the Mad River & Lake Erie was reorganized as the Sandusky, Dayton & Cincinnati. Several years after the Civil War the road was acquired by the "Big Four" and the New York Central.[15]

The Bellefontaine & Indiana was the fourth and last major road in Ohio destined for the New York Central sys-

"Old Number 9" was a Chicago & Alton day coach reconstructed in the late 1850s into a sleeping car following plans by George Pullman. (COURTESY, PULLMAN COMPANY.)

tem. This road was chartered in February 1848 by Ohio to build a road from Galion, Ohio, on the route of the Cleveland, Columbus & Cincinnati, westward to Union City, an unbuilt but staked-out town on the Ohio-Indiana border. In the same month the state of Indiana was chartering a companion line, the Indianapolis & Bellefontaine, to be built from Union City west to the state capital of Indiana. Construction on the line in Ohio started in 1852, and the first 20 miles of road were completed between Galion and Marion.

Soon the Cleveland, Columbus & Cincinnati was providing substantial financial support to the Bellefontaine and Indiana by endorsing its bonds and making cash loans. The 118-mile line to Union City was completed in 1854, via Bellefontaine, where it intersected the north-south road, the Mad River & Lake Erie. During the decade the road never prospered, even though it was part of a new through route to Indiana. In 1855 John Brough, Ohio lawyer, newspaper publisher, and former Democratic state official, was elected president of the I. & B. Since Brough was also president of the connecting line east of Union City, a joint working agreement was hammered out between the two lines, soon jointly known as the Bellefontaine Line. After the Civil War a series of mergers brought both roads into the New York Central's "Big Four" line.[16]

Four of the major lines operating in Ohio on the eve of the Civil War were eventually to be controlled by the Baltimore & Ohio. Two of them, the Central Ohio and the Marietta & Cincinnati, as east-west roads, were western extensions of B. & O. from terminal points on the Ohio River. The remaining pair, the Sandusky, Mansfield & Newark and the Dayton & Michigan, were north-south lines that were to extend B. & O. service northward to port cities on Lake Erie.

The Central Ohio was chartered by the state of Ohio in February 1847, more than five years before the B. & O. was to reach Wheeling on the Ohio River. The road was to be built from Columbus to Bellair on the Ohio. Construction started in 1852 in the center of the line, and by the end of

1853 track had been laid from Columbus to Zanesville, a distance of 59 miles. During 1854 the 78 miles of line on east to Bellair was constructed. At Bellair a 1,000-ton ferry gave service across the river to Benwood, four miles down river from Wheeling. No bridge across the Ohio was immediately contemplated by the railroad, but railway officials rather shied away from building at Wheeling—the 1,000-foot suspension bridge built there by John A. Roebling to carry the National Road over the Ohio had recently collapsed in a heavy windstorm.

Hugh J. Jewett, Zanesville lawyer, banker, and a former member of the Ohio state senate, became a director of the Central Ohio in 1855, vice-president in 1856, president in 1857. With a fairly large funded debt, the 137-mile Central Ohio had never been sufficiently prosperous to declare any dividends. Thus the Panic of 1857 brought financial difficulty, and in 1859 Jewett was appointed receiver for the road. Several years later, in 1869, the reorganized road was leased to the Baltimore & Ohio, which later took over full control.[17]

The Marietta & Cincinnati was the second east–west line across Ohio that eventually would come under B. & O. control. This road was an 1851 consolidation of two earlier projected lines, the Belpre & Cincinnati (chartered in August 1847) and the Franklin & Ohio. The proposed route ran from Cincinnati eastward to the Ohio River near Parkersburg, Virginia, the western terminal of a B. & O. subsidiary, the Northwestern Virginia Railroad. William Parker Cutler, a Marietta landowner and politician who later would be a Republican congressman during the Civil War, was the president of the Marietta & Cincinnati throughout the decade. By 1854 Cutler had managed to obtain stock subscriptions from towns, counties, and individuals in southern Ohio totaling nearly $3 million. Hoping that the road might be extended up to Wheeling, the Pennsylvania Railroad was also considering a large stock subscription.

The construction through the hills of southern Ohio was not easy, especially since the surveying engineers wished to have a maximum gradient of 52 feet to the mile. During 1855 a line of 100 miles was built from Loveland, 23 miles east of Cincinnati, to Byers, and a 21-mile branch was constructed to Hillsboro. In 1856 and the early months of 1857 the road was pushed on another 73 miles through Athens to the vicinity of Marietta, where a 9-mile ferriage connected with the Parkersburg Branch across the Ohio. Service from Loveland into Cincinnati was over the tracks of the connecting Little Miami.[18]

Thus by the spring of 1857 it was possible to travel by rail from Baltimore west to Cincinnati and Saint Louis. The B. & O. and the Marietta & Cincinnati (both built in standard gauge) and the 6-ft. gauge Ohio & Mississippi, recently completed from Cincinnati to East Saint Louis, provided a route of some 900 miles from the Atlantic to the Mississippi. This new through line was soon to be called the "American Central Route." Chauncy Brooks, president of the B. & O. since 1855, decided that a giant excursion was in order. The guest lists, special trains, banquets, and speechmaking were all reminiscent of the Erie festivities of 1851. President James Buchanan was unable to attend, but Secretary of State Lewis Cass, Henry Ward Beecher, George Bancroft, and former B. & O. presidents Philip E. Thomas and Thomas Swann all came. When the excursion left Baltimore early on the morning of June 1, 1857, hundreds of men, women, and children were crowded into the several trains.

At the first night's stop at Grafton, Virginia, the fine new hotel there found room only for the ladies in the party— most of the men were relegated to the bunks of several crude sleeping cars. Two days later at Cincinnati the celebration was marked by more speeches, marching bands, and demonstrations by several rival fire companies showing off their new equipment. Somehow an errant fire crew threw a stream of water into a carriage, dousing the secretary of state and sending his fine silk hat into a Cincinnati gutter.

The remaining two Ohio lines eventually under B. & O. control, the Sandusky, Mansfield & Newark and the Dayton & Michigan, connected the two east-west lines with Lake Erie.

Merged from several earlier chartered lines, the Sandusky, Mansfield & Newark was built between 1848 and 1851 from Newark on the Central Ohio up to Sandusky on Lake Erie. Even though it was built in the nonstandard gauge of 5 feet 4 inches, it was leased to the Central Ohio after the Civil War and thus came under B. & O. management. The other line, the Dayton & Michigan, was chartered in 1852, and between 1853 and 1859 built 144 miles of line from Dayton north to Toledo. During the Civil War it was leased to its connecting road to the south, the Cincinnati, Hamilton & Dayton, which in turn was later taken over by the Baltimore & Ohio.[19]

The last of the major Ohio roads was the Toledo, Wabash & Western, which would later form a major portion of the main line of the Wabash Railroad. Two separate connecting lines, the Toledo & Illinois, organized in Ohio in April 1853, and the Lake Erie, Wabash & St. Louis, organized in Indiana in August 1853, were to provide rail service from Toledo westward to Fort Wayne, Indiana, and thence down the Wabash Valley to the Indiana-Illinois border. The road was built from Toledo to Fort Wayne in 1855, and during the following year pushed westward via Peru, Logansport, and Lafayette to the Illinois state line. The two connecting lines were merged in June 1856 into the Toledo, Wabash & Western. The 243-mile line was built in standard gauge, as were all but one of the six roads that served Toledo. Even though the new railroad ran parallel to the Wabash & Erie Canal through much of its route, its traffic in the late 1850s included twice as much freight revenue as passenger. Since nearly two-thirds of the cost of the combined lines had been paid for with bonds rather than capital stock, the road was soon in default after the Panic of 1857. The first of several reorganizations came in 1858, and twenty years later it was included in the Wabash, St. Louis & Pacific, which later became the Wabash Railroad.[20]

Four of the six major lines in Indiana were eventually destined to be controlled by the Pennsylvania, the New York Central, or the B. & O. By far the longest was the Ohio & Mississippi, a 340-mile road running from Cincinnati across

Indiana and Illinois to East Saint Louis. According to the 1860 Census, Indiana was given "credit" for a line much of whose mileage was in Illinois. In the same fashion, of course, Ohio had been credited with the Indiana mileage of such roads as the Pittsburgh, Fort Wayne & Chicago and the Toledo, Wabash & Western.

The Ohio & Mississippi was chartered at midcentury in three states: in Indiana on February 14, 1848, in Ohio on March 15, 1849, and in Illinois on February 12, 1851. It included among its early sponsors Alphonso Taft, Cincinnati lawyer and father of a later American president; John O'Fallon, soldier-merchant of Saint Louis and nephew of George Rogers Clark; and Judge Abner T. Ellis of Vincennes, an early sponsor of river traffic on the Wabash. Cincinnati, by far the largest city in Ohio with a population of 115,000 in 1850, was especially eager to build a railroad westward to Saint Louis and the Mississippi. In 1849 its citizens voted to have their city subscribe to a million dollars of stock, and later the individual sponsors of the project subscribed to $80,000 of stock in a single hour. Construction was not fast, even with such support. The first segments of the road were built in 1854—27 miles west of Cincinnati and a 61-mile stretch over in southwestern Illinois. The following year another 87 miles were added in Illinois and an even 100 miles in Indiana. Early in 1857 the final 65-mile segment in Indiana, from Mitchell west to Vincennes, was built, and the entire 340-mile road was finished. The railroad mileage from Cincinnati west to East Saint Louis was roughly half of the river steamer distance via the Ohio and Mississippi.[21]

A few weeks after the Chauncy Brooks excursion, the business leaders of Saint Louis replied with a file of special trains sent eastward over the Ohio & Mississippi to Cincinnati and Baltimore. In Baltimore the B. & O. officials outdid themselves with a lengthy banquet that included four kinds of fish, nine relishes, and eleven different entrées. But the traffic on the 6-ft. gauge O. & M. was not so rich. Revenue for 1857–58 was under $900,000 for a road that had cost nearly $19 million, only a third of which was in capital stock.

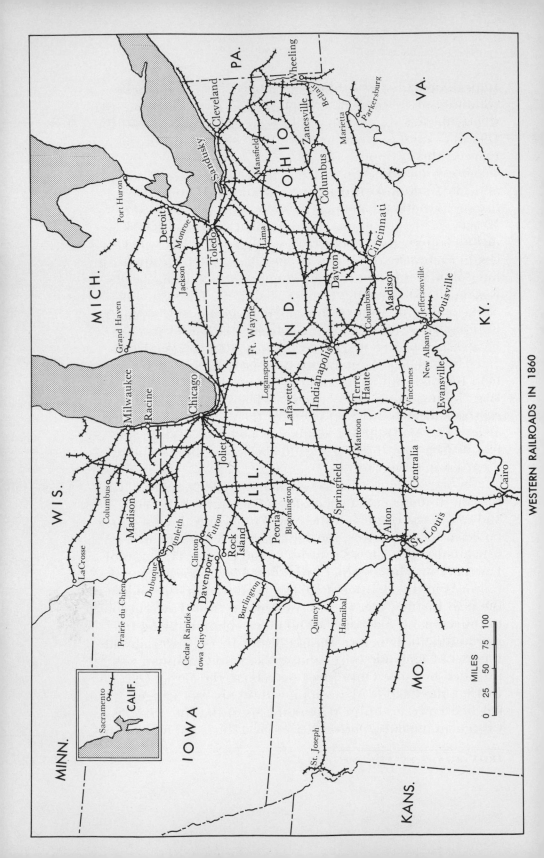

WESTERN RAILROADS IN 1860

With the Panic of 1857 the railroad was soon in financial trouble, and a receiver was appointed in 1860, the same year that George B. McClellan gave up his vice-presidency of the Illinois Central to move to Cincinnati as president of the Ohio & Mississipppi.[22]

Two major lines in Indiana, the Cincinnati & Chicago and the Madison & Indianapolis, would both eventually belong to the Pennsylvania. Between 1854 and 1858 the shorter of the two roads, the 108-mile Cincinnati & Chicago, was built from Richmond, Indiana, to Logansport, where it would eventually connect with the Chicago & Cincinnati running on into the Windy City. The Madison & Indianapolis was much older, having been started in the late 1830s as part of the ambitious Indiana internal improvement program. Completion of the road in 1848 from Madison to Indianapolis, a distance of 86 miles, was made possible by loans provided by James F. D. Lanier, a Madison financier, who was to help Indiana with its financial problems during the Civil War. John Brough, who later would be interested in the railroads of Ohio, was president of the railroad in the early 1850s. The Madison & Indianapolis had a small debt and had sufficient traffic to pay good dividends and also build a branch line to Shelbyville.[23]

A single major road in Indiana, the Indianapolis & Cincinnati, would eventually become a part of the "Big Four" and under the control of the New York Central. First proposed in the late 1830s, the Indianapolis & Cincinnati was organized in the late 1840s with Judge George H. Dunn of Lawrenceburg as the chief promoter. Long an advocate of railroads in the Hoosier state, Dunn was the first president of the line. In 1853 I. & C. was constructed from Lawrenceburg to Indianapolis, a distance of 90 miles, the road being finished just shortly before Dunn's death. In 1853 no railroad ran east of Lawrenceburg, and service into Cincinnati was provided by a fast Ohio River steamboat, the *Forrest Queen*. In 1854 the Ohio & Mississippi, with its six-foot gauge, reached Lawrenceburg. When officials of the Indianapolis & Cincinnati obtained permission to lay a third rail in standard gauge on the O. & M. track, direct train service between Indianapolis and the Queen City was possible. The new route did good business, and the road paid 7 percent dividends in the mid-1850s.[24]

The Evansville & Crawfordsville was one of two major Hoosier roads that did not succumb to the control of a giant eastern railroad system. This standard-gauge line was the consolidation of two earlier roads and was constructed from Evansville north to Terre Haute, a distance of 109 miles, between 1852 and 1854. The road crossed important east-west lines at Vincennes and Terre Haute. A further northern extension to Rockville was completed just before the Civil War. Even though the road quickly became one of the most important coal carriers in the state, it was unable to pay any dividends before the Civil War.

One of the longer railroads in Indiana was the New Albany & Salem, which by the eve of the Civil War was reorganized as the Louisville, New Albany & Chicago. Chartered in 1847 to connect two southern Indiana towns, the line by 1851 had been built from New Albany, on the Ohio River across from Louisville, through Salem to Orleans, 57 miles to the northwest. The president of the road was James Brooks, a New Albany businessman with a vision. Brooks insisted that his short southern Hoosier line should be extended up to Lake Michigan, and he proceeded to do it. During 1853 a 119-mile section of line was constructed from Crawfordsville north to Michigan City, and the following year almost as much was added as the gap was closed between Crawfordsville and Orleans. The entire 288-mile road from the Ohio to Lake Michigan was completed with the laying of the last rail on June 24, 1854.

By 1855 the line was operating 31 locomotives, 26 passenger cars, and 468 freight cars, but the interest charges on the large bonded debt were too great for the road to declare any dividends. Nor was service always of top quality. In 1853 Horace Greeley used the line during a temperance lecture tour in the West. The editor boarded the cars of the New Albany & Salem at Lafayette for LaPorte, his next tour stop in northern Indiana. Trouble plagued the whole 90-mile journey. Not far out of Lafayette the locomotive was derailed, and when once more on the track both water and wood soon were depleted. Greeley joined the crew who set out in the cold autumn night on a handcar in search of another engine. Finally he reached LaPorte some twenty-one hours after leaving Lafayette. With the Panic of 1857, the line was in growing financial trouble, and Brooks retired as president in 1859, the same year that the railroad was reorganized as the Louisville, New Albany & Chicago.[25]

As earlier noted, only two of the ten major lines in Illinois were destined to later come under the control of major eastern rail systems. The Logansport, Peoria & Burlington, with a 171-mile line built in the late 1850s from Logansport, Indiana, to Peoria, Illinois, was to come under the management of the Pennsylvania in the years after the Civil War. The Terre Haute, Alton & St. Louis, which gave service from central Indiana to the Mississippi River and Saint Louis, was reorganized during and after the Civil War and soon became part of the New York Central system serving Indianapolis and Saint Louis. Both the Logansport, Peoria & Burlington and the Terre Haute, Alton & St. Louis were built in standard gauge which, with the exception of the 6-ft. Ohio & Mississippi, was the only gauge found in Illinois.

During the 1850s the Illinois Central, the first railroad in the nation to receive a land grant, was probably the most important of the major railroads serving Chicago and Illinois. The I.C. was chartered in 1851 to build a road in the shape of a thin wishbone running the length of the state from Dunleith and Chicago in the north down to Cairo at the junction of the Ohio and Mississippi rivers. As the road was built across the virgin prairie land of Illinois in the early 1850s, it seemed to many observers that it was running the "wrong way." Most projected railroads in the upper Mississippi Valley ran from east to west to capture the trade of the expanding frontier, and once well under way they frequently added the word "Pacific" to the company name.

The construction of the Illinois Central was only well

started in 1853 when Robert Schuyler, the first president, resigned because of more pressing railroad commitments back in New England. His successors vigorously pushed construction, and under the leadership of Colonel Roswell B. Mason, engineer-in-chief of the Illinois Central, the entire road was completed in September 1856. At this time the cost of living was rising, and a bushel of potatoes or a gallon of whiskey might cost 40 to 50 cents in Illinois. Before the road was finished Mason was having to pay $1.50 a day to the Irish and German workers in his track gang. When completed, the 705-mile Illinois Central accounted for nearly 30 percent of all mileage in the state and was reported to be the longest railroad in the world. Even before the I.C. was fully built the roster of equipment included 62 engines, 42 passenger cars, and 1,250 freight cars. Gross revenue in 1856 was $2,476,000, and locomotives on the northern division alone were consuming about 3,000 cords of wood per month. The strongest of the early presidents of the Illinois Central was William H. Osborn, a New Englander who quickly became fully committed to honest and vigorous railroad administration. During his ten years in office (1855–65), Osburn faced problems of both depression and war.[26]

The substantial federal land grant held by the Illinois Central assisted in the fairly rapid completion of the road, since the directors were able to pay for much of the construction costs with bonds secured by the bulk of the grant. By 1859 the railroad had sold more than 1,280,000 acres of its land, at an average price of nearly $12 an acre, and was thus able to retire a considerable portion of its debt. Since the railroad was assuring itself of an increasing traffic with every farm it sold, the Illinois Central was an early promoter of agriculture, In the late 1850s it helped sponsor annual agricultural fairs, gave discount rates for fruit grown in and shipped from the southern counties of the state, and offered prizes for the invention of improved farm machinery.

Being of north–south line, the Illinois Central was to play a vital role in the movement and supply of Union troops during the Civil War. The southern portion of the road at Cairo was almost like a pistol aimed down the Mississippi at the lower Confederacy. The town of Cairo was well south of Louisville, Cincinnati, and Washington, D.C., and in fact was the farthest southern point among all the free states east of the Mississippi River. Several big names of Civil War fame were involved in the prewar management of the I.C. Abraham Lincoln was retained by the railroad throughout the 1850s and played a major role in winning for the railroad the "McLean County Tax Case," a legal victory that annually saved thousands of dollars for the railroad. Civil War military leaders who earlier had worked for the I.C. included George B. McClellan, chief engineer and vice-president (1856–60), Nathaniel P. Banks, resident director in Chicago (1861), and Ambrose E. Burnside, cashier and treasurer (1858–61).

Two other lines serving Chicago, the Galena & Chicago Union and the Chicago & Northwestern, would eventually be consolidated under the name of the latter road. The older, the Galena & Chicago Union, was first granted a charter in 1836, but for a decade no significant progress was made on the projected line. In 1846 the Galena line was revitalized with William Butler Ogden, Chicago's first mayor and a well-to-do real estate man, as the new president. Ogden at first found only modest support for the road in Chicago and Galena, but the farmers along the line of the road helped to fill the first subscription books. By 1850 the line was open to Elgin, 42 miles west of Chicago, and the road was grossing $1,000 a week. By 1853 the line had been extended westward to Freeport, where it connected with the Illinois Central for service into Galena. During the next two years a second line was built west to Fulton on the Mississippi.

Just as Ogden had foreseen, the road had a heavy traffic in farm produce. This grew during the decade, and by the eve of the Civil War nearly three-quarters of the line's traffic came from freight, much of it grain and livestock headed for Chicago markets. The Galena road was early a moneymaker. Since capital stock made up about two-thirds of the road's total cost, it soon was paying dividends: cash dividends were declared each year during the fifties, with an average annual yield of about 9 percent.[27]

Ogden had left the presidency in 1851, but remained a

director and retained an undiminished faith in the future of railroads serving Chicago. He was increasingly looking northward toward the rich timber, copper, and iron lands of Wisconsin and upper Michigan. In the mid-1850s several short lines were being chartered and built out of Chicago toward Janesville and Fond du Lac in Wisconsin. In 1855 these several lines were merged into the Chicago, St. Paul & Fond du Lac. When this road failed to meet some bond-interest payments in the depression of the late 1850s, Ogden was quick to move. With legislation both in Illinois and Wisconsin permitting the reorganization of the Fond du Lac road, the line was sold in June 1859 to a New York attorney, Samuel J. Tilden. A few days later Tilden conveyed the purchased property to the recently organized Chicago & Northwestern Railroad, of which Ogden was the newly elected president. Ogden's new property by the end of the year was operating a 213-mile road from Chicago north to Oshkosh, Wisconsin. In 1864 the Chicago & Northwestern took over control of Ogden's earlier line, the Galena & Chicago Union.[28]

Two of the major Illinois lines in 1860, the 138-mile Chicago, Burlington & Quincy and the 100-mile Quincy & Chicago, were to be merged in the mid-1860s to form the core of the later important Granger line, the Burlington. The 13-mile Aurora Branch Railway, chartered in 1849, and completed from Turner Junction on William Butler Ogden's Galena & Chicago Union to Aurora, was the first portion of the C. B. & Q. Having trackage rights over the Galena road, the Aurora Branch by October 1850 was able to offer service from Aurora into Chicago; the 43-mile trip required from two to three hours. By 1853 the line was extended from Aurora westward to Mendota, a distance of 46 miles. The Central Military Tract Railroad, chartered in 1851, continued the route southwestward to Galesburg, completing the 80-mile extension early in 1855. That same year the Illinois state legislature created the Chicago, Burlington & Quincy Railroad, which was in complete control of the several roads forming the 138-mile route from Turner Junction to Galesburg.[29]

The management of the roads merging into the C. B. &.

Q. was under the direction of the "Forbes group," including a trio of Yankees from New England, John Murray Forbes, John W. Brooks, and James F. Joy. Left fatherless at an early age, Forbes entered his uncle's counting house at 15 and soon was in China where he accumulated a fortune before the age of 25. A decade later, in 1846, Forbes and his friends purchased the Michigan Central from the state of Michigan, with Forbes as the new president. Once the Michigan Central had reached Lake Michigan and later Chicago, Forbes, Joy, and Brooks turned their attention to the financing and construction of connecting roads from Chicago to the Mississippi and beyond. Forbes was a serious businessman, but he could play the genial host at his summer home at Buzzard's Bay, Massachusetts, and he also was an avid yachtsman. He liked to make money, but he was often willing to wait. In a letter written shortly after the Panic of 1857, he assured his cousin that the bonds both of the C. B. & Q. and the Michigan Central could be sold "sooner or later at a good profit."[30] Certainly Forbes, and his associates, gave the growing C. B. &. Q. a stability of management rather unusual for that day.

The newly merged, 138-mile Chicago, Burlington and Quincy was a profitable line. Between 1856 and 1861 it paid dividends three years out of five, with an average yearly yield of 5 percent. In 1856, when James F. Joy took over as president, the Burlington represented a total investment of $6,991,000, and had an equipment roster consisting of 54 locomotives, 31 passenger cars, and 768 baggage and freight cars.[31]

At Galesburg the Burlington connected with two other roads, the Quincy & Chicago, and the Peoria & Oquawka. The 100-mile Quincy & Chicago, originally a portion of the Northern Cross Railroad, was completed from Galesburg to Quincy early in 1856. The Peoria & Oquawka in the mid-1850s was building a line west from Galesburg to the Mississippi River opposite Burlington, Iowa, and a second road from Galesburg east to Peoria. The 40-mile road to Burlington was completed in 1855; the 53-mile line to Peoria was in operation two years later.

Almost from the beginning the Forbes group had given

a substantial, and controlling, financial support to the Quincy & Chicago and the Peoria & Oquawka. Thus by 1856 the C. B. & Q. was essentially in control of a rail system from Chicago westward to two important points on the Mississippi, Burlington and Quincy. West of the Mississippi the Forbes group was projecting and building two additional lines: the Hannibal & St. Joseph in Missouri giving service west of Quincy, and the Burlington & Missouri River in Iowa providing an extension west from Burlington.[32]

Another major Illinois line connecting Chicago and the Mississippi was the Chicago & Rock Island, the first road to bridge successfully the "Father of Waters." The line was chartered February 7, 1851 by the Illinois state legislature, but with restrictive clauses favoring the competing and parallel Illinois and Michigan Canal. However, the railroad's first president, Judge James W. Grant of Davenport, managed to evade these charter restrictions, and construction west of Chicago was soon being pushed vigorously. By October 1852, track was laid out to Joliet, 40 miles west of Chicago, and the entire 181-mile line from Chicago to the Mississippi was completed by July 1854. Traffic on the Rock Island boomed, and the original equipment ordered for the road had to be substantially increased. From 1855 through 1860 the new road had revenues running well over $1 million a year, and paid dividends in four of the six years.[33]

By the time the bridge that Henry Farnam had built across the Mississippi was opened at Rock Island in the spring of 1856, the Mississippi & Missouri, a subsidiary line west of Davenport, had already been built 55 miles on west to Iowa City. The citizens of Davenport and eastern Iowa were soon to lose their new direct service to Chicago and New York City. Only two weeks after the festive opening of the Rock Island bridge, the *Effie Afton,* a new steamboat belonging to the New Orleans & Louisville Packet Company, swung into a central bridge pier. The crash upset a stove on the boat, and the fire quickly spread to the bridge. The efforts of local firemen saved the end spans of the railroad bridge, but the central span was lost.

Alleging that the Rock Island bridge was a menace to river navigation, the owners of the *Effie Afton* refused to pay damages for the "accident" and in fact filed a suit against the railroad. President Henry Farnam engaged a well-known trial lawyer from Springfield to help with the case. Abraham Lincoln studied a report on that part of the river made earlier by Robert E. Lee, and talked with a 12-year-old boy from Davenport about local river currents. In presenting his case at the Chicago trial, Lincoln argued that "people have as much right to travel east and west as north and south." The case moved slowly through the courts, finally being appealed to the United States Supreme Court, which held in favor of the railroad. Thus the Rock Island retained its right to bridge the Mississippi.[34]

On the eve of the Civil War the two major cities in the middle Mississippi Valley were joined by the Chicago, Alton & St. Louis, originally chartered as the Chicago & Mississippi in 1847. The first track on this line was laid in 1852. By 1854 the road had constructed 220 miles of line between Joliet and Alton. South of Alton riverboats gave service downstream 20 miles to Saint Louis. By 1855 service from Joliet into Chicago was provided by the Joliet & Chicago, which was later leased in perpetuity to the larger line. The road never paid any dividends during the 1850s and was reorganized in 1857.

The last remaining longer road in Illinois was the Great Western, which after the Civil War would be included in the Wabash system. The western portion of this road, the Northern Cross, had been commenced as a state work in the late 1830s. Illinois sold the Northern Cross in 1847 at auction for $21,000 to a local group under the name of the Sangamon & Morgan Railroad. In 1850 the Sangamon & Morgan claimed to have 60 miles of road running west from Springfield to Meredosia and Naples, but the entire line was very dilapidated and operations were most irregular. During the mid-1850s the line became known as the Great Western, and between 1854 and 1856 it was extended eastward from Springfield through Decatur and Danville to the Indiana state line, where it connected with the Toledo, Wabash & Western.

The Great Western had a large funded debt and never prospered during the fifties. It was this line that President-elect Lincoln used as he left Springfield in mid-February 1861 for his twelve-day preinaugural trip to Washington.[35]

Only four of the remaining seven western states had any substantial rail mileage on the eve of the Civil War. Michigan, Wisconsin, Iowa, and Missouri together could claim more than 3,000 miles of line, including eleven major roads of 100 miles or more, which made up well over two-thirds of the total mileage in the four states. The direction of the projected roads, and often the corporate title as well, indicated that the lines were headed for the West. In Michigan they ran from Detroit toward Chicago or Lake Michigan; in Wisconsin both Milwaukee and Racine desired rail connections with the Mississippi; and in Iowa and Missouri it was hoped that someday the railroad would reach the Missouri River. In Michigan and Wisconsin the new major roads started out as independent lines, while in Iowa and Missouri most of the longer roads were projected as western extensions of older, Chicago-based railroads. With the exception of the three Wisconsin lines, most of the remaining major roads would ultimately be merged with larger and older eastern or midwestern systems. The 11 major lines in the four states are listed in Table 5.3.[36]

In Michigan the two longest roads on the eve of the Civil War, the Michigan Southern & Northern Indiana and the Michigan Central, would both eventually be merged into the New York Central. Both lines were part of an overly ambitious plan for new railroads projected by the legislature of the Michigan Territory in 1836, months before Michigan was even admitted to statehood. The Michigan Southern was planned as a road from Monroe, on Lake Erie south of Detroit, running through the southern tier of counties, to New Buffalo on Lake Michigan. The state found it difficult to finance construction, and by 1843 only 68 miles of line had been built. Some of that had originally been laid with maple rails instead of strap iron, and in early passenger

| | | Length in 1850 | Length in 1860 | | |
| | | | 100–199 miles | over 200 miles | |
Railroad	State				Later Name
Detroit & Milwaukee	Mich.	25	188		Grand Trunk
Michigan Central	Mich.	226		284	New York Central
Michigan Southern & Northern Indiana	Mich.	103		484	New York Central
LaCrosse & Milwaukee	Wisc.	—		200	Milwaukee
Milwaukee & Mississippi	Wisc.	20		234	Milwaukee
Racine & Wisconsin	Wisc.		104		Milwaukee
Dubuque & Pacific	Iowa	—	111		Illinois Central
Mississippi & Missouri	Iowa	—	187		Rock Island
Hannibal & St. Joseph	Mo.	—		206	Burlington
North Missouri	Mo.	—	168		Wabash
Pacific	Mo.	—	189		Mo. Pacific

trains the engineer collected tickets in the absence of a conductor.

Eastern and local interests purchased the road from the
state in 1846 for $500,000, less than half of the state's origi-
nal investment. Under the new corporate title of the
Michigan Southern, the road had permission to head for
Chicago through northern Indiana. During the 1850s George
Bliss, the Yankee lawyer who earlier had been president of
the Western Railroad in Massachusetts, was twice president
of the Michigan Southern. Bliss and John B. Jervis, another
railroader from the East, built the road on to LaPorte,
Indiana, during 1851, and by the spring of 1852 had
reached Chicago. The line through Indiana was built by the
Northern Indiana Railroad, which soon merged with the
Michigan Southern to become the Michigan Southern &
Northern Indiana. In addition to the 243-mile line from
Monroe to Chicago, a second route from Toledo west to Elk-
hart, Indiana, was built. This plus several branches serving

southern Michigan gave the line a total of 484 miles by 1860. In the mid-1859s the Michigan Southern & Northern Indiana had the majority of its revenue from passenger rather than freight traffic; for several years it paid regular dividends. In 1869 when it was merged with other Ohio lines to form the Lake Shore & Michigan Southern, it became a portion of the main line of the New York Central.[37]

The second of the state rail projects in Michigan was a line projected from Detroit across the state to the shores of Lake Michigan. When the legislature refused any further financial support, the line had been built to Kalamazoo, 144 miles west of Detroit. In 1846 the Forbes group purchased the line from Michigan for $2 million and chartered the property as the Michigan Central. With Forbes as president, the road was pushed 84 miles further west to Michigan City, Indiana, by 1850, and two years later entered Chicago, using the tracks of the Illinois Central for the last few miles.

While the Michigan Central was being built toward Chicago, company officials back in Michigan were waging a "railroad war" with a number of farmers in Jackson County. The local farmers objected to being paid only half the market value of livestock killed by the small, woodburning locomotives of Forbes's railroad. The farmers retaliated by tampering with switches, greasing rails, firing buckshot at passing trains, and finally burning a railroad depot. John W. Brooks and the railroad's lawyer, James F. Joy, brought the farmers to trial, where they finally received jail sentences even though they were defended by William H. Seward, brought in specially from New York.

As on the Michigan Southern, traffic on the Michigan Central at midcentury consisted more of passenger than freight business. Very shortly after taking over the Michigan Central, Forbes had pointed out to Superintendent Brooks that it should be fairly easy for their railroad to capture the passenger traffic from the steamers on the Great Lakes. The well-established freight service on the Great Lakes, however, could generally undercut rail freight rates in the first years of competition. With the Forbes group increasingly interested in the expansion of the Burlington lines in Illinois, Iowa, and Missouri, John Murray Forbes gave up the presidency of the Michigan Central in 1855, to be succeeded by John W. Brooks. After the Civil War, Forbes and his eastern friends continued to give top priority to the Burlington, and in 1877 control of the Michigan Central passed to Vanderbilt interests and the New York Central.[38]

The last of the three major roads in Michigan was the Detroit and Milwaukee, originally chartered in 1834 as the Detroit & Pontiac. The 25 miles north to Pontiac was in operation by 1844, but additional construction was delayed more than a decade. Under the name of Detroit & Milwaukee, the line, between 1855 and 1858, was extended to Grand Haven, 188 miles from Detroit. Passage on to Milwaukee, 85 miles across the lake, was by steamer. Within a few years the line was leased to the Grand Trunk Railway of Canada.

All three of the major lines in Wisconsin on the eve of the Civil War would ultimately form a major portion of the Milwaukee, or more correctly, the Chicago, Milwaukee, St. Paul & Pacific. The oldest was the Milwaukee & Mississippi, the name given in 1850 to the earlier chartered Milwaukee & Waukesha. The first president of the Milwaukee & Mississippi, Byron Kilbourn, mayor of Milwaukee, had considerable legal and engineering experience with plank roads and canals both in Ohio and Michigan. By 1850 Kilbourn was pushing railroads and hoped to see Milwaukee rival and surpass Chicago in building a line to the Mississippi. The extent of his dream was revealed by a graphic map hung on the wall of his office. It showed Milwaukee's future rail lines stretching out to Saint Paul, LaCrosse, Dubuque, Saint Louis, and western points beyond.

But in 1850 Kilbourn only had a few miles of grade running west of Milwaukee, and much of it paid for in kind, harness, oats, timber, and manual labor. If iron was to be put down, hard cash was needed. At a gathering of the sponsors of the line in the spring of 1850, Joseph Goodrich, a farmer with real imagination, suggested that his farm might be

mortgaged to help finance the road's construction. This plan
appealed to the directors of the railroad, and they soon were
inviting farmers living along the projected right-of-way to
buy railroad stock paying 10 percent dividends. The farmers
would pay for the stock with their personal notes, secured by
mortgages on their farms, payable in ten years and bearing 8
percent interest. The company promised to pay the interest
on the farm mortgages and to accumulate a fund to help pay
off the principal debt. In the prosperous early fifties the plan
seemed to be foolproof—the Wisconsin farmer figured that
within a decade both his stock certificate and his farm would
appreciate in value. This opportunity to get railroad stock for
next to nothing appealed to hundreds of farmers, and soon
other railroads in Wisconsin were also trying comparable
farm-mortgage stock plans. Between 1850 and 1857 about $5
million of railroad stock was obtained in this way by nearly
6,000 farmers in the state.

Kilbourn disposed of the mortgages back East and soon
had his needed rail. Waukesha, 20 miles out of Milwaukee,
was reached early in 1851, and Madison, halfway across the
state, was reached by May 1854. In the mid-1850s the road
managed to declare a few dividends. Construction also continued, and Prairie du Chien, 225 miles west of Milwaukee
on the Mississippi, was reached in the spring of 1857. Later
that same year the Panic of 1857 forced many railroads in
Wisconsin to the verge of bankruptcy. The farmers' stock
certificates became nearly worthless, and when hard-pressed
railroads failed to meet bond-interest payments, eastern
bankers started to seek foreclosures on the farms of Wisconsin. The anger of the distressed farmers was even greater
where altered routes or frauds had resulted in the total
absence of any rail line in their community. The farm-
mortgage stock purchase fiasco in Wisconsin did much to
deepen the antirailroad attitude in the state.[39]

The second Wisconsin road, the LaCrosse & Milwaukee,
was also associated with Byron Kilbourn, farm mortgages,
and financial problems. In the early 1850s Kilbourn had
resigned the presidency of the Milwaukee & Mississippi

under something of a cloud. Kilbourn, however, was not one to stay out of railroading. Soon he was president of the road projected from Milwaukee to LaCrosse. In the mid-1850s he was just as successful in getting farmers to mortgage their farms to help with the road to LaCrosse as he had earlier been in getting their aid for the Milwaukee & Mississippi. The LaCrosse & Milwaukee was chartered in 1852, and between 1855 and 1858 constructed its 200 miles of road from Milwaukee to LaCrosse on the Mississippi. Just as the road was being finished, it was revealed that back in 1856 Byron Kilbourn had been guilty of wholesale bribery in obtaining a state land grant for the LaCrosse & Milwaukee. He had delivered more than $800,000 to the greedy state officials in Madison; $335,000 went to fifty-nine assembly-men, $175,000 was divided up among thirteen state senators, and $50,000 was given to Coles Bashford, the Republican governor of the state, who not long after shifted his political base out to the Arizona Territory.[40]

The last and shortest of the major roads in Wisconsin was the Racine & Mississippi, an 1855 consolidation of two projected but unbuilt roads in southern Wisconsin and north-ern Illinois. Between 1855 and 1859 the Racine & Mississippi built 104 miles of road from Racine, a lake port 25 miles south of Milwaukee, to Freeport, Illinois. The road was quite well financed with a modest funded debt, but it paid no divi-dends in the late fifties. Like the other two major Wisconsin roads, the Racine & Mississippi by the late 1860s was firmly controlled by the Milwaukee & St. Paul, a growing line whose president was Alexander Mitchell, a poor Scottish immigrant who had prospered in banking and insurance in Milwaukee.

In Iowa two major roads, the Mississippi & Missouri and the Dubuque & Pacific, were the westward extensions of the Rock Island and the Illinois Central respectively. Two other Chicago lines, the Burlington and the Chicago & North Western, also had shorter (under 100 miles) subordinate lines building west from the Mississippi River. All four roads were aided by the land grants provided in legislation approved by President Pierce in May 1856.

The Mississippi & Missouri River was chartered in 1852. When it was organized some time later, Thomas A. Dix of New York was president, William B. Ogden of Chicago was vice-president, and Henry Farnam was chief engineer. By 1855 Farnam had pushed the road 23 miles west to Wilton and then on south to Muscatine. The citizens of Iowa City, 30 miles west of Wilton, fearful that the branch down to Muscatine might become the main line to the West, made an attractive offer to Henry Farnam: if Farnam would build the track to the Iowa City depot by December 31, 1855, they would give the railroad a $50,000 cash bonus. At first Farnam's work crews made good progress, but cold weather in late December slowed them down. On December 31 the temperature dropped to 30° below zero and the new wooden depot was still 1,000 feet away. The tired track crew desperately laid ties and iron rail on the frozen ground, and a track of sorts soon lay in front of the new depot. As the church bells marked the end of the old year, the exhausted workers used pinch bars to push the frozen locomotive into town. Farnam and his men had earned the bonus.

In the summer of 1856 the Mississippi & Missouri had its portion of the federal land grant approved by the state of Iowa, and construction continued on west toward Des Moines and Council Bluffs on the Missouri River. The Panic of 1857 naturally slowed construction, but by 1860 the road was built to a point 75 miles west of Iowa City and was nearing Des Moines. Moreover, a 50-mile branch via Muscatine to Washington, Iowa, was in operation. On the eve of the Civil War Farnam's western extension of the Rock Island in Iowa represented more than a quarter of the total mileage in the state.[41]

The other major road in Iowa, the Dubuque & Pacific, was not originally backed by the Illinois Central but was to come under its control shortly after the Civil War. Dubuque, second largest town in the state with 3,100 inhabitants at midcentury, became actively interested in railroad promotion in the early 1850s once it was learned that the Illinois Central would have a northern terminal across the Mississippi River at Dunleith, Illinois. In April 1853, the Iowa legislature granted a charter to the Dubuque & Pacific Railroad, and a company was soon organized with Captain Jesse P. Farley, steamboat builder and operator and former Dubuque mayor, as the first president. Ground was broken on October 1, 1855, and a year later, in September 1856, the road's first motive power—the little woodburner the *Dubuque*—was delivered by ferry across the river from Dunleith. Construction was aided by the 1856 land-grant act, and by May 1857, 29 miles of road was finished out to Dyersville. In 1859 the road had a roster of 8 locomotives, 8 passenger cars, and 85 freight cars. By the eve of the Civil War the line had been extended westward to Cedar Falls, six miles west of Waterloo.[42]

Two shorter Iowa roads, the Burlington & Missouri and the Chicago, Iowa & Nebraska, also were being built in the late 1850s with help from the land-grant legislation of 1856. The Burlington & Missouri was chartered on January 15, 1852 by several businessmen of Burlington, Iowa, who desired better transportation for their river town than toll roads. In little more than a year John Forbes and his associates were offering financial backing to the line, since it could provide a westward extension for their C. B. & Q. Construction west of Burlington started in earnest in 1856, and by the eve of the Civil War the B. & M. had constructed 93 miles of line with the western railhead several miles west of Ottumwa. The second line, the Chicago, Iowa & Nebraska, was chartered in 1853, and built from Clinton, on the Mississippi, 82 miles westward to Cedar Rapids by 1859. During the Civil War the Chicago, Iowa & Nebraska was leased to the Galena & Chicago Union.[43]

The three major roads in Missouri, the Hannibal & St. Joseph, the Pacific Railroad of Missouri, and the North Missouri, together accounted for about two-thirds of the state's rail mileage on the eve of the Civil War. All would later form major portions of larger midwestern lines. The first two of the three were aided by federal land grants made available by congressional legislation in 1852.

The Hannibal & St. Joseph, the longest of the three roads in 1860, was also the oldest, having received its charter on February 16, 1847. Colonel Robert Marcellus Stewart, active railroad promoter and later governor of Missouri, was the first president. Despite his best efforts, progress on the Hannibal line was slow until the federal land grant was obtained in 1852. John M. Forbes, John W. Brooks, and James F. Joy, the promoters of the Burlington, soon became interested in the road and by 1854 had a substantial investment in the project. In the fall of 1854 Forbes was writing his cousin that the Hannibal road ran through farming land superior to that of Illinois, and that the east-west line, unlike the Illinois Central, ran in the "right direction." [44]

Construction of the railroad was pushed at both ends of the route, and by November 1858 the road was completed 100 miles west of Hannibal and 46 miles east of Saint Joseph. When construction crews proved hard to find, the managers of the line used several Otis steam excavators, steam shovels that were among the first used on western railroads. On February 13, 1859, the final spike on the 206-mile road was driven near Cream Ridge, Missouri, and a few days later the arrival of the first through passenger train in Saint Joseph was celebrated by emptying a jug of water from the Mississippi into the muddy Missouri. Connecting service to the Burlington at Quincy was soon provided with the completion of a short road, the Quincy & Palmyra. In 1860 the Hannibal & St. Joseph graphically revealed its location as the westernmost extension of the nation's iron network, when in April it carried mail sacks from the Burlington at Quincy to Saint Joseph for the first Pony Express service to the far Pacific. The speedy, 204-mile run from West Quincy to Saint Joseph was made in less than five hours, twice as fast as schedules typical of the early post–Civil War years. [45]

The other two major Missouri lines both served Saint Louis. The older, the Pacific Railroad of Missouri, received a charter on March 12, 1849 to build across the state from Saint Louis to the Kansas border. Senator Thomas Hart Benton, a major proponent of a railroad to the Pacific starting in his adopted state, was an early supporter, as was Colonel John O'Fallon, a wealthy Saint Louis merchant and a veteran of the Battle of Tippecanoe. The Saint Louis convention of 1849 generated interest, but little construction was possible until the federal land grant of 1852. Substantial loans from the state also helped, and 125 miles of line were constructed by 1856. In the late 1850s gross revenue was over $600,000 a year, but the line was not clearing enough to pay the interest on its large debt. By the early months of the Civil War the road was in operation to Sedalia, 189 miles west of Saint Louis and two-thirds of the way to Kansas City. After the war the line became a part of the Missouri Pacific Railway.[46]

The last of the major Missouri roads was the Northern Missouri, which was chartered March 1, 1851, and projected from Saint Louis to a connection with the Hannibal & St. Joseph. Colonel O'Fallon was also a promoter of the line, but more important were the Missouri state bonds made available to the project. Construction started in May 1854, and by February 1859 the road was constructed 168 miles to Macon, where it connected with the Hannibal road. After the Civil War the Northern Missouri was merged into the Wabash, St. Louis & Pacific.

In the antebellum years such public figures as Asa Whitney, Stephen A. Douglas, Thomas Hart Benton, and Jefferson Davis all had planned and sponsored the construction of a railway to the far Pacific from some favorite terminal point in the Mississippi Valley. When the guns of war first sounded in the spring of 1861, none of these promoters had seen their dream fulfilled. But other railroad builders, perhaps lesser men, had constructed much new mileage in the middle and upper Mississippi Valley during the fifties. Each of the seven western states (old Northwest plus Iowa and Missouri) had constructed 400 miles or more of new railroad during the decade, and some of the states much more. During the 1850s Illinois had added over 2,600 miles of line, Ohio some 2,300 miles, and Indiana more than 1,900 miles.

Western steamboat tonnage expanded by nearly 50 percent, while rail mileage increased more than sevenfold. Merchants and farmers alike welcomed the new railroads. In the decade the production of corn climbed by 45 percent, and that of wheat by nearly 75 percent. Much of this increase was in the very region of rapid rail construction. Certainly as America approached the years of sectional and military conflict many new iron roads had been built in the West.

CHAPTER SIX

Victory over Road, Canal, and Steamboat

IT WAS A pleasant and warm July 4 in Lafayette, Indiana, and the citizens of that bustling Hoosier town were celebrating the official opening of their canal—the Wabash & Erie. Started on Washington's birthday in 1832, the canal had been built down the Wabash Valley, reaching Peru in 1837 and Logansport in 1839. Now it was finished all the way from Lafayette to Fort Wayne, and then on through Ohio to Toledo at the western end of Lake Erie. Banners in Lafayette carried the legend, "Lafayette to New York City." The first portion of that trip, the 240-mile ride on a luxurious canal packet boat to Toledo, cost seven dollars and took the remarkably short time of only two days and eight hours—more than 100 miles a day. In Fort Wayne the high point of this special Hoosier Independence Day was an address by General Lewis Cass of Michigan, former secretary of war under Andrew Jackson, who had just returned from six years as the nation's minister to France.

The extension of the Wabash & Erie to Lafayette was big news in Indiana in 1843. Down in Indianapolis Calvin Fletcher, lawyer and banker, noted in his diary that nearby merchants and farmers were sending wagon freight north to Lafayette since the new canal provided the most economical route to eastern markets. In the early 1840s Indiana had no more than 30 miles of railroad, all in the south near the Ohio River. Ohio had only 84 miles of railway, and Illinois a mere 22 miles. During the 1840s the National Road was being built across Indiana, and other roads were also in use north and south out of Indianapolis. Slow but adequate stagecoach service from Lafayette to Indianapolis, 65 miles to the southeast, could be had for three dollars. Lafayette was the effective head of steamboat navigation on the Wabash, and in an average year perhaps a hundred steamboats arrived or departed, most in the spring months of ample water. Few of the boats on the Wabash were much above 125 tons, and few went beyond the Ohio River.[1]

However, the canal boom in Lafayette lasted only a few years. The Wabash & Erie was built on down the Wabash Valley, reaching Terre Haute in 1849 and Evansville in 1853. But the open season on the canal was only from March to November, and frequently it was closed even in those months because of low water, flooding, or needed repairs. Canal traffic was suffering a serious decline well before the Civil War. In 1852 Lafayette obtained rail service to Indianapolis, and a year later a line was completed north to Michigan City on Lake Michigan. In 1857 a railroad running parallel to the upper Wabash River was built from Fort Wayne west through Lafayette on into central Illinois. This new service rather quickly brought gloom to the Wabash & Erie Canal. Very soon rail travel from Lafayette to Toledo, only 203 miles by train, was possible in less than nine hours, six times as fast as the canal packet. As the Hoosiers built nearly 2,000 miles of new railroad in the 1850s, the highways of the state were relegated to the status of feeder routes. Hoosier canals also quickly were bested by the Iron Horse, and even some captains of steamboats on the Wabash began to hedge their bets on the future. Commerce in Lafayette and Indiana, and indeed all across the nation, was changing as Americans built more rail lines. By the eve of the Civil War highways, canals, and steamboats everywhere were falling victim to the railroad.[2]

The victory of railroads over highways and turnpikes was the earliest and the most complete. Wherever the railroad made any substantial appearance, both the toll road and the common country road were relegated to positions of secondary importance. This shift in use was not too harmful for the public or common roads, but it often was the final blow for the toll road or turnpike.

The success of the Lancaster Turnpike, built in the 1790s, resulted in a rage for turnpikes that lasted until the mid-1820s. Most of the hundreds of projected toll roads were proposed for the New England and mid-Atlantic states. Dozens of different turnpike companies planned and built roads in New England, especially in the three southern states. By 1821 some 150 different companies had been given charters in Pennsylvania, and New York had nearly 4,000 miles of completed toll roads. In most of the southern states there was more promotion and planning than accomplished construction. Similarly, the states of the Old Northwest planned many turnpikes during the 1820s and 1830s, but few roads were completed, except in Ohio.

Very few of the new turnpikes, North or South, ever made the profits promised by their promoters. The story of New England is typical: only half a dozen of the 230 turnpikes in the area ever returned to their owners a reasonable dividend on their investment. The competition from canals, and from the railroads a few years later, brought disaster to the turnpike era. A single canal boat could haul a load ten times that of a four-horse Conestoga wagon on the best of the toll roads. Freight rates on the turnpike ranged from 12 to 18 cents a ton-mile; even the first railroads could provide faster service at much lower rates. When rail service between Boston and Worcester started in 1833, the freight rate was just over six cents a ton-mile. On the competing turnpike it was 17.5 cents a ton-mile.[3]

Turnpike after turnpike succumbed to the railroads. West of Worcester, Massachusetts, Thomas B. Wale's Western Railroad increasingly took passengers away from stagecoach and turnpike as the line was built to Springfield and Albany in the late 1830s and early 1840s. Further south, other new rail lines took business away from other Concord

The *Pacific*, the first locomotive west of the Mississippi, was shipped by steamboat from New Orleans to St. Louis in August 1852, and early in December was operating on the freshly laid rails of the Pacific Railroad. (COURTESY, MISSOURI PACIFIC RAILROAD.)

The first railroad bridge over the Mississippi River was completed at Rock Island in April 1856 by the Chicago & Rock Island Railroad. Shortly thereafter the steamboat *Effie Afton* "accidently" struck a bridge pier and the resulting fire destroyed the bridge. (COURTESY, ASSOCIATION OF AMERICAN RAILROADS.)

coaches as they followed the middle or lower routes of the Old Post Road between Boston and New York City. Sometimes an upstart village, not on a turnpike, would successfully bid for a place on a projected railroad, at the expense of a complacent older town. Once the new town had obtained the steamcars with all its new passenger traffic, the older "turnpike village" was left to decay along with its empty stables and languishing stage taverns.

It was much the same in New York and Pennsylvania. At one time the stage lines west of Albany had been very busy. In 1830 the several daily stage lines out of Albany for the Mohawk Valley had to add extra coaches to take care of the traffic. Then came the railroads. Long before Erastus Corning or Cornelius Vanderbilt controlled the New York Central, the several short roads that together gave rail service between Albany and Buffalo had stolen away most of the turnpike traffic. In Pennsylvania the railroad being built west of Philadelphia, the Philadelphia & Columbia, took away much of the stagecoach passenger traffic from the nearby Lancaster Turnpike. This was especially true when steam locomotives replaced horsepower on the new rail line in 1836. West of Harrisburg a few years later J. Edgar Thomson and his Pennsylvania Railroad were just as destructive of turnpike passenger traffic on the several toll roads that had been built across the mountains from the state capital to Pittsburgh.

In the western states the construction of both turnpikes and railroads came several years later than in the East. The National Road was completed to Columbus, Ohio, in 1833, and pushed on to its final terminus, Vandalia, Illinois, by midcentury, just a few years before the western states seriously turned to railroad building. As the nation became disenchanted with turnpikes, some areas became enthusiastic about plank roads, intended for short- and moderate-distance transportation. This innovation, much like the construction principle of wooden sidewalks, was borrowed from Russia and appeared in upper Canada in the mid-1830s.

When William B. Ogden started to talk up railroads in

the late 1840s, Chicago was already served by a growing network of new plank roads. The success of Ogden's Galena & Chicago Union, and the other rival roads that soon followed, quickly dampened the enthusiasm for plank roads. Other western efforts at building plank toll roads instead of railroads were no more successful. Between 1849 and 1851 William F. Coolbaugh and James W. Grimes, businessmen of Burlington, Iowa, led in the construction of a 28-mile toll road from Burlington west to Mount Pleasant. The newness had hardly worn off the stout white-oak planks before the same men were projecting the Burlington & Missouri Railroad to serve the same region.[4]

The story of the decline of the turnpike at midcentury is graphically illustrated by the two trips Abraham Lincoln took, one in March 1849 and the second in February 1861. On his return to Springfield from Washington, D.C., in 1849 Lincoln had no choice but to take a stagecoach over the National Road from Cumberland to Wheeling, and he may have completed his homeward trip on another stagecoach, from Saint Louis to Springfield. A dozen years later his entire preinaugural trip from Springfield to Washington, D.C., was by railroad.

The supremacy of the railroad over the canal did not come as easily as the victory over the turnpike. Although several canals were projected and built in the late eighteenth century, the total canal mileage in existence by the second decade of the nineteenth century was still quite limited. In 1817, the year of the Bonus Bill, legislation sponsored by President James Madison, John C. Calhoun, and Henry Clay, there were only about 100 miles of completed canal in the country. In that same year Governor DeWitt Clinton succeeded in getting New York State to start the Erie Canal, a 364-mile project that would require unprecedented feats of engineering, $8 million, and eight years to complete. Finished in 1825, the new water route from Albany to Buffalo, an immediate financial success, sparked the canal craze.

The rate of canal building greatly accelerated during the

1820s, especially after 1824. By 1830 canal mileage in the nation had increased to 1,277 miles, close to forty times the total railroad mileage. More canal construction occurred in the 1830s, but in volume it did not match the building of new rail lines. By 1840 total canal mileage was 3,326 miles, while that of railroads stood at 3,328 miles. Between 1824 and 1840 a total of perhaps $125 million had been invested in American canals. Probably another $75 million had gone into canal construction by the eve of the Civil War. At least a third of this new money went into the enlargement of the Erie Canal.

Fewer than 400 miles of new canal were added during the 1840s, and in 1850 the total canal mileage was 3,698 miles, as compared with 9,000 miles of railroad. During most of the 1850s, more miles of canal were abandoned than constructed; certainly total canal mileage did not increase. On the other hand, as already noted, railroad mileage increased more than threefold; the national total on the eve of the Civil War was well over 30,000 miles.[5]

In 1850 the 3,698 miles of American canals were located in twenty different states. Only six states east of the Mississippi (Florida, Michigan, Mississippi, New Hampshire, Tennessee, and Wisconsin) lacked that first mile of man-made waterway. At midcentury eight states (Illinois, Indiana, Maryland, New Jersey, New York, Ohio, Pennsylvania, and Virginia) had 100 miles or more of canal, and in general these same states were leaders in rail mileage. Most of the canals were located in the Northeast, and three states, Pennsylvania (954 miles), New York (803 miles), and Ohio (792 miles) together possessed about 70 percent of the total mileage.

The dozens of canals projected and built in the third, fourth, and fifth decades of the nineteenth century were generally of three types: (1) *tidewater* canals to serve the coastal regions of eastern states; (2) *trans-Allegheny* canals to furnish transportation from eastern cities to the West; and (3) *western canals* in the Old Northwest to connect the Great Lakes with the Ohio and Mississippi rivers. Tidewater canals were chiefly found in southern New England and the mid-Atlantic states; several were "anthracite canals," built to transport coal to Philadelphia or New York City. Trans-Allegheny canals, such as the Erie and its later rivals, were found in New York, Pennsylvania, Maryland, and Virginia. The western canals were almost entirely in Ohio and Indiana.

Canals were expensive to build. First-class, hard-surfaced turnpikes could be constructed for $5,000 to $10,000 a mile, whereas many canals cost $20,000 to $30,000, or even more, for each completed mile. Since many canals were also longer than the typical toll road, most of the waterways could not be privately financed. The federal government did not help finance the Erie, but later it granted about 4 million acres to canal projects in the Old Northwest and made substantial subscriptions to the stock of several canal companies. Far more important were the canal investments of several states. New York, Pennsylvania, Ohio, and Indiana each spent millions of dollars in building their own major systems of artificial waterways. The anthracite canal frequently was built with little financial support from the state, however. These coal-bearing canals often were financially successful. After being enlarged to accommodate coal barges of up to 140 tons, the 106-mile Delaware and Hudson Canal, where John Jervis had tried out the English-built *Stourbridge Lion*, was able to pay yearly dividends of 8 percent or higher during the forties and fifties.

Many of the trans-Allegheny and western canals were completed and in full operation shortly before the midcentury upsurge of rail construction. The Erie was opened by 1825, but the Pennsylvania Main Line was not opened until 1834, and in 1850, the Chesapeake & Ohio was finished 184 miles to Cumberland, and the James River & Kanawha at mid-century was completed only to Buchanan, 200 miles above Richmond. The two major north–south canals in Ohio were opened in 1833 and 1845, and Indiana's Wabash & Erie reached its Ohio River terminal only in 1853.

Some canals, especially the first ones to be completed, had several years of good business and prosperity, but they could not compete with railroads. Canals were stymied by hills of any size. They were built where geography favored them rather than where man wanted them. Rail lines could be projected and built in many locations that could never be served by canals. Most hills, and many mountains, could be crossed by a railroad if a civil engineer was given the task of surveying and laying out a modest gradient. And a railroad could provide a more dependable service since it could operate all year. The typical canal was closed from three to five months a year because of cold weather, and frequently was often closed because of needed repairs, low water, or flooding.

Even the Erie Canal, the original and by far the most profitable of the trans-Allegheny waterways, succumbed to the railroads during the 1850s. Of course the Erie had never attempted to give year-round service. Throughout the 1830s and 1840s the canal normally was open fully only in May through November, being closed most of the rest of the year.[6]

The real and relative decline of the New York waterway can be seen in the comments of the *American Railroad Journal* at the beginning and end of the 1850s. In January 1850, the journal reviewed the canal traffic in 1849: "Notwithstanding . . . the cholera the annexed figures show that the past season has but one equal in the history of our State canals; and that year can scarcely be taken as a criterion for others, we allude to the ever memorable 1847. . . ." In 1849 the total Erie canal traffic moving eastward to the Hudson River came to 1,580,000 tons, with 90 percent consisting of either forest or agricultural products.[7]

Ten years later, in the spring of 1860, the *Journal* was telling a far different story. In reviewing the increasing traffic of the New York Central and the Erie railroads in the middle and late 1850s the *Journal* wrote:

> One of the most marked features in the internal commerce of the country is the steadily increasing traffic of our railroads, and corresponding diminution on all our water lines. Perhaps the most striking evidence of this tendency is

afforded by the traffic of the Erie and New York Central Railroads and the New York Canals. Notwithstanding the enlargement of the canals, the number of tons moved one mile upon them is about 25 per cent less than it was seven years ago, while upon the two roads named, the increase, in the aggregate, has been one hundred per cent. . . .

During the seven years covered (1853 through 1859) the New York Central traffic increased from 54 to 157 million ton-miles and the Erie Railroad's traffic grew from 101 to 147 million ton-miles, while that of the Erie Canal dropped from 700 to 544 million ton-miles.[8]

Since the rail freight rates were much higher than the combined tolls plus freight rates on the Erie Canal, in 1859 the two railroads each had gross revenues about equal to the total charges for the canal traffic. The New York Central grossed $3,337,000 with an average rate of 2.13 cents a ton-mile; the Erie Railroad made $3,195,000 with a 2.17 cents a ton-mile rate, and the Erie Canal had revenues of $3,467,000 at an average cost of only .63 cents a ton-mile. Costs per ton-mile in each case had declined since 1853, when the New York Central rate was 3.36 cents, the Erie Railroad 2.49 cents, and the Erie Canal .91 cents. In fact tolls and freight rates on the canal had been declining for a generation. Charges per ton for canal freight from Albany west to Buffalo had been $20 in 1830, $16.60 in 1840, $7.20 in 1850, and $2.80 by 1858. Down freight, from Buffalo to Albany, cost $9.07 a ton in 1830, $7.50 in 1840, $5.48 in 1850, and $3.14 in 1858. For both movements the tolls paid the canal and the freight paid the boat operators had been roughly equal. As tolls declined, the size of the canal boat increased. In 1844 the average boat on the Erie had a capacity of 64 tons, but by 1852 this was up to 90 tons, more than six times the capacity of the normal railroad car.[9]

During these same years the origin of Erie Canal traffic moving eastward (Buffalo to Albany) experienced a great change. As the freight rates dropped in the 1830s and 1840s, the traffic coming from western states rapidly expanded, growing from 54,000 tons in 1836 to 158,000 tons in 1840

The steamboat *Denver* was used in 1860 to ferry the U.S. mail from St. Joseph, western terminal of the Hannibal & St. Joseph Railroad, across the Missouri River to the riders of the Pony Express in Elwood, Kansas. (COURTESY, ASSOCIATION OF AMERICAN RAILROADS.)

and 778,000 tons in 1850. By midcentury western states were providing the great bulk of the eastern canal traffic. But the rate of growth slowed during the 1850s, as the canal boats shared an increasing share of the freight with newly completed railroads. From 778,000 tons in 1850, canal freight grew only to 1,092,000 tons in 1855 and 1,273,000 tons in 1858. During the 1850s the population of the western states nearly doubled, and the increase of the domestic trade in the region grew even faster. For example, between 1854 and 1860 Chicago's shipment eastward of corn doubled while that of wheat increased fivefold. Certainly traffic on the canal in the mid-1850s in no way was keeping up with the buoyant economy of the West. In the same years ton-mileage carried by Erastus Corning's New York Central tripled while its freight revenue doubled, increases far above those of the Erie Canal.[10]

The Erie Canal suffered not relative, but real, losses in its carriage of eastern merchandise and manufctured goods to western states. The tonnage going to western states via the canal averaged 127,000 tons a year between 1849 and 1851 and peaked in 1853–54 with nearly 300,000 tons. From then on such traffic was increasingly lost to the New York Central and the Erie Railroad, and the share moving by the Erie Canal was down to a yearly average of 90,000 tons for the years 1859–61. Railroads tended to carry the lighter, more valuable merchandise, while the bulkier, less valuable freight was left to the slower canal boats. Some estimates suggest that canal freight on the average was worth but two cents a pound, while that traveling by rail was valued at about ten cents a pound.[11]

Of course the railroads had taken passenger traffic away from the Erie Canal even earlier. The several connecting railroads paralleling the canal by the 1840s had taken away the cream of the passenger traffic, even from the newest and most luxurious of the canal packets. In the mid-1830s half of the boats on the Erie were either packets or carried passengers along with the freight. By 1842 only a fifth of the Erie boats could carry passengers.

Before midcentury the threat of the railroads to the canal's freight traffic was postponed and delayed by the New York State law that required competing rail lines to pay canal tolls when carrying freight. When this restriction was removed on December 1, 1851, railroad freight at once increased. Some local newspapers claimed the Erie Canal would soon be a "useless ditch." This prediction never came true, but such lines as the New York Central rather quickly added many more freight trains. In 1853 New York Central passenger revenue was still 50 percent greater than that from freight, but by 1858 freight revenue was a third larger.[12]

The victory of the trunk line railroads over the other trans-Allegeheny canals was even quicker and easier. Certainly this was true in the case of the Pennsylvania Canal System, a route from Philadelphia to Pittsburgh consisting of a 75-mile railroad to the Susquehanna, a 173-mile Grand Canal on to Hollidaysburg, a system of inclined planes (the Portage Railroad) ascending and descending the Appalachians between Hollidaysburg and Johnston, and a western slope canal on into Pittsburgh. This 394-mile Main Line was built across the state between 1826 and 1834 and cost Pennsylvania originally about $10 million.

The Pennsylvania system provided much slower service than the Erie, required twice as many locks, and was forced to hoist its canal boats to an elevation of 2,200 feet above sea level in using the inclined planes of the Portage Railroad. Between 1834 and 1857 it yielded total revenues of $3,648,611, but had operating expenses of $4,876,334. In spring 1857 Pennsylvania offered to sell the entire system for $7.5 million—about half of the state's investment. Shortly thereafter, J. Edgar Thomson purchased the system for his Pennsylvania Railroad. By this time the Pennsylvania Railroad had double-tracked most of its line from Philadelphia to Pittsburgh, had annual revenues of nearly $4 million, and was operating 133 locomotives and 2,000 freight cars. Its total freight movement was far larger than that of the ill-fated canal system that had tried to cross the mountains of Pennsylvania.[13]

South of the Mason-Dixon Line, canals were even less successful in their efforts to cross the Alleghenies. Certainly the Chesapeake and Ohio Canal neither lived up to its name nor gave the railroads in the region much competition by midcentury. President John Quincy Adams, using a ribbon-bedecked spade, had turned the first earth of the projected canal in 1828. The first time Adams dug into the soil he struck a root. He tried a second and a third time before he finally got a full shovelful of dirt. His troubles were to be symptomatic of the canal's later history. Construction was plagued by sickness and labor trouble, and building costs soon were running at $60,000 a mile, nearly three times the cost of the Erie. The Blue Ridge proved to be too high an obstacle. About $11 million were spent, but when construction stopped in 1850 the canal was completed only 184 miles to Cumberland. In 1854 the C. & O. Canal earned only $120,000 in tolls, perhaps a tenth of the total interest due on the investment and debt. The canal was never to reach the Ohio River, which the rival Baltimore & Ohio Railroad had done in 1852. And the B. & O. ran twelve months a year—even in the early 1830s the railroad was closed but a single day out of 365. Further south in Virginia, the railroads were just as successful in competing with the James River and Kanawha Canal, which at midcentury was stalled on the upper James River at Buchanan, only 200 miles above Richmond.[14]

At midcentury most of the canal mileage west of the Allegheny Mountains was located in Ohio and Indiana. Ohio had been an early leader in canal building, with 245 miles in 1830, 744 in 1840, and 792 miles in 1850. In the generation before the Civil War only New York and Pennsylvania had more canal mileage. But in the 1850s Ohio became even more enthusiastic about railroads. Her 575 miles of railway in 1850 placed her fifth in the nation, but the nearly 2,400 miles of construction in the decade gave her first place among the states in 1860 with a total of 2,946 miles. By this time Alfred Kelley, long a proponent of canals in Ohio, had shifted his allegiance to railroads.

The bulk of the Ohio canal mileage was in two north–south canals connecting the Ohio River with Lake Erie. On July 4, 1825 Governor DeWitt Clinton left the Erie Canal long enough to break ground on the Ohio and Erie Canal, a 308-mile route from Portsmouth, on the Ohio River, to Cleveland on Lake Erie. At a total cost of $8 million, this canal was completed in 1833. Further west the 244-mile Miami and Erie, from Toledo, via Dayton, to Cincinnati was not finished until 1845. Both canals were well planned and built. By 1846 these canals, along with branch routes and lesser works in the state, were bringing in annual total revenues of $611,000, a figure which grew to $833,000 for the year 1851. These revenues had dropped to less than $500,000 a year for the years 1854 to 1856, and the editors of the *American Railroad Journal* in March 1857 wrote: "It is true that the nearly three thousand miles of railroads in this State [Ohio] operate to the disadvantage of the canals in the general freight. . . ."[15]

Ohio canals had lost much of their packet-boat passenger traffic even earlier, mostly to the first railroads, and the peak of the passenger traffic on some Ohio canals was past by midcentury. Even deluxe packet boats, with a top speed of more than four miles an hour, had little appeal when the steam cars offered travel six times as rapid. By the mid-1850s Ohio rail passenger travel was many times the peak years of canal passenger business.

In the late 1840s several projected Ohio railroads were subjected to special taxes on all freight carried, the money to be used to reimburse the state for canal tolls that were lost. These restrictions were soon given up, however, and within a few years the Ohio canals started to reduce their tolls in order to meet the increasingly severe railroad competition. Many of the railroads had shorter routes than those available by canal, and all provided year-round service in contrast to the seven- or eight-month service available on the canal freight boat.[16]

As a result many major canal terminals in the state saw traffic decline during the 1850s. Between 1852 and 1860 canal commerce arriving at Cleveland dropped from 425,000 tons to only 122,000 tons; clearances in the same years declined from 67,000 to 34,000 tons. During the same years, arriving and departing canal tonnage at Toledo dropped more than 50 percent. This trend did not hold true at Cincinnati, where canal tonnage, both arrivals and departures, remained fairly stable during the decade. By contrast, the estimates of the traffic growth of Ohio railroads between 1849 and 1859 reveal a sixteen fold increase in total receipts, a fourteen fold increase in passenger traffic, and an eighteen fold growth of freight.[17]

As earlier noted, Indiana was much slower in canal construction than Ohio. Thus the major Indiana canal, the Wabash and Erie, had very serious competition from railroads almost before it was finished. Total canal expenditures were greater than receipts in 1851, when there was still relatively limited rail mileage in the state. Canal tolls in Indiana reached their peak in 1852. The Wabash & Erie was pushed on to the Ohio River at Evansville by 1853, and the Hoosiers could boast of a completed waterway of 450 miles, the longest canal in the nation. But the expected traffic never appeared on the lower reaches of the canal. Floods, inadequate funds for repair work, and fierce competition from new rail lines all plagued the canal. By 1860 all operation ceased on the lower sections of the canal: in Indiana the 2,100 miles of railroad were triumphant.[18]

During the 1850s the trunk line railroads and other roads operating in the area from New York and Pennsylvania westward to the Mississippi faced serious competition from the substantial commerce on the Great Lakes. The registered tonnage of vessels operating in the five lakes had increased from 48,000 tons in 1840 to 186,000 tons in 1850 and 450,000 tons in 1860. On the eve of the Civil War, sailing vessels still outnumbered steamers on the Great Lakes, but they were smaller in size. The 369 steamers averaged 370 tons each, while the 1,207 sailing vessels averaged only 210 tons.[19]

Rail mileage in the Old Northwest certainly had grown

The *Pioneer*, the first locomotive to operate in California, belonged to the Sacramento Valley Railroad, a short line built in the mid-1850s. (COURTESY, SOUTHERN PACIFIC COMPANY.)

American "Express" Train. The print makers, Currier and Ives, were also aware of the expanding rail service in western states in the 1850s, a growth much greater than that of the rival river steamboats. (CURRIER & IVES PRINT OF 1855, AUTHOR'S COLLECTION.)

more rapidly in the 1850s than had lake navigation. However, the rapid population growth of the western states and the still greater expansion of the domestic commerce in the area meant that there was traffic enough for both the railroads and the Great Lakes. A larger and larger share of the passenger traffic shifted away from the lakes to the railroads. The growing number of rail lines had the advantage of more direct routes, faster schedules, and year-round service. Lake vessels had an open season typically from April into early December. From 1850 through 1858 the date of the first spring boat ranged from March 25 to May 1, and the average of annual days of navigation was 216. The accident rate for lake navigation was definitely higher in the early spring and late fall.[20]

By the eve of the Civil War much of the lake-borne freight moving east consisted of bulky products such as wheat, corn, coal, lead, and lumber. Such commerce was not much injured by the winter closing of the lakes, and much of this freight continued on eastward via the Erie Canal. By the end of the 1850s the eastbound rail freight included livestock, dressed meats, hides, general merchandise, and flour. These more valuable products were more apt to require the year-round service available by rail. During the decade western railroads were capturing an increasing share of the growing commerce with eastern states.[21]

During the 1850s the railroad also challenged the steamboats. In the New England and the mid-Atlantic states, the steamboat traffic of Long Island Sound, the lower Connecticut, the Hudson, the Delaware, and Chesapeake Bay continued without any serious competition from the railroad. In the South the often inferior quality of the railroads, the general absence of industrial growth, and the great abundance of navigable rivers resulted in only a moderate shift from river to rail transport. But the challenge of the railroad to the stately white side-wheeler on the Ohio and upper Mississippi rivers in the 1850s was more successful, especially in the states west of Pittsburgh and north of the Ohio River. As earlier noted, the rail mileage in these western states increased eightfold in the 1850s. In the long run, the steamboats of the Ohio and upper Mississippi were destined to fall to the rail network. The rapid success of the railroad in these years was not immediately obvious, since the tide of settlement was so rapid in the upper Mississippi Valley. Between 1850 and 1860 the population of Illinois, Wisconsin, Iowa, and Minnesota increased from a total of 1.3 to 3.3 millions. This growth plus the general industrial prosperity of the decade meant that both steamboats and the railroads were often taxed to carry the expanding traffic.

As the railroads in the region of the Great Lakes and the upper Mississippi Valley successfully challenged the river-borne commerce, they also succeeded in diverting more and more of the internal commerce of the region from the South toward eastern markets. The bulk of the 8,000 miles of railroad built in the Old Northwest ran from east to west rather than from north to south. The four great trunk lines (New York Central, Erie, Pennsylvania, and Baltimore & Ohio) and their extensions in western states were built to serve eastern rather than southern markets.

A railroad map of 1860 reveals that north–south lines in the Old Northwest touched the Ohio River at only four places: Cairo, Evansville, New Albany-Jeffersonville, and Cincinnati. The most important of the north–south railroads was the "wrong way" Illinois Central. A comparable stretch of the middle Mississippi in 1860 shows east–west lines touching that river at nine points: Saint Louis, Alton, Quincy, Burlington, Davenport, Clinton, Dubuque, Prairie de Chien, and La Crosse. The major thrust of the rail construction of the decade had clearly been from east to west.[22]

Historians of the western steamboat do not all agree as to the degree, or the timing, of the steamboat's decline and the triumph of the railroad. But Louis C. Hunter, in his *Steamboats on the Western Rivers* (1949), sees the decline as being well under way in the 1850s. In his chapter entitled "The Critical Decade," he wrote:

> . . . But fundamentally the decade of the fifties, for the steamboat interest as a whole, was marked by depression and misfortune and by the beginning of the trend which within a

few years was to relegate steamboats to a minor role in the economic life of the West. The increasing diversion of traffic to the railroads, the shifting routes and changing direction of internal commerce and, stimulated by these conditions, the growing severity of competition among steamboatmen themselves were the basic factors in this decline.[23]

More recent authorities on western steamboating do not all agree with Hunter. Erik F. Haites, James Mak, and Gary M. Walton, in their *Western River Transportation* (1975), write: ". . . our findings show that steamboating had not entered a period of absolute decline prior to the Civil War. Undoubtedly, the railroad was making inroads during the 1850s, first in passenger service and later in freight, but by our estimates total steamboat tonnage continued to expand right up to the outbreak of hostilities."[24] Haites, Mak, and Walton estimate that during the 1850s the number of western steamboats increased 28 percent (from 638 to 817) while total tonnage grew by 45 percent (from 134,566 to 196,022 tons).[25] These riverboat increases did not match the 48 percent population growth in the twelve-state trans-Appalachian region, and they certainly were much lower than the commercial expansion of the area in the 1850s. During that decade the increase in rail mileage in the twelve-state region was more than 800 percent! These figures clearly suggest that while western river traffic may not have suffered a *real* decline, it suffered a serious *relative* loss to the railroad during the prewar years.

For three decades prior to midcentury western steamboats had a real monopoly of transportation in the Mississippi-Ohio basin. Many westerners saw any improvement in transportation across the Appalachians as a challenge to the traditional river traffic that flowed south to New Orleans and the Gulf. In a speech before the Senate in 1830, Thomas Hart Benton had denounced improved transportation across the mountains: "Every canal, and every road, tending to draw the commerce of the western states across the Allegheny Mountains, is an injury to the people of the West." A decade and a half later Benton was to become a proponent of western railroads. Certainly by the 1850s western railways were proving to have several competitive advantages over the side-wheelers and stern-wheelers of western rivers.[26]

Frequently the distance by rail between two given cities was much less than the river distance between the same two points. The rail distance from Pittsburgh to Cincinnati was 316 miles, whereas by the twisting Ohio River it was 470 miles. The rail mileage from Cincinnati to New Orleans was 922, while that via the Ohio-Mississippi rivers was 1,484. The steamboat trip from Cincinnati to Nashville, via the Ohio and Cumberland rivers, was 644 miles long; in 1859, when James Guthrie had completed the L. & N., the rail distance was only 301 miles. The indirect steamer trip from Cincinnati west to Saint Louis was listed as 702 miles, while Joseph Alsop's broad-gauge Ohio & Mississippi, once it was finished in 1857, required only 339 miles of travel. These savings in distance available by rail went far to offset the advantages of the lower freight rates per to-mile quoted by the steamboat captains.

These shorter rail distances, plus the faster speed of the railroad, meant that both passenger travel and freight service by rail was much quicker than that available by the steamboat. Travelers, especially businessmen, were quick to note the faster schedules available by rail. In the late 1850s steamboat travel from Cincinnati to Pittsburgh took something over three days—by railroad it was only fifteen hours. The downstream trip from Cincinnati to New Orleans took eight days on the average, and low water might lengthen that. By rail the same trip took only two and a half days. The river trip from Cincinnati to Saint Louis took nearly three days; by rail on the Ohio & Mississippi it took only sixteen hours. The *American Railroad Journal* in June 1857 noted the effect of the completion of the Ohio & Mississippi upon the steamboat packet line:

> A few years ago we had a daily line of splendid steamboats running between this [Saint Louis] and Louisville. They went and came filled with people, carried the U.S. Mail, and did a smashing business. But the completion of the Ohio and Mississippi Railroad, by which passengers are carried to Louis-

ville and Cincinnati in less than twenty hours, has broken up the business of the daily line, and now the passenger trade between St. Louis and the Ohio is worth precious little.[27]

Freight trains were naturally slower than passenger service but still quite a bit faster than the riverboats. On the eve of the Civil War, freight from Cincinnati to Saint Louis took just under three days when sent by the river. A freight train would take less than half as long, perhaps thirty hours. Riverboat freight up the Ohio from Louisville to Pittsburgh required four days, while rail freight was twice as fast, requiring only two days.

Another major advantage of the railroad was its ability to enlarge the area served through the building of new lines and branches. The shallow-hulled western steamboats, especially the smaller stern-wheelers, required a remarkably modest depth of water, but even so there were real limits to the navigable portions of the Mississippi-Ohio river system. Only the lower portions of the tributaries of the two rivers were deep enough to permit any substantial steamboat navigation. In April 1831, the citizens of Indianapolis noisily greeted the *Robert Hanna,* but upon the start of her trip downstream the small boat promptly went aground in the shallow White River, remaining there for six weeks. In the 1830s and 1840s the Indianapolis lawyer-banker Calvin Fletcher had to travel to and from the Hoosier capital by horseback or stage, not by steamboat. Many interior towns in Ohio, Indiana, and Illinois started to grow and prosper only with the coming of the railroad.

Columbus, Ohio, and Springfield, Illinois, state capitals to the east and west of Indianapolis, never possessed any significant steamboat service. These cities began to grow as they obtained their first railroads. Columbus, hometown of Alfred Kelley, obtained its first railroad in 1850. Indianaplis received its first rail line three years earlier, and in the 1850s its population promptly boomed from 8,000 to 18,000. Further west Springfield had had a short railroad of sorts for several years, but Abe Lincoln could not take a train to Chicago and points east until 1853. The interior of the five states

Railroad suspension bridge, near Niagara Falls. When completed in early 1855, this two-level 822-foot structure was easily one of the major engineering feats of the decade. (CURRIER & IVES PRINT OF 1856, AUTHOR'S COLLECTION.)

of the Old Northwest, along with Iowa and Missouri, bene-
fited greatly with the expansion of the western rail network.

Rail travel was available in more cities than were served
by the stately white steamers, and was speedier, but still many
travelers preferred the comfort of water travel. In his extensive travels before the Civil War, Dr. Thomas Low Nichols,
journalist and pioneer dietician, invariably found the river
steamer more comfortable than the railroad.[28] Train travel
could be noisy, dirty, and tiresome. The best passenger cars
were far more cramped than riverboats and were subjected
to jolting and extremes of temperature. There were few
sleeping cars on the rails before the Civil War, and dining
facilities were normally much better on the boat than by rail.

Accidents were common on both the railroad and the
river in the early years, but by the 1850s rail travel was probably considered safer by the general public. Railway accidents
tended to be more frequent, but the loss of life generally was
greater when disaster struck the steamboat. During 1853 rail
accidents were reported as killing 227, while 359 lost their
lives in steamboat travel. The average rail accident that year
took fewer than two lives, while the death toll for the steamboat was nearly a dozen per accident.[29]

Rail service had other advantages. Riverboat traffic was
very competitive whereas railroads had a near monopoly of
the immediate market area, with no competition from other
railroads or riverboats. As a consequence, the railroads early
set up and maintained regular schedules and quickly separated passenger and freight service. These facts meant that
rail service, both passenger and freight, avoided the delays so
common on the river. Furthermore, the railroad had greater
flexibility, since, within limits, cars could be added or taken
off to fit more nearly the available traffic on a particular day
or at a given station. In contrast, riverboats had to carry the
same hull weight regardless of the size of the cargo.
Railroads also gave much better service than steamboats in
arranging for forwarding and transshipping freight, and in
providing single, through passenger tickets.[30]

A final, and extremely important, advantage of the

railroad was its year-round availability. Unusual droughts in 1854 and again in 1856 caused long periods of extremely low steamboat activity on the Ohio River. These deficiencies in navigation were so great on the upper Mississippi above Saint Louis that the typical season of navigation was little more than six months out of the year. Only during the season of unrestricted navigation did the lower river freight rates give the steamers an advantage over the railroad. And even then the rail advantages of greater speed, shorter distances, and more regular schedules to a great extent offset the rate advantages. Frequently the traffic lost by steamboats in seasons of low water was retained permanently by the railroad.[31]

Since a majority of the railroads in the western states were east–west rather than north–south roads, the decline in river traffic was more pronounced on the Ohio than the Mississippi. This trend can be seen by noting the annual steamboat arrivals in the leading river cities. During the dozen years before the Civil War, annual steamboat arrivals in New Orleans increased from 2,800 or 2,900 in the early and middle fifties to a little more than 3,000 arrivals a year in the late 1850s. Further north at Saint Louis, the annual arrivals also increased by perhaps 10 percent during the decade. By the end of the decade the great bulk of the river traffic at Saint Louis came from the upper or lower Mississippi, and less than 10 percent came from the Ohio River or its tributaries.[32]

Steamboat traffic actually declined on the Ohio River during the 1850s. Between 1848 and 1859 the annual arrivals at Cincinnati, the principal Ohio River port, dropped from a yearly average of 3,649 steamboats for 1848 through 1851 to only 2,961 in 1856 to 1859. The available data also suggest that there was no growth in river traffic at either Pittsburgh or Louisville. Such a decrease is not surprising since each of the three cities had achieved abundant rail service during the decade.[33]

The victory of the western railroad over the steamboat is illustrated by the contrasting development of Chicago and Saint Louis. Chicago, a railroad town, had its first rail service in 1848 with the building of William Ogden's Galena & Chicago Union. By 1860 the city was the center of a widespread iron network, being directly served by eleven different railroads. Saint Louis, a steamboat town for several decades, did have a short railroad heading westward in 1852, but on the eve of the Civil War it was the focal point of only a modest amount of rail mileage.

In 1850 Saint Louis had a population of 79,000, nearly triple the 30,000 in Chicago. In the following ten years Saint Louis doubled its population, while that of Chicago increased nearly fourfold. During the last six years of the decade, the quantities of flour sent from Chicago to eastern markets increased sixfold, wheat increased fivefold, and corn doubled. The commerce of Saint Louis did not begin to increase to this extent. Clearly such Chicago leaders and railroad promoters as William B. Ogden, John Wentworth, and Stephen A. Douglas had been better judges of the commercial future of railroads than such Saint Louis businessmen as Thomas Allen, John O'Fallon, and James H. Lucas had been.[34]

Geography also played a part in the success of Chicago. Located at the southern end of Lake Michigan, Chicago became a natural transfer point for land and lake shipping. This was especially important as the growing commerce in the decade sought eastern rather than southern markets. Chicago was in an excellent position to capture the bulk of the trade of Illinois, eastern Iowa, and even northern Missouri. In these years many eastern Iowa towns shifted from river to rail service. By 1856 Burlington, Iowa, was shipping fifteen times as much wheat, and twice as much corn, by rail as by the Mississippi. At the end of the 1850s the newly completed 206-mile Hannibal & St. Joseph Railroad in northern Missouri was sending far more of its traffic northeast to Chicago than southeastward to Saint Louis.[35]

During the 1850s the production of wheat more than doubled (41 to 95 million bushels) in the ten western states and territories, and that of corn nearly doubled (222 to 406 million bushels). Certainly the Saint Louis river traffic south to New Orleans grew very little during these years. The

amount of western foodstuffs received at New Orlenas was
only slightly larger in the late 1850s than in the early 1850s.
New Orleans in 1851–52 received from the north 927,000
barrels of flour. In 1859–60, it received 973,000 barrels. The
railroads of the Old Northwest, plus the Great Lakes, not the
steamboats of the Mississippi, were moving the increased
western farm production to market.[36]

A decade after the Civil War Mark Twain in his *Life on
the Mississippi* described the decline in the western river traffic
since the lush days of the 1850s. The former riverboat pilot
wrote:

> Boat used to land—captain on hurricane roof—mighty
> stiff and straight—iron ramrod for a spine—kid gloves, plug
> hat, hair parted behind—man on the shore takes off his hat
> and says:
> "Got twenty-eight tons of wheat, cap'n—be a great favor
> if you can take them."
> Captain says:
> "I'll take two of them"—and don't even condescend to
> look at him.
> But nowadays the captain takes off his old slouch, and
> smiles all the way around to the back of his ears, and gets off
> a bow which he hasn't got any ramrod to interfere with, and
> says:
> "Glad to see you, Smith, glad to see you—you're looking
> well—haven't seen you looking so well for years—what you
> got for us?"
> "Nuth'n," says Smith; and keeps his hat on, and just turns
> his back and goes to talking with somebody else.[37]

The river traffic had not collapsed on the eve of the Civil
War to the degree that Twain described in the mid-1870s.
Nevertheless, by 1860 the commerce of side-wheelers and
stern-wheelers were in a relative, if not an absolute, decline.
The western railroad was gaining the same victory over the
western riverboats that it earlier had achieved over the turnpike and the canal.

CHAPTER SEVEN

Technical Advances in Antebellum Railroads

THE RAILROADS that were taking traffic away from canal boat and side-wheeler were the talk of the nation in 1850. Ralph Waldo Emerson saw railroads as the chief topic of conversation at midcentury, of interest to such diverse groups as farmers, merchants, and small boys. Farmers in Wisconsin were mortgaging their farms to finance new lines, the money made by merchants in the China trade helped build new rail lines in Michigan and Illinois, and the first train out of Indianapolis had seen Calvin Fletcher's son get a free ride on the cars "by assisting the engineer by handing a bucket of water at intervals."[1]

The American people were proud as they saw the railroads of their nation expand and advance technically. Many improvements in the comfort and convenience of railroad travel appeared during the 1850s. By the end of the decade a passenger could purchase a through coupon ticket from eastern cities to the "Far West." Arrangements for long-distance baggage checking were established on many lines.[2] Train speed had increased, and one could travel from Saint Louis to Boston in forty-eight hours, or from Charleston to Memphis in 42. The best chair cars were equipped with water tanks, corner toilets, and newsboys. In the North many of the best trains might include crude "sleepers." Night travel was prevalent, but Sunday trains were still a matter of dispute, especially in the South. No dining or restaurant cars were yet available, and travelers had to buy hurried snacks at railroad eating houses during scheduled 15- or 20-minute meal stops.

However, the improvement in railroad technology did not assure any real uniformity in service and equipment. Certainly there was diversity rather than uniformity in the matter of railroad gauge. It is not surprising that no real trend toward the acceptance of a single uniform gauge had been achieved during these years, since the typical railroad projected and built in the 1840s and early 1850s was originally planned to fill only local needs. Five different gauges, ranging from 4 feet 8½ inches to 6 feet, were found in five states or more on the eve of the Civil War. The variety of gauges in the several states are shown in Table 7.1.[3]

As Table 7.1 indicates, at least half a dozen different gauges were in use in the thirty-one states having mileage on the eve of the Civil War. Fifteen of these states had all of their mileage in a single gauge, eight states having the "standard" 4 feet 8½ inches gauge, five states, chiefly in the South, having the 5-ft. gauge, and two states having the broader gauge of 5 feet 6 inches. In the other sixteen states the "dominant" gauge in nine states was the 4 ft. 8½ in. gauge, while the 5-ft. width was found in three southern states.

Each of the six states with the greatest mileage—Ohio, Illinois, New York, Pennsylvania, Indiana, and Virginia—had at least two different gauges within their borders. While Ohio, the first state in mileage, favored the gauge of 4 feet 10 inches, each of the other five states had the standard 4 ft. 8½ in. gauge as the dominant type. Clearly the 4 ft. 8½ in. gauge was very common in the North, while the 5-ft. gauge was popular in the South. The 4 ft. 10 in. gauge was popular in New Jersey and Ohio, while the 5 ft. 6 in. width was found in the Southwest. A summary of the major gauges found in the several states is shown in Table 7.2.

The two major authorities on railroad gauges of a century ago, George Rogers Taylor and Irene D. Neu, have estimated that on the eve of the Civil War the standard gauge

TABLE 7.1
VARIETY IN GAUGE IN THE RAILROADS OF THE UNITED STATES IN 1860

New England and Mid-Atlantic States	Mileage in 1860	Only Gauge in the State	Dominant Gauge	Other Major Gauges
Maine	472		4'8½"	5'6"
New Hampshire	661		4'8½"	5'6"
Vermont	554		4'8½"	5'6"
Massachusetts	1,264	4'8½"		
Rhode Island	108	4'8½"		
Connecticut	601	4'8½"		
New York	2,682		4'8½"	6'0", 4'10"
New Jersey	560		4'10"	6'0", 4'8½"
Pennsylvania	2,598		4'8½"	4'10", 6'0"
Delaware	127	4'8½"		
Maryland	386	4'8½"		
Southern States				
Virginia	1,731		4'8½"	5'0"
North Carolina	937		4'8½"	5'0"
South Carolina	973	5'0"		
Georgia	1,420	5'0"		
Florida	402	5'0"		
Kentucky	534		5'0"	4'8½"
Tennessee	1,253	5'0"		
Alabama	743		5'0"	4'8½"
Mississippi	862		5'0"	4'10", 4'8½"
Louisiana	335		5'6"	5'0", 4'8½"
Arkansas	38	5'6"		
Texas	307		5'6"	4'8½"
Western States				
Ohio	2,946		4'10"	4'8½", 5'4"
Indiana	2,163		4'8½"	4'10", 6'0"
Illinois	2,790		4'8½"	6'0"
Michigan	779	4'8½"		
Wisconsin	905	4'8½"		
Iowa	655	4'8½"		
Missouri	817	5'6"		
California	23	5'0"		

TABLE 7.2
SUMMARY OF MAJOR GAUGES, BY STATES

Gauge	Only Gauge in the State	Dominant Gauge	Other Gauges	Total Listing
4'8½"	8	9	7	24
5'0"	5	3	3	11
5'6"	2	2	3	7
4'10"	0	2	4	6
6'0"	0	0	5	5
5'4"	0	0	1	1

was used by more than 200 lines, with a total of more than 17,000 miles, or a majority of the national rail network. They found the 5-ft. gauge in a strong second position with more than 7,000 miles of line. Next in popularity in 1860 would be the 4 ft. 10 in. gauge (nearly 3,300 miles), the 5 ft. 6 in. gauge (nearly 2,900 miles), and the 6-ft. gauge (more than 1,700 miles). These five gauges together accounted for about 99 percent of all the American trackage in 1860.[4]

These extensive differences in gauge meant that the iron network in the nation was far from fully integrated. The interchange of cars and engines was impossible, and "through traffic" as Americans were to know it in later decades did not exist. The lack of connecting lines across such cities as Philadelphia and Richmond, plus the absence of bridges across many major rivers, also kept rail service from being fully integrated. Uniformity in gauge and the building of bridges across such streams as the Potomac, the Ohio, and the lower Mississippi would have to wait until the early post–Civil War decades.

The costs of engineering and surveying, of laying out, grading, and bridging the route, plus the cost of rail, represented a major portion of the money needed to construct a new road in the 1850s. Few lines spent much money for fencing their route, but still the right-of-way was sometimes put to good use. In the late 1850s a portion of the New York Central right-of-way, which was generally fenced, was planted in potatoes; the "railroad farms" were tended by the wives of railroad workers. The Illinois Central early in 1855 had completed about three quarters of its 705 miles of charter line with a total expenditure of more than $17 million. Between 1851 and 1855 about $1 million had been spent for charter expenses, company and legal expenses, and additional lands needed beyond the generous Illinois Central land grant. The actual construction of the roughly 500 miles of completed road, including engineering costs, all labor, bridging, grading, spikes, ties and needed construction machinery came to more than $10 million. The railroad iron imported from England, and including transportation and insurance, had cost just under $4 million. Several years of interest on the bonds amounted to about $.8 million. The equipment for the road, including 62 engines, 1,250 freight cars, and 42 passenger cars, had cost $1.7 million. Total construction costs for the Illinois Central to the end of 1854 represented about four-fifths of all expenditures to that date.[5]

By the 1850s most of the iron land on American roads was the rolled, wrought-iron T rail. The earlier strap-iron rails and the U rail were found on only a few branch lines or on an occasional southern railroad. The T rails ranged in length from 18 to 24 feet and in weight from 35 to 68 pounds to the yard. During the Civil War some roads in New England as well as the Pennsylvania Railroad were laying rail weighing as much as 80 pounds to the yard. All the rail before the Civil War was iron rather than steel. J. Edgar Thomson of the Pennsylvania laid a bit of English-made steel rail during the war, but the first domestic steel rail was available only after the war.[6]

Many of the new roads constructed relied upon rail imported from England. Even though there was a great desire to use American rail if possible, at midcentury the importation of English rail had reached 100,000 tons a year. The English rail paid a duty of $16 a ton in the early 1850s, but it remained competitive in price. When a company found financing available in England, as the Illinois Central did, it was natural and normal to use English manufactured rails.[7]

Trestle and bridge in California in the 1850s. Railroad trestles were one of the quickest and cheapest means of crossing valleys and small streams. (COURTESY, SMITHSONIAN INSTITUTION.)

In building the 705 miles of charter lines between 1851 and 1856, the Illinois Central purchased about 80,000 tons of English iron, paying an average of just over $ 40 a ton, free on board, shipped from Wales or Liverpool. Over 200 cargoes of English iron crossed the Atlantic, with the normal cargo ranging from 300 to 500 tons. Since a mile of track laid with 50-pound rail required about 90 tons of iron, a 300-ton shipment could provide the rails for a bit more than three miles of track. William Osborn, the Illinois Central president from 1855 to 1865, found the English rail to be of top quality, and some of it was to remain in use for 30 years.

As the nation added more and more mileage in the decade, an increasing share of the rail laid was manufactured in the United States. By the mid-1850s the New York Central stated that it was saving a great deal of money each year by manufacturing its own rails. In 1859 the South Carolina Railroad decided to make a test of imported and domestic iron. On a mile of track one side was laid with imported English iron while the other side was laid with domestic iron from the Lackawanna Iron Works of Scranton, Pennsylvania. President John Caldwell of the South Carolina hoped that the experiment would test the wearing characteristics of the English and Lackawanna iron.[8]

By the mid- 1850s the Lackawanna Iron Works was one of the three or four largest rail mills in the United States. The great majority of the large rail mills (producing at least 3,000 tons a year) were in Pennsylvania; the other major mills were located in Massachusetts, New Jersey, Ohio, and Virginia. By 1854 American mills represented a total investment of perhaps $10 million, with an annual production of 100,000 tons of rail. The amount of railroad iron imported in 1854—most of it from England—amounted to 282,000 tons.[9]

Much of the American-produced iron was used for track maintenance and repair, rather than the laying of original line. Quite a large amount of rerolled rail was produced in the American mills, and much of this was used in track repair and maintenance. Maintenance of way was a major operating expense in the 1850s: on the Illinois Central it averaged just under 25 percent of all expenses, and on the New York Central expenses were about as great. Most experts believed that rails had to be replaced in somewhere between ten and twenty years depending upon the volume of traffic. Railroad ties, which cost no more than 25 cents per tie late in the decade, were expected to have a life expectancy of at least seven years. Certainly many of the poorer roads did not begin to replace them that frequently. Even before the Civil War a few lines were beginning to inject their ties with creosote.[10]

All roads had at least a minimum amount of additional line in the form of sidings or second track. In 1856 the editors of the *American Railroad Journal* estimated that in addition to the 21,440 miles of main line or first track in the country, there was an additional 3,749 miles of sidings and second track. This extra trackage was much more plentiful on the northern and eastern roads than in the southern states.

There was much double trackage in New England, especially in Massachusetts and Connecticut. New York State in 1860 probably had 1,000 miles of second track and sidings in addition to 2,600 miles of first track. The Pennsylvania Railroad as early as 1852 planned to double-track its main line from Philadelphia to Pittsburgh, and much of the 350-mile route was laid before the Civil War. But in the South, the light traffic justified very little double trackage, and even sidings were short and infrequent. One of the stronger southern lines, the Virginia & Tennessee, had only 10 miles of "turnouts" in the 204-mile route from Lynchburg to Bristol. Further to the west, Vernon K. Stevenson's Nashville & Chattanooga had only 8 miles of sidings along the 150-mile route between those two Tennessee cities.[11]

The American rail network on the eve of the Civil War also lacked bridges over many important streams. No railroad bridge crossed the Hudson at Albany or any point down to the New York harbor. At the nation's capital, the Long Bridge across the Potomac was not sturdy enough to bear the weight of trains. Below Pittsburgh no single railroad bridge spanned the Ohio River, even though both Cincinnati and Louisville had made plans to build bridges during the decade. Late in 1854 the *Louisville Journal* even reported plans for a double-track, 2-mile tunnel to be built under the river at a cost of $1.2 million.[12]

At the mouth of the Ohio a two-hour ferry connection was required between William Osborn's Illinois Central at Cairo and the northern terminal of the Mobile & Ohio at Columbus, Kentucky. Bridge building across the lower Mississippi had hardly reached the dreaming stage at such river towns as Memphis, Vicksburg, Baton Rouge, or New Orleans. No bridges spanned the Mississippi at Saint Louis, Alton, Hannibal, or Quincy. The only rail line across the Mississippi during the entire decade was the Rock Island bridge, completed in 1856.

Of course many lesser streams were spanned by railroad bridges. The Baltimore & Ohio completed the Thomas Viaduct in 1835, and today this strong stone structure carries trains many times the weight of those of the 1830s. A dozen years later the Scottish engineer James P. Kirkwood, with 800 men and $ 300,000, completed the equally sturdy Starrucca Viaduct for the Erie Railroad. But most bridges were only temporary wooden structures. In 1839 a wooden bridge over the Delaware River at Trenton was altered to permit the passage of steam-drawn trains. And in 1849, under the direction of J. Edgar Thomson, a multispanned wooden bridge was completed over the Susquehanna River a few miles above Harrisburg.

Many of the wooden railroad bridges were Howe truss bridges, patented in 1840. William Howe, a Yankee and uncle of the sewing machine inventor, designed a bridge truss with wooden diagonals and vertical iron tie rods. Unfortunately, the Howe truss bridges were more popular than safe. Frequently they grew tired and worn, the heavy trains fell through, and car stoves ignited the resulting debris.

The two major bridges built during the 1850s were the

Types of railroad signals in use at mid-century. (COURTESY, UNION SWITCH & SIGNAL COMPANY.)

railroad suspension bridge built near Niagara Falls and Henry Farnam's Rock Island bridge across the Mississippi, discussed earlier. The suspension bridge was built by John Augustus Roebling, who had received an excellent technical education in his native Germany before coming to America in 1831. After failing at farming in western Pennsylvania, Roebling shifted to engineering and in 1841 succeeded in manufacturing the first wire rope made in America. He built several suspension highway bridges and canal aqueducts before beginning the Niagara Falls bridge in 1851. The work on the Niagara bridge was started by a boy on the Canadian side flying a kite that carried a string over to the New York shore. The construction itself was slow, and was further delayed by a cholera epidemic in 1854.

The two-level, 822-ft. Niagara bridge was finally opened in March 1855, and included a wagon road below with the railroad track above. The rail was laid in three gauges (4 ft. 8½ in., 5 ft. 6 in., and 6 ft.). Twin stone towers carrying four wire cables, each of 10-in. diameter, supported the bridge structure, which was designed to carry a maximum load of 1,250 tons. The beauty of the suspension bridge was such that some visitors found it almost as great an attraction as the Falls itself. But the practical builder Roebling concerned himself with such theories as that a public procession marching to music or a troop of soldiers keeping regular step could be more injurious to the bridge than a heavy train crossing over to Canada at the speed of 20 miles per hour.[13] After the Civil War Roebling was to design and plan the construction of the Brooklyn Bridge between lower Manhattan and Brooklyn.

Significant improvements in locomotive design and performance appeared during the 1850s. Changes in boiler design, cylinders, fuel, and general weight and size of the engine all took place. In matters of basic wheel arrangement there was little change, since the American-type engine (4–4–0) continued to be the most popular until well after the Civil War. A few railroads such as the Baltimore & Ohio and the Delaware, Lackawanna & Western, tried different

designs. In summer 1853 the officials of the Delaware, Lackawanna & Western proudly announced that their new ten-
wheeler, the *Ontario,* had pulled a coal train, consisting of 90
four-wheeled cars with a gross weight of 720 tons, up a 21-
foot-per-mile grade at a speed of 5 to 7 miles an hour. The
Ontario had six 54-in. drivers, and with its loaded tender
weighted more than fifty tons. But most lines continued to
use the familiar American type eight-wheeler (four drivers
plus a bogie truck) both for freight and passenger service.[14]

As the national mileage more than tripled during the
decade, the total number of locomotives in use also increased. The annual manufacture of locomotives reached
500 or more engines per year. The total number of locomotives operating in the country increased from about 3,000
in 1850 to 5,000 in 1855 and probably 8,500 by 1860.[15]

During the 1850s the typical American locomotive grew
in weight and steam pressure even though there were no
changes in wheel arrangement. These increases are shown in
Table 7.3.[16]

TABLE 7.3
TYPICAL AMERICAN LOCOMOTIVES AT MIDCENTURY

Year	Wheel Arrangement	Size of Cylinders	Driver Size	Weight (tons)	Steam Pressure (pounds)
1845	4–4–0	13" x 18"	54"	13	80
1850	4–4–0	15" x 20"	60"	15	100
1855	4–4–0	15" x 20"	60"	20	100
1860	4–4–0	16" x 22"	60"	25	110

Several improvements in locomotive performance and
appearance were achieved during the decade. Thomas
Rogers, a Connecticut Yankee who had been a carpenter and
blacksmith before starting to manufacture locomotives in
New Jersey, had by midcentury one of the largest locomotive
plants in the country. By 1850 Thomas Rogers was introducing the "wagon top" boiler, a design that provided for an
enlarged conical boiler section just in front of the cab. This
enlarged boiler area provided for greater steam space,

allowed more water surface over the fire, increased the engine weight over the drivers, and made easier interior boiler repairs. Within a very few years nearly all locomotive boilers were using the wagon-top design.[17]

A second major change in engine design in the 1850s was the relocation of the cylinders in a lower and level position, made possible by spreading or increasing the wheelbase of the leading or bogie truck. By the mid-1850s this design was appearing in the locomotives coming out of the shops of Thomas Rogers, Septimus Norris, and William Mason. It permitted a much more secure mounting of the cylinders upon the frame and also improved the general appearance of the engine. By mid-decade the Stephenson link valve gear was also being widely adopted. This type of link motion, with its axle-mounted eccentrics, was most effective when used on the American 4–4–0 locomotives. During the decade "inside" valve connections were going out of favor; soon all locomotive shops were producing engines with "outside" connections. By late 1853 the outside connections were being used by builders by a ratio of nearly six to one.[18]

During the decade the American-type locomotives improved in beauty and symmetry as well as performance. William Mason, who like Thomas Rogers produced textile machinery before turning to locomotives, built some of the most beautiful locomotives appearing before the Civil War. Mason was not a major manufacturer of motive power, but he fully succeeded in his belief that beauty and strength could be merged in a steam engine. He once wryly commented that locomotives should look somewhat better than cookstoves upon wheels.

During the 1850s the cost of a first-class American-type locomotive ranged from $8,000 to $10,000. In the spring of 1854 the *American Railroad Journal* predicted that increased labor and material costs might soon push the price of a good locomotive as high as $12,000. This guess was not accurate; most domestic-built engines continued to sell for $10,000 or less. In the fall of 1856 William Osborn, president of the Illinois Central, was expecting to pay Morris K. Jesup of New

York City only from $9,000 to $9,500 for each of twenty "coal burners with copper furnaces." Earlier that fall Osborn had obtained from the Rogers Locomotive Works four switching engines priced at $6,500 each.[19]

The price of engines remained fairly constant despite their increasing weight and complexity and some increases in labor and the cost of material. There were a great number of engine building works in the New England and the mid-Atlantic states, and the competition among them was active. The makers of English-built locomotives found it difficult to understand the low prices prevalent in America. But the overhead costs in England were higher, and often the British used more expensive materials: for example, they used wrought iron while the American builders favored cast iron. At the same time the reputation of American-built engines was good, and a fair number were being exported abroad in the years before the Civil War.[20]

During the 1850s the three major locomotive plants were owned by Thomas Rogers, Matthias Baldwin, and the three Norris Brothers, Richard, Septimus, and William. Each of the three shops had produced a total of about 1,000 locomotives by 1860. Baldwin and the Norris Brothers each manufactured nearly 600 engines, during the 1850s, while the shop of Thomas Rogers delivered nearly 750. Rogers made money from the business—when he died in 1856 he was reported to be worth nearly a million dollars. The Norris shops would go out of existence shortly after the Civil War, but Matthias Baldwin's was destined to dominate the field long before 1900. All three shops were in the mid-Atlantic states; Baldwin and the Norris boys were in Philadelphia, while Rogers was in Patterson, New Jersey. The fourth largest company, that of Holmes Hinkley, matched only half the production of Rogers. Hinkley, originally a carpenter like Rogers, was based in Boston and by midcentury was the largest of the engine makers in New England.[21]

At midcentury wood was the universal fuel for the locomotives with their huge balloon or turnip-shaped stacks. But by the mid-1850s many of the more progressive roads in the

North were already experimenting with coal, and some were considering complete conversion to the new form of fuel. By 1859 the Philadelphia & Reading had entirely given up cord-wood for coal.

The price of wood varied greatly from road to road and from time to time during the decade. In 1854 the Indianapolis & Cincinnati figured that the more than 5,000 cords of wood on hand were worth only $1.25 per cord. In the tree-less prairies of Illinois, John Griswold and William Osborn, at the helm of the Illinois Central in the mid-1850s, were paying $5.00 to $5.25 per cord. In the winter of 1856–57 Osborn was complaining to a subordinate that no cord-wood was available for sale within 30 miles of Chicago. On the eve of the Civil War the Baltimore & Ohio was paying from $3.25 to $4.50 a cord, the New York Central was buying it in northern New York for under $4.00 a cord, and the Pennsylvania figured its average cost at $3.00 a cord, delivered on the tender. In New England, where many forests had disappeared, the Boston & Worcester was paying $5.65 a cord in 1859–60. Both hard woods and pitch pine were considered prime fuel. At the end of the decade the New Jersey Railroad was paying $4.35 a cord for hickory or oak and $4.61 for a cord of pine.[22]

During the 1850s the size and weight of the locomotive tender increased, but most tenders were built to carry from 1,000 to 2,000 gallons of water for the boiler, plus from one to two cords of wood for the firebox. The tenders were designed to use water and fuel at an equivalent rate, and a full tender would normally run an engine between 30 and 60 miles, depending upon load and grade. In 1853 the *Equinox*, a Rogers-built locomotive with large drivers, pulled a Buffalo & State Line 3-car passenger train 69 miles in three hours, consuming in that period a tender loaded with 1,152 gallons of water and 98 cubic feet of cord-wood (about three-quarters of a cord). Water consumption was thus about 17 gallons per mile while each milepost saw the burning of about 1.4 cubic feet of cord-wood.[23]

In the early 1850s some railroads were already success-

Interior of passenger coach operating on Grand Trunk in the late 1850s. Note the wood-burning stove, shutters, improved lighting, and quaint and rather small baggage racks. (COURTESY, CANADIAN NATIONAL RAILWAYS.)

fully using coal as a fuel. On the Baltimore & Ohio Ross Winans had produced a successful coalburning engine as early as the mid-1840s, and by the early 1850s much of the B. & O. freight was moving behind coal-fired engines. Even so, many railroads were reluctant to use the new fuel. In the summer of 1855 the *American Railroad Journal* wrote: "Up to the present time, great difficulty has been experienced in all attempts to substitute coal for wood."[24]

By midcentury it was generally agreed that coal, if it could be used, would be a more efficient fuel than wood. The experts figured that a ton of coal had the heating value of about 1¾ cords of wood. Since a cord of wood weighed about 3,000 pounds, a ton of coal was equal to 5,250 pounds of cord-wood. Thus the use of coal would provide savings in weight as well as bulk. By the 1850s many new mines were being opened that produced soft coal, a fuel much better suited for a locomotive than anthracite. And by the mid-1850s it was discovered that fireboxes of normal design were capable of burning coal. Thus the production of coal increased and the price began to fall, dropping to $3 a ton in many areas.[25]

As more and more railroads successfully tried coalburning engines, fuel costs per mile declined. In 1859 the New Jersey Railroad had fuel costs of less than 10 cents a mile for coal and nearly 20 cents a mile for wood. The New York Central figures were nearly 11 cents a mile for coal and about 14 cents for wood. Fuel costs per mile on the Boston and Worcester were under 11 cents for coal (at $5.78 a ton) and about 17 cents a mile for wood (at $5.65 a cord). The Baltimore & Ohio, which had many new coal mines opening along its main line in the mid-1850s, had a still lower rate of less than 6 cents a mile for coal. John W. Garrett, president of the B. & O., was buying some coal for as little as a dollar a ton in 1860.[26]

By late 1857 the *American Railroad Journal,* basing its estimates upon the fuel costs of several major northern and western lines, was predicting that each of the roads would achieve substantial savings through the use of coal. In 1860 the Illinois Central kept very careful performance statistics upon two groups of freight locomotives, sixteen woodburners and sixteen coalburners. Each group ran a total of 376,000 miles during the year, pulling average trains of 15.3 cars for the woodburners and 16.6 cars for the coalburners. President Osborn was able to report that fuel costs for the woodburners were 13.4 cents a mile but only 6.2 cents a mile for the coalburners. Repair costs per mile were slightly higher for the coalburners, but the total operational savings for the coalburners were still nearly 6.5 cents a mile. Even with these proven savings, most locomotives in the country were still using wood on the eve of the Civil War, with an estimated annual consumption of more than 3,700,000 cords of wood. However, by the end of the 1860s probably half of the motive power in the nation had converted to coal.[27]

Freight and passenger cars together far outnumbered the locomotives on the typical railroad. For the entire nation in the late 1850s there was probably one locomotive for every 15 to 18 cars. In New England and the mid-Atlantic states, where the heavier population created a large passenger traffic, the normal line had more passenger cars than locomotives. In the South and West locomotives typically were more numerous than passenger cars. On all roads freight cars far outnumbered passenger cars by a ratio ranging from six to one up to ten to one or even higher.[28]

The typical freight car had two four-wheel trucks, was from 26 to 34 feet long and had a capacity of from eight to ten tons. Not too many cars were fully loaded, and the average load per car was well below the rated capacity. Freight trains rarely were longer than 15 or 20 cars, and a pay load of as much as 150 tons per train was thus quite rare. The average freight train speed of 12 miles per hour reported by the railroads in Massachusetts in 1852 was probably somewhat above the national average for the decade. First-class freight cars seldom cost more than $500 per car, and frequently cars were built in company shops for much less.[29]

Most company freight equipment rosters consisted of

only three types: box or housecars, flat or platform cars, and gondola cars. Some Eastern coal roads had far more gondola or coal-carrying cars than any other type. Some roads also had a limited number of stock cars for the shipping of cattle to market. When Illinois Central officials realized that farmers were ready to market a large crop of hogs in 1855, they constructed movable decks for some of their cattle cars to increase their hog-carrying capacity. That same summer the Illinois Central built special small doors at the ends of several "house" cars to facilitate the loading and unloading of lumber. By the end of the decade at least one eastern railroad was experimenting with a refrigerator car, lined with zinc and cooled with ice. Such a car reached Indianapolis in April 1860, filled with fresh shad, lobsters, and oysters.[30]

Passenger cars in the 1850s were constructed of wood, and were normally about 50 feet in length, 9 to 10 feet in width, with a seating capacity of fifty to sixty. The type of seats varied from road to road, but many cars had seats with cushioning. Several types of reclining seats were being invented. Most cars depended for illumination upon candles, often limited to a single candle or two at either end of the car. Oil lamps, which were common for home illumination, were frowned upon by most railroad officials because of the danger of fire. In 1856 the Galena & Chicago Union introduced new lighting in passenger cars: a lamp burning a type of compressed coal gas. The passenger cars pleased some foreign visitors. When the large family of J. Richard Beste returned to London after their American tour, the children complained about the confinement of the English carriages, and the lack of movable seats permitting one to ride looking in either direction.[31]

By midcentury and before most passenger cars had a toilet plus a drinking water tank at one end of the car, a convenience quite rare on the passenger trains of England. The visitor from England, J. Richard Beste, was happy to discover a water closet in his New York Central coach since it "removed one great difficulty, which the father of eleven children could not but have foreseen in the journey of three hundred and twenty-five miles. . . ." Heat was provided by a wood or coal-burning stove (or stoves) often with one located at each end of the car. Many inventions were being patented for improved car ventilation, but few of the expensive devices were ever adopted or put into use. The average traveler remained dependent upon the occasionally opened door or the open window, which provided dust, smoke, and soot along with fresh air. Fresh air could also be enjoyed on the open platform of the cars, but passengers were generally enjoined from moving from car to car while the train was in motion. The frequently uneven roadbed plus the inadequate car springs meant that a passenger train moving at a top speed of 25 miles per hour rarely provided smooth rides. Many lines boasted of their speedy "on-time" schedules, but many trains ran late. Horace Greeley grumbled about missed connections and late trains in his travels in northern states, and Frederick Law Olmsted was just as unhappy about slow or late trains in the South. The English novelist Anthony Trollope, who came to America in 1861, was in general displeased with passenger service in the United States.[32]

In the antebellum years railroads in the South often designated their best coaches as "Ladies' Cars," reserved for women, children, and men traveling with them. This practice was tried by some northern railroads but soon discontinued because of the additional equipment required.

These antebellum passenger cars, imperfect and uncomfortable as they often were, were still not inexpensive. A first-class coach could cost from $2,000 to $5,000 each. Some of the expense went for ornamentation and elaborate painting on both the interior and exterior of the cars. Exterior body colors frequently were pale yellow, light blue, pea green, or Indian red.[33]

Of course the new sleeping cars were even more expensive. In the 1830s two railroads in Pennsylvania had introduced crude sleeping cars. Late in the decade the Cumberland Valley Railroad had introduced bunk cars, used only for night travel and only by male passengers. In 1838 the Philadelphia, Wilmington & Baltimore Railroad introduced a car with longitudinal seats which could be converted into two-tier berths for night travel.

Only in the 1850s did sleeping cars in any way comparable to those of the twentieth century appear. In the antebellum years porters were not provided. All the inventors stressed that their inventions were so simple that any traveler could change the seat into a berth. In 1854 Henry B. Myer received a patent that allowed ordinary car seats to be arranged to form an unbroken line of berths along the length of the car. To Myer ventilation must have been more important than privacy, since his system provided neither curtains nor partitions.[34]

In 1856 Theodore T. Woodruff invented the first two-passenger sleeping compartment. Woodruff, as a young wagon maker in New York, had first advanced his ideas back in the 1830s. In the mid-1850s, as a master-car builder for the Terre Haute & Alton Railroad, he designed a sleeping car with twelve sleeping sections, six on each side. His cars were first tried on the New York Central, and later on the Pennsylvania and several western roads. Woodruff believed in not wasting space, and he managed to place three berths between the floor and the ceiling of the car; that economy may explain the nightly charge of 50 cents. During the late 1850s other versions of sleeping cars were invented by Webster Wagner, C. M. Mann, Plymon B. Green, and Edward C. Knight. The most famous provider of sleeping cars, George M. Pullman, did not successfully enter the field until the 1860s.[35]

By 1860 many different lines were using sleeping cars produced by one of the several companies making such equipment. Some of the new cars were quite luxurious, containing mahogany woodwork, damask curtains, fancy cushions, and marble washbowls. Some such cars cost as much as $8,000. Luxurious or spartan in design, none of the sleeping cars managed to solve the problem of adequate ventilation at night. After a rail trip from New York City to Chicago in May 1859, Horace Greeley wrote bitterly of the bad nighttime ventilation in a sleeping car: "After gasping awhile like a netted fish on a hot sandbank I rose to enter my solemn protest against all sleeping-cars not provided with abundant and indefeasible means of ventilation." However, that same spring Richard Cobden, the English statesman, spent two nights in sleeping cars between Chicago and New York City "with little fatigue." Anthony Trollope was also pleased with American sleeping cars.[36]

None of the sleeping cars, passenger coaches, or freight cars had anything better than hand brakes in the 1850s. However, the brakemen on passenger trains had the relative safety of open platforms for their braking operations, while freight train crews were forced to work upon the tops of moving cars, often in inclement weather. All cars were equipped with the link-and-pin coupler, which increased the hazards of a brakeman's life. The automatic coupler and the air brake would not appear until the 1870s and 1880s.

During the decade cooperation was growing between the railroad and the relatively new telegraph industry. In 1844 the first experimental telegraph line had been constructed along a railroad route, that of the Baltimore & Ohio, between Washington, D.C., and Baltimore. Several years went by before anyone realized the potential usefulness of the "talking wires" to railroad operation. One of the officials on board the special Erie excursion train, which opened that completed road in mid-May 1851, was the portly, efficient, and occasionally hot-tempered Charles Minot. Benjamin Loder, president of the Erie, had recently hired Minot away from the Boston & Maine to become his general superintendent. During his first months with the Erie, Minot had persuaded Ezra Cornell, a telegraph promoter in New York, to string telegraph wires along a portion of the Erie route. On the first day of the excursion trip, when one of the locomotives failed, Minot at once used the new telegraph line to wire ahead for a replacement engine.

Earlier in England, on New Years Day 1850, a runaway locomotive headed for London had been stopped by a warning sent ahead by telegraph. In America the first train dispatching by telegraph was on September 22, 1851, when an

Erie westbound passenger train superintendent Minot was riding was delayed at Turners (now Harriman), New York. Minot at once wired ahead to stop the eastbound train at Goshen. When the engineer of Minot's train refused to proceed on to Goshen by telegraphic order, Minot took over the engineer's seat and ran the train eventually into Port Jervis, where they met the opposing train. Some railroad officials, such as Herman Haupt, superintendent of transportation on the Pennsylvania, and John W. Brooks, president of the Michigan Central, were reluctant to accept the telegraph, but within a few years most railroads had adopted the practice of telegraphic train control.[37]

During the decade most new railroads made arrangements to have a telegraph line built along their new right-of-way. The telegraphic service generally gave priority to the needs of the railroad, with the station agent also serving as the commercial representative of the telegraph company. The revenues resulting from the commercial usage were divided between the railroad and the telegraph company. Often the telegraph served the railroad very well. In March 1855, Miss Lillian Foster was made happy when a helpful station agent in Georgia used the telegraph to locate and return her trunk. Later that same year an Illinois Central official wrote to President Osborn about an irate passenger who claimed his baggage was lost because of a careless train crew: "To appease him I immediately sent a message to every telegraphic office on the line from Dunleith to Cairo, and in three hours the wires had grabbed the lost baggage and it was on its way from Cairo to Chicago, to the great relief of the gentleman."[38]

But despite the improved train control that came with the greater use of the telegraph, railway accidents were frequent. In 1853, 11-year-old Benny Pierce, sole surviving child of Franklin and Jane Pierce, was killed before his parents' eyes in a railway accident, an event that would leave a mark of sadness upon the Pierce years in the White House. Rail accidents were so frequent in the fifties that a humor magazine of that day spoofed railroad directors who were

Accident on the Camden & Amboy Railroad, August 29, 1855. Twenty-one passengers were killed and seventy-five injured. (COURTESY, SMITHSONIAN INSTITUTION.)

often reluctant to ride in their own passenger trains. Early in 1860 the *American Railroad Journal* reported that from 1853 through 1859 there had been a total of 903 railroad accidents causing 1,109 deaths and 3,611 injuries. As a general rule, far more crew members or employees than passengers were killed or injured. In the same seven years steamboat accidents had numbered only 213, but 2,304 deaths had resulted. A variety of causes, including collision, bridge failure, faulty track, excessive speed, and boiler explosion, caused the numerous railroad accidents, which, year in and year out, averaged between two and three every week. Various efforts were made to reduce the accident rate. The *American Railroad Journal* urged stiffer qualifications for engine drivers, while a railroad in Ohio presented a silver pitcher and goblet to the two engineers who had run their locomotives the greatest distance without an accident. As a safety measure the New York & New Haven started checking the soundness of the cast-iron car wheels at each station stop by tapping each wheel with a small hammer.[39]

But the accidents and wrecks continued and even increased as more and more travelers and additional freight moved over the expanding iron network. Accidents sometimes resulted from disputes between rival roads over grade track crossings. In Illinois in the early 1850s the Illinois Central and the Michigan Southern had such a disputed crossing several miles south of Chicago. Both lines proceeded to operate trains over the crossing as if the other line, and its scheduled trains, simply did not exist. A year later came the inevitable: two trains tried to use the crossing at the same time, killing 18 and injuring 40. Several months later human error was the cause of the Camp Hill, Pennsylvania, accident on July 17, 1856, when a local mixed train of the North Pennsylvania Railroad met head-on an excursion train carrying hundreds of children to their annual Sunday School picnic. The final count of "the picnic that never was" came to 60 killed and 60 injured. Less serious was the accident suffered by Charles R. Weld, an Englishman taking a vacation tour through the United States and Canada in 1855. Weld's

B. & O. train jumped the track between Cumberland and Harper's Ferry as an overzealous train crew attempted to make up lost time on the winding track along the Potomac. The shaken but uninjured Weld observed, "Accidents on railways are thought so little of in America it is useless to remonstrate."[40]

Many Americans *were* willing to remonstrate about the operation of trains on Sunday. In 1854 the *American Railroad Journal* complained bitterly about Sunday railroad operations:

> Such is the result that follows every violation of a known and acknowledged duty as is the keeping of the Sabbath day. The moment a railroad company commences its violation, they put their employees to a school of vice. The very fact that labor on the Sabbath is considered disreputable, must degrade the person performing such labor in his own estimation. His self-respect becomes lost, his moral stamina is destroyed. . . .

There was much support for this point of view in New England, in much of the South, and on many western lines as well. Erastus Fairbanks, Vermont scale manufacturer and president of the St. Johnsbury & Lake Champlain, was adamant on the subject. Jonathan Blanchard, devout clergyman, staunch abolitionist, and president of Knox College in Galesburg, Illinois, tried and failed to stop Sunday trains in Galesburg. In nearby Chicago the Illinois Central officials generally did not operate trains on Sunday, except where the movement of certain stock trains might maintain the safety and health of the transported animals.[41]

In the mid-1850s the major trunk lines in the mid-Atlantic states split on the Sunday train issue. The two major roads in New York state, the Erie and the New York Central, both basically operated on a six-day week with no Sunday trains. Where no Sunday train was permitted, long-distance passengers often had to spend the Sabbath at an inn or hotel in the town where the train stopped on Saturday night. Further south, the Pennsylvania and the Baltimore & Ohio ran their trains on the Sabbath. A major argument used by railways favoring Sunday service was the need to maintain the speedy and continuous movement of the U.S. mails. This point plus other commercial reasons would later make regular Sunday railroad service a normal procedure.[42]

During the 1850s railroads did not use a standard time. Each railroad tended to use the local sun time of its major city if it was a short road, or that of several cities if a longer road. The Baltimore & Ohio used Baltimore time for trains running out of that city, Columbus time for operations in Ohio, and Vincennes time for everything west of Cincinnati. There naturally was a crazy-quilt variation of dozens of local sun times across the country. In 1857 *Dinsmore's American Railroad Guide* showed that when it was noon in Washington, D.C., it was 12:24 P.M. in Boston, 12:12 in New York, 12:02 in Baltimore, 11:48 A.M. in Pittsburgh, 11:53 in Buffalo, 11:31 in Cincinnati, and 11:07 in Saint Louis. Some cities served by more than a single railroad actually had several different times. The Buffalo station had three clocks, one for the New York Central, a second for the Lake Shore & Michigan Southern, and a third set to local sun time. Everyone admitted the system was confusing, but there was little enthusiasm for the *American Railroad Journal* suggestion that the nation should use only the local sun times of three or four key cities. As with standard gauge, automatic couplers, and better brakes, the adoption of standard time would be delayed until well after the Civil War.[43]

Railroad workers certainly were in no position to complain about dangerous equipment, the lack of a standard time, or the necessity of working on Sunday. Labor unions would not appear until the Civil War and after—the locomotive engineers first organized in 1863, conductors in 1868, firemen and engineers in 1873, and trainmen in 1883.

During the decade the number of men employed by railroads increased so rapidly that the report totals often were out of date. The 1860 Census reported that 36,567 persons were working on railroads in 1860, up from 4,831 a decade earlier. Certainly the figure was much too low. In 1860 Massachusetts alone had more than 6,000 railroad workers—in a state with more than 1,200 miles of road. In

1853 the Central of Georgia, with 257 miles of line, had 927 employees, while in 1856 the 705-mile Illinois Central employed 3,581 men. The ratio of four to five workers per mile of road, as shown on these two lines, was probably high, since both the Central of Georgia and the Illinois Central had more traffic than many lines. Using a more reasonable figure of three employees for a mile of line would suggest that the total for the nation in 1860 may have been close to 90,000 workers.[44]

Naturally there was a great variation in the salaries and wages paid the workers. The top executives were often quite well paid. In 1857 the *American Railroad Journal* noted the unprecedented salary of $25,000 paid Charles Moran, the newly elected president of the Erie. More typically, presidents' salaries ranged from $3,000 to $6,000. Moran defended his high salary, which was $15,000 above that of his predecessor, Homer Ramsdell, by pointing out that he was also general superintendent of the road. On some lines general superintendents had salaries almost as high as that of the president. In the mid-1850s, when the Illinois Central was one of the longest railroads in the nation, that line was paying its 30-year-old vice-president, George B. McClellan, $3,000, and $2,500 to James C. Clarke, superintendent of the northern division. President William H. Osborn was also willing to pay fairly high salaries to the station agents in the larger towns up and down the line of the Illinois Central. Several in the mid-1850s were receiving from $1,200 to $1,400 a year.[45]

The operating personnel were generally paid by the day but often had their wages reported as monthly averages. In 1852 the Reading was paying $3.00 a day to engineers, $1.50 daily to firemen and conductors, and $1.25 to brakemen. In the same year the Central of Georgia reported that the monthly income of engineers ranged from $40 to $90 and conductors from $40 to $60. Most firemen were paid a dollar a day. Daily average rates on the New York Central in 1855 were $2.50 for engineers and under $2.00 for conductors.

In the early 1850s many conductors wore no distinctive

clothing except for a special cap. The *American Railroad Journal* in 1855 commended the Erie for introducing uniforms for passenger train conductors.

The reliability and trustworthiness of the workers varied more than their rates of pay. In 1852 the Rochester & Buffalo was calling Jeremiah Guile a "model engineer" since in fifteen years of steady service in a locomotive cab he had pulled trains a total of 488,000 miles with no serious mishaps and only one passenger killed—and he fell off the car's platform because of intoxication. In contrast, Vice-President Tom Scott of the Pennsylvania in 1860 discovered that some of his conductors were guilty of fraud—retaining for themselves a major portion of the cash receipts received from passengers who boarded trains without tickets. In one instance a conductor with no visible income other than his year wages of $700 was spending $800 yearly for rent.[46]

Since so much new mileage was being built in the decade, a fair fraction of the rail employees were construction workers, among the first of the railroad "boomers," or transient employees. Even though the heavy immigration from Europe in the fifties brought tens of thousands of Germans and Irish to American shores, rival railroad contractors in Illinois in the early fifties often found their construction crews shorthanded. Colonel Roswell B. Mason, engineer-in-chief of the Illinois Central, believed that 10 cents an hour was a fair wage for unskilled day labor, but in the spring of 1853 he feared he might have to raise the daily rates since builders near Saint Louis were paying $1.37½ a day.[47]

Clearly the level of wages and salaries in the mid-nineteenth century were well below those of our day. However, freight rates and passenger fares have not greatly changed since the 1850s. Freight rates of from 2 to 5 cents a ton-mile and passenger fares of from 2 to 4 cents a mile, typical of the 1850s, are not too different from those of the present day. Thus, while prices generally, along with the cost of living, have greatly increased in the last century, the increased productivity and operating efficiency of the railroads have often permitted reductions, rather than increases, in fares and

Stock Exchange. In June 1853, the *American*
rnal began to print periodically a "Railway Share
railroads of the United States, giving "a complete
ir financial condition, as well as the current value
res." The first such list in the issue of June 11,
154 different lines. Only 54 of these lines, or 35
ere paying dividends in 1852. The dividend
m 2.5 to 12 percent, with an average rate of 7 per-
t half of the roads located in New England or the
ic states were paying dividends, while only about a
lines in the South and West were able to do so.
those roads in the South and West paying divi-
the average, paid higher dividends than the north-
1

ividend record, in general, did not improve during
the decade. In 1855 the "Share List" showed 57
3 percent) of 173 companies paying dividends,
om 2.5 to 17 percent, with an average rate of 7.3
gain southern and western lines lagged behind in
dividends but paid slightly higher rates. In the
f 1857, before the Panic, 55 lines (32 percent) of
anies were paying dividends, ranging from 2.5 to
t, with the average rate of nearly 8 percent. In the
about 40 percent of the roads were paying divi-
ile just over a quarter of the southern and western
able to do so. The Panic of 1857 forced many
etrench and reduce or eliminate dividends. In the
59 only 80 (23 percent) of 340 roads listed in the
Railroad Journal "Share List" were reported as pay-
nds. These ranged from 2 to 10 percent and
not much above 6 percent. Only a third of the
ern lines were paying dividends in 1859, and in the
e country only one road in seven could do so. By
many railroad experts were saying that America had
its rail network.[52]
ng the 1850s the investment in railroads had grown
h the increase in mileage and the number of indi-
mpanies. Between 1850 and 1860 the investment in

rates. During the decade sor
larger carriers to fix or stabi
did these efforts succeed for

Both fares and rates dec
passenger fares in 1850 rang
in New England and the mid
more than 4 to5 cents in the
southern roads were generall
the North. By the late 1850s
down to two cents a mile or l
ticket from New York City to
could be purchased for $25.2
Erie Railroad was offering rai
Chicago, nearly 1,000 miles, f

Freight rates also fell in tl
average rail freight rates drop
in 1851 to 2.2 cents in 1860. I
freight rates on the New York
cents a ton-mile to 2.06 cents;
1.84 cents; and on the Pennsyl
cents. Bulk products such as co
able to get lower rates, especia
When a shipper in Mattoon, Ill
nois Central for special rates fc
bushels of wheat south to Cairo
him a 2.5 cents a ton-mile rate,
figure.[49]

During the decade the num
along with the growth of mileag
more than tripled from 9,000 to
period the number of individua
increasing from 172 companies
New England and the mid-Atlar
than half of the total, 235 lines;
remaining 113 were located in tl

Less than half of these lines
pay regular dividends. However,
had capital stock, and many of tl

New York
Railroad Jo
List" of th
view of th
of their sh
1853, liste
percent, w
ranged fr
cent. Abo
mid-Atlan
fifth of th
However,
dends, on
ern lines.[5]

The c
the rest o
lines (or s
ranging f
percent. .
declaring
summer c
172 comp
20 percei
Northeas
dends, w
lines wer
roads to
fall of 18
American
ing divic
averagec
northeas
rest of tl
1859–60
overbuil

Dui
along wi
vidual cc

American railroads had grown from $296 million to $1,151 million. The new money invested in railroads during the decade, something more than $800 million, was several times the total capital invested in canals during the first half of the nineteenth century.[53]

This new capital invested in railroads during the decade came from a variety of sources: (1) state and local governmental aid, (2) federal land grants, (3) private investors along the line of the road, (4) the sale of securities to eastern bankers, and (5) securities sold to foreign investors. In the first half of the nineteenth century the newness of the governmental units made them rather willing to try new ways of aiding internal improvement. Certainly in the antebellum years politicians and the promoters of rail projects were quite resourceful in thinking up ways for the several levels of government to help in the building of new railroads. Southern states, as well as some western states, were quite generous in the support of new construction. In the decade and a half before the Civil War, several states had borrowed more than $90 million, much of it being used to finance new railroads. In the West counties especially, towns and cities had also advanced additional funds to help support new construction. As earlier noted, federal land grants in the 1850s also had aided construction in such states as Michigan, Wisconsin, Illinois, Iowa, Missouri, Mississippi, and Alabama.[54]

Most of the new capital was private money, either from those living along the projected route or from eastern men of money. Farmers, tradesmen, merchants, and businessmen living along the road could often be persuaded to buy some capital stock or bonds. The promoters of a new road generally sought both the good will and the financial support of local leaders. John Murray Forbes wrote to James W. Grimes, senator from Iowa, that the Burlington extension in Iowa "needs . . . the friendship of all influential people along its lines to keep up its credit." But far more rail securities were sold to investors and bankers in such eastern cities as Philadelphia, Boston, and New York. In the 1830s and 1840s the banks and bankers of Philadelphia and Boston marketed the bulk of the securities that made possible the modest rail construction of those decades. At midcentury, as the pace of new construction increased, the banks and money markets of New York City came to the fore as the major source of capital funds for the expanding iron network.[55]

Some of the capital required for American railroads came from Europe, especially from England. (The German and Dutch investment in American railways was much smaller than that of the English.) Much of the English investment at midcentury was the result of paying for English rails with crisp new railroad bonds. This was especially true of several southern lines that strongly preferred English rather than American rails. The English investors were certainly not interested in all American railroad bonds. One cautious British investor wrote: "Were the bonds *good*, they would be salable in the United States, it would be unwise in us having anything to do with them."[56]

In 1853 the secretary of the treasury estimated that the total foreign holdings of American rail securities amounted to just over $ 52 million out of a total American railroad investment of perhaps $550 million. Most of the securities held, nearly $44 million, were railroad bonds, while just over $8 million were shares of capital stock. These foreign holdings in 1853 would account for no more than a quarter of all railroad bonds, and well under 5 percent of the total capital stock issues. While foreigners held securities in more than 200 different railroads, only 10 roads had as much as $1 million of their securities held abroad. Major companies with a substantial foreign interest included the Philadelphia & Reading, the Erie, the Western of Massachusetts, the Pennsylvania, the Camden & Amboy, the Ohio & Mississippi, the South Carolina, the Illinois Central, and the Baltimore & Ohio. In the mid- and late 1850s the portion of the railroad investment held abroad did not increase, and it may have declined a bit following the Panic of 1857. On the eve of the Civil War the American rail system—an iron network reaching to the Mississippi and the near frontier—belonged to, and was controlled by, Americans.[57]

CHAPTER EIGHT

Railroads on the Eve of War

IN THE mid-1850s the Athens (Tenn.) *Post,* like
many newspapers of that day, was writing proudly of its new
railroad. Athens was located halfway between Chattanooga
and Knoxville on the 111-mile East Tennessee & Georgia, a
line completed during the early 1850s. Boasting of what the
new iron road was doing for the farmers of eastern Tennessee, the *Post* pointed out that before the road had been built
the farmers of three nearby counties were yearly growing
fewer than 25,000 bushels of wheat, worth less than 50 cents
a bushel. The harvest season of 1855 found the same three
counties producing a wheat crop of 400,000 bushels, which
was selling for a dollar a bushel. Certainly the`farmers of
Tennessee, and the entire economy of the state, had bene-
fited greatly from the more than 1,200 miles of railroad
built. Thousands of farmers living north of the Ohio River
also experienced the same good fortune in the antebellum
years.[1]

During the 1850s the railroads of the nation had helped
the entire national economy achieve a new orientation and
posture. Agriculture, both in the North and the South, had
experienced several significant changes because of the
expanding railroads. Large eastern cities gave a new attention to their growing domestic trade with the fast-rising population in the West. The first maturing of American industry
accompanied the construction of many new rail lines. The
thousands of miles of new railroad between the Hudson and
the Mississippi rivers resulted in a new east–west trade axis

which was replacing the earlier north–south trade of the Mississippi and Ohio steamboats. This shift goes far in explaining the loyalty of the Old Northwest to Lincoln and the Union during the Civil War. By 1860 the western boundary of the iron network was very near the moving edge of the American frontier in Wisconsin, Iowa, and Missouri. Rail developments of the decade suggested that American railroads during the Civil War and after would enter a golden age.

In the midcentury years a number of changes, most of them favorable, were coming to the American farm. Famine in Europe in the late 1840s plus the Crimean War half a dozen years later created favorable prices for the farmer's bumper crops in the early and mid-1850s. The general prosperity and surge of farm production was accelerated by the appearance and acceptance of several new or improved farm implements. In the same years, as tens of thousands of immigrants from Europe pushed into the frontier of the middle and upper Mississippi Valley, farmers in that area discovered rather quickly that prairie soil would grow crops just as lush as the wooded acres further east. Finally, thousands of miles of iron track laid in the heartland states of Ohio, Indiana, and Illinois made it easy for many farmers to shift from subsistence to an early form of commercial agriculture.

In the 1850s the farmer was the prototypical American. His was the dominant occupation in the nation: about two-thirds of the gainfully employed labored in agricultural or rural pursuits. Both the total agricultural investment and the crop production increased greatly in the decade: wheat production climbed by 73 percent while the corn crop increased by nearly 42 percent.[2]

In the twenty years between 1840 and 1860 there was a marked shift westward of the center of grain production in the nation. In 1840 the New England and mid-Atlantic states together produced a third of the nation's wheat, just a bit more than produced in the Old Northwest and trans-Mississippi area. Twenty years later, in 1860, wheat production in the Northeast had dropped slightly, providing only a seventh of the national total. But the 1860 wheat crop in the midwestern states was up nearly fourfold, to 95 million bushels, about 55 percent of the national production. A comparable shift from East to Midwest also appeared in the production of corn during the two decades. In 1860 Illinois led the nation in both wheat and corn production: Chicago forwarded to eastern markets 700,000 barrels of flour, 12,400,000 bushels of wheat, and 13,700,000 bushels of corn.[3]

As the center of farming shifted to the West, so did the growth of population. During the 1850s the population of the Old Northwest and the states just to the west simply exploded, increasing by 68 percent, nearly double the rate for the entire nation. The population of Illinois and Wisconsin both doubled; that of Iowa increased threefold. On the even of the Civil War the population of the northcentral area (Old Northwest plus Missouri, Iowa, Minnesota, and Kansas) was just over 9 million, roughly equal to that of the Confederacy. Of course, the fertile soil in the region, especially in Ohio, Indiana, and Illinois, contributed greatly to the rapid expansion of the population.

The new farming region was increasingly using new and improved farm implements. Between 1850 and 1860 more and more midwestern farmers were buying John Deere's wrought iron and steel plow and Cyrus McCormick's reaper. In these years the value of farm machinery in the nation increased by 62 percent, climbing to a total of $246 million by the eve of the Civil War.[4]

The railroad was also a major contributor to the booming agricultural economy. A review of the early business career of Cyrus McCormick reveals that in Illinois during the 1850s there was a close correlation between the sale of reapers, the increased production of wheat, and the building of railroads: western rail mileage increased about eightfold, and nearly 7,000 miles of new track was laid in the three states of Ohio, Indiana, and Illinois. By the eve of the Civil War very few farmers in those three states were more than fifteen or twenty miles from a railway. Directness of route plus year-round service were other major advantages offered by the new mode of transport.

The railroads were friendly to farmers in the antebellum years. As he pushed the Michigan Central toward Indiana and Chicago at midcentury, John Murray Forbes rated the good will of midwestern farmers well above that of grain-forwarding merchants. The Illinois Central helped sponsor state agricultural fairs in Illinois throughout the 1850s, and in cooperation with the State Agricultural Society offered a $3,000 prize for the invention of a steam-driven plow. The natural cooperation between prairie railroads and agriculture in the region was noted by the English traveler James Stirling:

> . . . the prairies absolutely make their own railways without cost to anyone. The development of the country by the means of a railway is such, that what was yesterday a waste land is today a valuable district. There is thus action and reaction: the railway improves the land; the improvement pays for the railway.[5]

The urban, industrial population in the New England and mid-Atlantic states grew while much agricultural production was shifting to western states. Between 1840 and 1860 the number of American cities over 50,000 in population increased from five to sixteen, with most of this expansion in the Northeast. Many farms in the Northeast shifted from grain to truck, dairy, or orchard production, crops that needed rapid rail transportation to New York City, Philadelphia, and other urban markets. By midcentury both the Erie and the Harlem railroads were bringing millions of quarts of milk yearly into New York City. Soon the growing industrial cities of the East were buying more and more food from afar. Quickly the expanding grain and meat crops of the western states became a reciprocal exchange operation for the growing industrial production of the Northeast. During the 1850s, as the major trunk lines built westward to the Ohio River and beyond, this east–west exchange of food for manufactured goods rapidly increased.[6]

A reclining car seat of 1856. Before sleeping cars were common, such inventions as the reclining seat made night-time coach travel somewhat more bearable. (FROM THE *American Railroad Journal*, JANUARY 1856.)

The expansion of industrial and manufacturing activity in the northeastern states easily matched the agricultural surge of the Old Northwest and the upper Mississippi Valley. The total investment in manufacturing in the nation increased nearly 90 percent in the decade, from $533 million in 1850 to $1,009 million in 1860. There was also a significant increase in the total value of American manufactured goods, which by 1860 had grown to $1,885 million. Northeastern states on the eve of the Civil War were far ahead of the rest of the nation, especially the South, both in industrial growth and in urban population. In 1860 the New England and mid-Atlantic states had a population that was more than 35 percent urban, while in the South the urban population was well under 10 percent. Few factories were located in the South, and most of them were small with limited production. In 1860 the 20,000 factories in southern states represented only a seventh of the national total. But in capital invested and factory employees the southern share was less than 10 percent, while the value of their product was no more than 8 percent of the total for the country.[7]

At midcentury America had available immense deposits of both coal and iron, the "warp and woof" ingredients of nineteenth-century industrial growth. But the exploitation of these vital resources had been quite slow, and as of 1850 the nation was easily a score of years behind British production and development. Even so, there was a notable growth in the use of coal and iron during the 1850s. Between 1850 and 1860 the number of coal mines in the nation increased by more than a fifth, the production of Pennsylvania anthracite rose by 150 percent, and the mining of soft coal more than doubled. In the half-century prior to the Civil War the use of iron in the nation increased five times as rapidly as the population. By 1860 there were 256 rolling mills in the country, most of them in northeastern states. The rapid extension of rail mileage plus the growing acceptance of coal as a locomotive fuel meant that the railroad industry itself was a major factor in the growing use of both iron and coal.[8]

The growing American manufacturing of the 1850s was

An artist's impression of night-time travel on a New York Central coach in the late 1850s. (FROM *Harper's Illustrated Weekly*, OCTOBER 2, 1858.)

rich in its variety, was gaining fame for its quality, and was marked by the economy and speed of its production. By mid-century invention was so common in the nation that some saw it almost as a form of recreation. In the decade and a half prior to the Civil War the annual rate of patent issuance in the United States roughly doubled every five years (502 in 1845, 986 in 1850, 1,992 in 1855, and 4,589 in 1860), a rate of increase never again to be equaled. Visitors to Washington flocked not to the Capitol, but to the U.S. Patent Office, to view the latest models of looms, locks, plows, pistols, and sewing machines. The general high quality of American manufactured goods was noted by visitors to the Crystal Palace Exhibition in London in 1851, where the American exhibits of shovels, churns, ice-cream freezers, locks, roadscrapers, and other illustrations of Yankee ingenuity were acclaimed. Visitors to factories back in the United States were often surprised at the economical and rapid rate of American production. Dr. Thomas L. Nichols of England was amazed at the automatic machinery and versatility he found in American factories. During his visit on the eve of the Civil War Nichols saw a machine in Pittsburgh turn out 50 eight-ounce railroad spikes each minute, bricks shaped for the kiln at the rate of 2,000 an hour, and an automatic machine cut wooden shingles at the rate of 10,000 a day.[9]

The railroad spikes made in Pittsburgh, the brass clocks produced in Connecticut, the sturdy picks and shovels manufactured by Oakes and Oliver Ames in Massachusetts, the popular Concord coaches out of New Hampshire, and the plows pouring out of John Deere's factory in Moline, Illinois, all were produced in such quantity that they required a mass market. Such a market needed reliable and economical transportation, and the same year-round service that railroads were giving the farmers of the West.

The iron roads to the West soon appeared. Early in 1853 Henry V. Poor wrote:

> The past year has been signalized by a number of important events in the history of roads: among which have been the completion of the Baltimore & Ohio, the opening of a

through line through Pennsylvania, and the union of the roads of the two divisions of the country by the completion of the Lake Shore roads. All the most important western cities have new railroad connections with the East . . . and the Mississippi river is nearly reached at two points.

But most of the roads to the West were located in northern rather than southern states. The Virginian Matthew F. Maury, naval officer and oceanographer, believed that the South was well behind in railroad construction. In 1854 he wrote: "Now, take Poor's railroad map and glance your eyes over it. Ohio and Indiana exhibit a perfect network of railways and canals. . . . Now cast your eyes upon Virginia and her neighbors . . . see how blank they look. . . ."[10]

The rail network in Ohio, Indiana, and other western states was to favor some cities over others. In 1852 James DeBow wrote that Cincinnati and Saint Louis would become "the primary cities of the central United States." He was proven wrong, for Chicago rather quickly assumed a position of preeminence in western rail development. In 1857 the *Missouri Democrat* (published in Chicago's rival, Saint Louis) admitted that the granaries, storehouses, and railroad depots of Chicago were "scarcely surpassed by any city in the Union." By 1860 Chicago was a city of 109,000 with eleven different railroads; boosters claimed that 100 trains à day served the city. Chicago was indeed the major western terminal of the east–west rail network, a system described by Horace Greeley as "long iron arms extending far into the productive West."[11]

During the 1850s the Baltimore & Ohio, the Erie, the New York Central, and the Pennsylvania, the most important long iron arms to the West, all enjoyed a major increase in their freight and passenger revenues. Their connecting lines west of Buffalo, Pittsburgh, and Wheeling—such as the Pittsburgh, Fort Wayne & Chicago, and the Ohio & Mississippi—were also expanding. As the exchange of eastern factory goods for western farm produce grew during the 1850s, the older merchant capitalism gave way to an emerging national economy more centered on domestic than foreign trade. The

A Wagner sleeping car on the New York Central. The width of the aisle, as drawn by the illustrator, somewhat exceeds reality. (FROM *Frank Leslie's Illustrated Weekly,* APRIL 1859.)

men of business and commerce in Boston, New York City, Philadelphia, and Baltimore, no longer preoccupied with foreign trade, were increasingly shifting their attention from dock and wharf to the railroad depot and freight yard. During the decade this east–west axis of domestic trade was well established between the northeastern states and the Old Northwest. On the eve of the Civil War a strong economic alliance existed between these two regions.[12]

The Civil War found the western states allied politically as well as economically with the Northeast. During the mid-1850s the Republican party had been formed in a series of spontaneous meetings in several midwestern states. In the elections of 1860 and 1864 the five states of the Old Northwest voted for Lincoln and the Republican party. Even though the Copperheads were strong in the southern parts of Ohio, Indiana, and Illinois, those three states strongly supported Lincoln's call for troops. During the four years of the war the total Illinois enlistments in the Union army came to more than 15 percent of that state's population. In Indiana the figure was over 14 percent, and in Ohio it was more than 13 percent. All three states responded to the call to the colors better than most northern states, where the average ratio of enlistments to population was 12 percent.

Many things contributed to the basic decision of the West to ally itself with the North rather than the South during the sectional political struggle of the 1850s. Certainly the building of thousands of miles of east–west railroads between the Mississippi and Pennsylvania was a major factor. Direct rail traffic with the East meant that the West was no longer totally dependent upon the riverboats of the Ohio and Mississippi rivers. This point is graphically made by William and Bruce Catton in their *Two Roads to Sumter:* "Southerners who dreamed that the Northwest might be neutral or even an ally in the event of civil conflict should have looked more closely at the endless parade of freight trains clattering across the mountains between the ocean and the Lakes."[13]

With the exception of minor activity in the Mexican War

and the Crimean War, the Civil War was the first conflict in which railroads played a vital role. During the four years thousands of freight and passenger trains served the Union and Confederate forces. In 1861 there was a tremendous disparity in motive power, rolling stock, number of skilled employees, and repair facilities between the rival systems. Southern production of new rails in 1860 was only one-ninth that of the North, and a dozen Yankee locomotive plants could be found for every one in the Confederacy.

The contrast in the two wartime rail systems is illustrated by incidents that occurred in the fall of 1863 and in the spring of 1865. Late in September 1863, Secretary of War Edwin M. Stanton proposed to Lincoln's inner cabinet that the War Department should send 30,000 men by railroad from the nearby Army of the Potomac to help lift the siege of Chattanooga. Stanton estimated the total move might be done in five days. General Henry W. Halleck thought the idea preposterous, and Lincoln was so skeptical that he said to Stanton: "I will bet that if the order is given tonight the troops could not be got to Washington in five days." Stanton proved more correct than the president. In 11½ days nearly 25,000 men and ten batteries of artillery, with all their horses, were moved by rail 1,200 miles from Washington to the banks of the upper Tennessee. The route of nearly 600 cars making up 30 trains was by the way of Harper's Ferry, Columbus, Indianapolis, Louisville, and Nashville. The northern rail network remained strong throughout the conflict, and by 1865 had actually added more than 4,000 miles of new line, chiefly in the mid-Atlantic and western States.[14]

In contrast, in the spring of 1865 Confederate rail lines were as crippled and defeated as the Southern armies they had vainly tried to support. Four long years of war had completely destroyed about half of the railroads of the South, with losses running into tens of millions of dollars. Gutted stations, destroyed bridges, twisted rails, burnt ties, and lost or dilapidated engines and cars scattered from Virginia to Louisiana was the heritage of most southern railroads. Their condition was illustrated during the visit of Chief Justice

Ten Minutes for Refreshments. Before dining cars appeared in the early 1860s, many trains scheduled brief stops at railroad lunch counters. (COURTESY, NEW YORK CENTRAL SYSTEM.)

Salmon P. Chase to North Carolina in May 1865. The best facility that the Union troops could find for Chase was a train that the Washington correspondent Whitelaw Reid described as "a wheezy little locomotive and an old mail agent's car, with all the windows smashed out and half the seats gone." [15]

The decade prior to the Civil War had been one of the most dynamic periods in the history of American railroads. In 1850 a broken skein of short iron lines served the area between Maine and Georgia with a few stray strings of rail connecting the Ohio River and the Great Lakes. By the eve of the Civil War more than 30,000 miles of railroad served quite adequately all the states east of the Mississippi, and few areas of substantial population were much removed from the sound of the locomotive whistle. By the years of the war the railroad reached nearly to the moving edge of the frontier. In the generation after the Civil War, the rapid transcontinental rail expansion moved well ahead of the frontier line and quickly pulled millions of Americans into the western territory.

The most significant railroad construction in the 1850s occurred in the West and in the upper Mississippi Valley, especially in Ohio, Indiana, and Illinois. Since the new railroads in their trunk-line region offered significant advantages in speed, directness of route, and the seasonal and geographical availability of service, they took an increasing amount of business away from the canals and steamboats. These iron roads to the West rather quickly became an east–west axis of commerce between the industrial and mercantile East and the agricultural West.

American railroads achieved a measure of maturity in the expansion of the 1850s and the challenges of war that followed. In the half-century after Appomattox they would experience their golden age as the nation became the industrial giant we know today.

Notes

CHAPTER 1. THE IRON HORSE AT MIDCENTURY

1. Basler, ed., *Collected Works of Abraham Lincoln*, II, 31–38; Baringer and Miers, eds., *Lincoln Day by Day*, II, 8–10; *American Railroad Journal* (hereafter, *ARJ*), March 10, 1849, p. 159; Hunter, *Steamboats on the Western Rivers*, pp. 658–61.

2. Searcher, *Lincoln's Journey to Greatness*, map on inside cover.

3. Taylor and Neu, *American Railroad Network: 1861–1890*, maps at end of book.

4. Poor, *Manual of the Railroads of the United States for 1890*, p. vi; *Chronology of American Railroads, Including Mileage by States and by Years*, pp. 1–2, 7.

5. Kirkland, *Men, Cities, and Transportation;* I, 156.

6. Poor, *Manual for 1890*, p. vi; *Chronology of American Railroads*, pp. 1–3, 7.

7. Poor, *Manual for 1890*, p. vi; *Chronology of American Railroads*, pp. 2–4, 7.

8. *Eighth Census of the United States, 1860*, "Mortality and Property", p. 331.

9. *ARJ*, November 9, 1850, p. 703.

10. Durrenberger, *Turnpikes*, pp. 130–43.

11. Taylor, *Transportation Revolution*, p. 79; *Chronology of American Railroads*, p. 7.

12. *ARJ*, February 2, 1850, p. 69; Hunter, *Steamboats on the Western Rivers*, pp. 481–519.

13. Poor, *Manual for 1890*, p. vi.

14. *ARJ*, January 10, 1857, p. 27.

15. Fishlow, *American Railroads and the Transformation of the Ante-Bellum Economy*, pp. 322, 326, 328, 337.

16. *ARJ*, July 4, 1857, p. 429; December 23, 1854, p. 806.

17. *Ibid.*, November 27, 1852, p. 758; December 11, 1852, p. 790.

18. *Ibid.*, July 27, 1850, pp. 472–73.

19. Ringwalt, *Development of Transportation Systems in the United States*, p. 163.

20. Poor, *Manual for 1901*, p. xvii.

CHAPTER 2. YANKEE RAILROADS

1. Poor, *Manual for 1890*, p. vi; *Eighth Census, 1860*, "Mortality and Property," p. 331.

2. Robert B. Shaw, "The Profitability of Early American Railroads," pp. 56–69.

3. *ARJ*, March 29, 1856, p. 197; August 11, 1860, p. 701; February 19, 1859, p. 116; Kirkland, *Men, Cities, and Transportation*, I, 336–40.

4. *Eighth Census, 1860*, "Mortality and Property," pp. 325–26.

5. *ARJ*, March 2, 1861, pp. 169–70; Salsbury, *The State, the Investor, and the Railroad*, pp. 307–10.

6. *ARJ*, December 16, 1854, p. 789.

7. *Ibid.*, January 11, 1851, p. 29; May 29, 1852, p. 343; July 21, 1860, p. 637.

8. Griswold, *Train Wreck*, pp. 7–16.

9. *ARJ*, July 14, 1855, p. 439; September 8, 1860, p. 792; Poor, *Manual for 1869–1870*, pp. 22–23.

10. *ARJ*, April 2, 1859, pp. 212–13; July 21, 1855, p. 450; June 4, 1859, p. 360; Poor, *Manual for 1869–1870*, pp. 8–9, 40–41.

11. *ARJ*, August 18, 1860, pp. 724–25; Poor, *Manual for 1869–1870*, pp. 54–55.

12. *ARJ*, August 18, 1860, pp. 724–25.

13. *Ibid.*, April 1, 1854, p. 205; March 31, 1855, p. 199; April 12, 1856, p. 229; March 31, 1860, p. 275.

14. Harlow, *Steelways of New England*, pp. 411–32.

15. *Eighth Census, 1860*, "Mortality and Property," pp. 326–27.

16. *ARJ*, July 4, 1857, p. 428; Neu, *Erastus Corning, pp.* 67–71.

17. *ARJ*, December 27, 1851, p. 824.

18. *Ibid.*, December 19, 1857, p. 801; July 4, 1857, p. 429; December 20, 1856, p. 804; August 25, 1860, p. 747.

19. Poor, *Manual for 1882*, pp. 137–42.

20. Neu, *Erastus Corning*, pp. 181–85.

21. Poor, *Manual for 1882*, pp. 137–42.

22. *ARJ*, March 26, 1853, p. 195; September 7, 1861, p. 633.

23. *Ibid.*, March 22, 1856, p. 181.

24. Poor, *Manual for 1887*, p. 216.

25. Poor, *Manual for 1882*, p. 268.

26. *ARJ*, February 7, 1857, p. 89; August 31, 1861, p. 618; Burgess and Kennedy, *Centennial History of the Pennsylvania Railroad*, p. 799.

27. *ARJ*, August 18, 1855, p. 514; April 16, 1859, p. 242.

28. Poor, *Manual for 1869–1870*, pp. 197–99.

29. Hungerford, *Story of the Baltimore & Ohio Railroad,* I: 240–67.

30. *ARJ,* October 27, 1855, p. 676; June 14, 1856, pp. 371–72.

31. *Ibid.,* January 15, 1853, p. 35; September 22, 1860, pp. 837–38.

32. *Ibid.,* September 22, 1860, pp. 837–39.

33. *Ibid.,* February 26, 1859, p. 136; March 10, 1860, p. 260; March 9, 1861, p. 189.

34. Poor, *Manual for 1882,* pp. 237–38.

35. *ARJ,* February 10, 1855, p. 92.

36. *Ibid.,* March 13, 1852, p. 173; Poor, *Manual for 1887,* p. 233; Poor, *Manual for 1901,* p. 35.

CHAPTER 3. THE RAILROADS OF DIXIE

1. Phillips, *History of Transportation in the Eastern Cotton Belt,* pp. 303–35, 391–93; Ward, "J. Edgar Thomson and the Georgia Railroad," p. 28.

2. *De Bow's Review,* December 1866, p. 635.

3. Poor, *Manual for 1890,* p. vi; *Eighth Census, 1860,* "Mortality and Property," p. 331.

4. *Eighth Census, 1860,* "Mortality and Property," pp. 325–29.

5. *ARJ,* June 11, 1853, p. 376; May 20, 1854, p. 312; September 15, 1855, p. 582.

6. Ringwalt, *Development of Transportation Systems,* p. 150.

7. *Eighth Census, 1860,* "Mortality and Property," pp. 327–28.

8. Cleveland and Powell, *Railroad Promotion and Capitalization in the United States,* pp. 213–14; Couper, *Claudius Crozet,* pp. 133, 146.

9. Poor, *Manual for 1882,* p. 397; *ARJ,* November 14, 1859, p. 730; January 15, 1859, p. 41; Black, *Railroads of the Confederacy,* pp. 26–27; Johnston, *Virginia Railroads in the Civil War,* p. 11.

10. Poor, *Manual for 1882,* p. 380; *ARJ,* October 6, 1860, p. 889.

11. Poor, *Manual for 1882,* p. 407; *ARJ,* March 21, 1857, p. 182; January 1, 1859, p. 6; January 7, 1860, p. 8; Black, *Railroads of the Confederacy,* p. 31; Lefler and Newsome, *North Carolina,* pp. 348–49.

12. *ARJ,* November 28, 1857, p. 763; December 3, 1859, p. 782; January 7, 1860, p. 8; December 22, 1860, p. 1121.

13. *Ibid.,* December 12, 1857, p. 789; December 10, 1859, p. 808.

14. *Commercial and Financial Chronicle,* March 6, 1869, p. 295.

15. Poor, *Manual for 1887,* p. 645.

16. Phillips, *Transportation in the Eastern Cotton Belt,* p. 203; *ARJ,* February 1, 1851, p. 68; February 12, 1859, p. 99.

17. Poor, *Manual for 1887,* pp. 582, 578; *ARJ,* July 25, 1857, p. 470; January 1, 1859, p. 6; November 19, 1859, p. 743.

18. Phillips, *Transportation in the Eastern Cotton Belt,* p. 386.

19. *ARJ,* November 28, 1857, p. 753.

20. Phillips, *Transportation in the Eastern Cotton Belt,* pp. 244–45; *ARJ,* November 4, 1854, pp. 691–92.

21. Poor, *Manual for 1887*, p. 986.

22. *Ibid.*, p. 987; Phillips, *Transportation in the Eastern Cotton Belt*, pp. 275–80, 294.

23. *Commercial and Financial Chronicle*, May 19, 1866, p. 612; Phillips, *Transportation in the Eastern Cotton Belt*, pp. 309–18.

24. Phillips, *Transportation in the Eastern Cotton Belt*, pp. 319–21; Black, *Railroads of the Confederacy*, p. 108; *ARJ*, November 28, 1857, p. 753.

25. Poor, *Manual for 1878–1879*, p. 517; *Manual for 1888*, p. 584.

26. *Eighth Census, 1860*, "Mortality and Property," pp. 328–29.

27. *ARJ*, March 12, 1859, p. 170; March 31, 1860, p. 263; June 16, 1860, p. 510; May 25, 1861, p. 393; Poor, *Manual for 1887*, pp. 693–94; Cotterill, "Southern Railroads, 1850–1860," pp. 396–400.

28. *ARJ*, August 4, 1854, p. 493; July 28, 1860, p. 646.

29. Poor, *Manual for 1874–1875*, p. 736; *Manual for 1878*, p. 534; *ARJ*, July 28, 1860, p. 648.

30. *ARJ*, May 17, 1851, p. 314.

31. *Ibid.*, February 4, 1860, p. 100; August 4, 1860, pp. 669–70.

32. Corliss, *Main Line of Mid-America*, pp. 385–92; Poor, *Manual for 1877–1878*, p. 396; *Manual for 1893*, p. 1228.

33. *Commercial and Financial Chronicle*, February 8, 1868, p. 168.

34. Poor, *Manual for 1869–1870*, pp. 70–71; *Manual for 1882*, p. 482; *ARJ*, October 1, 1859, p. 633; September 22, 1860, p. 840; October 3, 1857, pp. 626–27.

35. *ARJ*, March 14, 1857, p. 168; February 23, 1861, p. 163.

36. Poor, *Manual for 1882*, p. 480.

37. Cotterill, "Southern Railroads, 1850–1860," pp. 402–5; Klein, *History of the Louisville & Nashville Railroad*, pp. 6–29.

38. Black, *Railroads of the Confederacy*, p. 15.

39. *ARJ*, January 7, 1860, pp. 6–9; October 6, 1860, pp. 886–89.

40. *Ibid.*, pp. 886–89.

41. Taylor and Neu, *American Railroad Network*, pp. 43–44.

42. *ARJ*, August 5, 1854, p. 493; February 12, 1859, p. 99.

CHAPTER 4. UNCLE SAM AND THE RAILROADS

1. *ARJ*, April 17, 1852, p. 267; Stephen A. Douglas to Citizens of Chicago, October 1850, in Johannsen, ed., *The Letters of Stephen A. Douglas*, p. 197; Corliss, *Main Line of Mid-America*, pp. 21–22.

2. Donaldson, *Public Domain*, pp. 269–70.

3. *Historical Statistics of the United States, Colonial Times to 1957*, p. 711.

4. Poor, *Manual for 1887*, p. x.

5. Donaldson, *Public Domain*, p. 258.

6. *ARJ*, September 28, 1850, p. 616; October 5, 1850, pp. 628–29; Hibbard, *History of the Public Land Policies*, pp. 241–45; Gates, *Illinois Central Railroad and Its Colonization Work*, pp. 21–43.

7. *ARJ*, September 28, 1850, p. 616; Sanborn, *Congressional Grants*, pp. 36–37.

8. Sanborn, *Congressional Grants*, p. 38; *ARJ*, March 13, 1852, p. 162.

9. Donaldson, *Public Domain*, p. 269; *ARJ*, September 28, 1850, p. 616.

10. Donaldson, *Public Domain*, p. 269; *ARJ*, May 31, 1856, p. 340; Overton, *Burlington West*, pp. 73–81.

11. Donaldson, *Public Domain*, pp. 269–70.

12. Stephen A. Douglas to Asa Whitney, October 15, 1845, in Johannsen, ed., *Letters of Stephen A. Douglas*, pp. 127–33.

13. Riegel, *Story of Western Railroads*, pp. 17–19; Paxson, *History of the American Frontier*, pp. 402, 411–13; Cotterill, "Southern Railroads and the Western Trade," pp. 432–34; *ARJ*, October 20, 1849, p. 663.

14. Rowland, ed., *Jefferson Davis*, II, 310–16.

15. *Ibid.*, III, 456.

16. *Ibid.*, III, 93.

17. Stephen A. Douglas to James Washington Sheahan, January 18, 1855, in Johannsen, ed., *Letters of Stephen A. Douglas*, p. 333; Johannsen, *Stephen A. Douglas*, pp. 436–37.

Chapter 5. Iron Roads in the West

1. *ARJ*, October 15, 1853, p. 663; September 27, 1856, p. 617; Belcher, *Economic Rivalry between St. Louis and Chicago*, pp. 62–63; Hayes, *Iron Road to Empire*, pp. 44–45.

2. *ARJ*, November 16, 1850, p. 727.

3. Poor, *Manual for 1980*, p. vi; *Eighth Census, 1860*, "Mortality and Property," p. 331.

4. *Eighth Census, 1860*, "Mortality and Property," p. 331.

5. *Ibid.*, pp. 329–30.

6. *ARJ*, May 9, 1857, pp. 289–90; Poor, *Manual for 1887*, p. 517; Burgess and Kennedy, *Centennial History of the Pennsylvania Railroad*, pp. 76–77.

7. *ARJ*, May 9, 1857, pp. 289–90; Poor, *Manual for 1887*, p. 517; Schotter, *Growth and Development of the Pennsylvania Railroad*, pp. 37–38; Paxson, "The Railroads of the Old Northwest Before the Civil War," XVII: 260, 271.

8. *ARJ*, September 7, 1861, p. 646; Burgess and Kennedy, *Centennial History of the Pennsylvania Railroad*, pp. 176–77.

9. *ARJ*, May 12, 1860, p. 391; Poor, *Manual for 1887*, p. 517.

10. *ARJ*, June 18, 1859, p. 387.

11. Poor, *Manual for 1882, p.* 545.

12. *Ibid.*, pp. 544–45; Harlow, *Road of the Century*, pp. 265–74.

13. Harlow, *Road of the Century*, pp. 274–79; *ARJ*, July 17, 1857, p. 435.

14. *ARJ*, April 15, 1854, p. 231; May 2, 1857, p. 280; August 27, 1859, pp. 547–78; Harlow, *Road of the Century*, pp. 344–53.

15. *ARJ*, June 2, 1855, p. 340; Paxson, "The Railroads of the Old Northwest," pp 268–69.

16. Paxson, "The Railroads of the Old Northwest," pp. 268–71; *ARJ*,

April 5, 1856, p. 213; May 26, 1860, pp. 453–54; Poor, *Manual for 1887*, p. 427.

17. Poor, *Manual for 1882*, p. 514; Hungerford, *Story of the Baltimore & Ohio*, I, 266, 292, 317, 325.

18. Hungerford, *Story of the Baltimore & Ohio*, I, 293, 298, 299; II, 110, 220; Poor, *Manual for 1882*, pp. 554–55; *ARJ*, March 4, 1854, p. 142.

19. Poor, *Manual for 1882*, pp. 521, 572–73.

20. *ARJ*, January 31, 1857, p. 65; January 12, 1861, p. 26; Poor, *Manual for 1883*, pp. 674–76.

21. *ARJ*, April 14, 1849, p. 233; May 31, 1851, p. 341; Poor, *Manual for 1886*, pp. 155–56; Hungerford, *Story of the Baltimore & Ohio*, I: 301–4.

22. Hungerford, *Story of the Baltimore & Ohio*, I, 312–14; *ARJ, June 25, 1859*, p. 402.

23. *ARJ*, September 25, 1852, p. 613; April 21, 1855; p. 246.

24. *Ibid.*, September 15, 1855, p. 582; July 25, 1857, p. 470.

25. *Ibid.*, September 20, 1856, p. 596; Poor, *Manual for 1887*, p. 485; Paxson, "Railroads of the Old Northwest," pp. 269–71; Hargrave, *Pioneer Indiana Railroad*, pp. 121–25, 128.

26. *Annual Report of the Illinois Central Railroad, 1856;* Stover, *History of the Illinois Central Railroad*, pp. 59–64.

27. *ARJ*, March 5, 1859, p. 152; February 11, 1860, p. 127; March 16, 1861, pp. 209–10.

28. Poor, *Manual for 1882*, pp. 671–72; Casey and Douglas, *Pioneer Railroad*, pp. 75–81.

29. Poor, *Manual for 1887*, p. 390.

30. John Murray Forbes to Paul S. Forbes, December 22, 1851, quoted in Cockran, *Railroad Leaders*, p. 331.

31. *ARJ*, July 18, 1857, p. 452; October 19, 1861, p. 731.

32. Poor, *Manual for 1887*, p. 390; Overton, *Burlington Route*, pp. 39, 63, 71.

33. *ARJ, November 2*, 1861, p. 762; Poor, *Manual for 1887*, p. 996; Hayes, *Iron Road to Empire*, pp. 15–32.

34. *ARJ*, September 27, 1856, p. 617; John W. Starr, Jr., *Lincoln and the Railroads*, pp. 92–116.

35. Poor, *Manual for 1877–1878*, p. 492; Poor, *Manual for 1883*, p. 675; Paxson, "Railroads of the Old Northwest," pp. 271–72.

36. *Eighth Census, 1860*, "Mortality and Property," pp. 330–31.

37. Poor, *Manual for 1882*, pp. 544–45; *ARJ*, March 6, 1852; p. 148; April 23, 1859, p. 261.

38. *ARJ*, January 3, 1852, p. 9; July 22, 1854, p. 460; July 18, 1857, p. 450; John Murray Forbes to John W. Brooks, April 27, 1847, in Cockran, *Railroad Leaders*, p. 326.

39. Paxson, "Railroads of the Old Northwest," pp. 269–73; *ARJ*, February 4, 1854, p. 76; June 28, 1856, p. 406; Derleth, *Milwaukee Road*, pp. 25–26.

40. Derleth, *Milwaukee Road,* pp. 81–82; Poor, *Manual for 1882,* p. 713.

41. Poor, *Manual for 1882,* pp. 679–81; Hayes, *Iron Road to Empire,* pp. 39–43.

42. *ARJ,* October 6, 1860, p. 886; Poor, *Manual for 1887,* pp. 809–10.

43. *Eighth Census, 1860,* "Mortality and Property," p. 331; Poor, *Manual for 1882,* p. 751.

44. John Murray Forbes to Paul S. Forbes, October 13, 1854, in Cockran, *Railroad Leaders,* p. 328.

45. Poor, *Manual for 1882,* pp. 788–89; Overton, *Burlington Route,* pp. 53–56.

46. Poor, *Manual for 1882,* p. 800; *ARJ,* April 9, 1859, p. 232; Ringwalt, *Development of Transportation Systems,* p. 145.

CHAPTER 6. VICTORY OVER ROAD, CANAL, AND STEAMBOAT

1. Thornbrough and D. Riker, eds., *Diary of Calvin Fletcher,* 2:82, 510–11; Poor, *Manual for 1869–1870,* p. xxvi; Hunter, *Steamboats on the Western Rivers,* p. 39; Waggoner, *Long Haul West: The Great Canal Era,* p. 247.

2. Paxson, "The Railroads of the Old Northwest," pp. 257, 259, 262.

3. Durrenberger, *Turnpikes,* pp. 130–43; Taylor, *Transportation Revolution,* p. 134.

4. Overton, *Burlington Route,* pp. 22–23.

5. Taylor, *Transportation Revolution,* pp. 52–53, 79; Ronald E. Shaw, *Erie Water West,* p. 396.

6. *ARJ,* May 1, 1852, p. 279.

7. *Ibid.,* January 5, 1850, p. 3.

8. *Ibid.,* May 12, 1860, p. 404.

9. *Ibid.,* May 12, 1860, p. 404; November 12, 1859, p. 721.

10. *Ibid.,* November 12, 1859, p. 722; May 12, 1860, p. 404; Taylor, *Transportation Revolution,* pp. 173–74; Chase, "Foreign and Domestic Commerce of the United States," p. 148.

11. Chase, "Foreign and Domestic Commerce of the United States," pp. 133, 135, 181; Taylor, *Transportation Revolution,* pp. 164–65.

12. *ARJ,* December 20, 1856, p. 804; December 17, 1859, p. 828; Ronald Shaw, *Erie Water West,* pp. 293–94, 371.

13. Ringwalt, *Development of Transportation Systems,* p. 53; *ARJ,* February 7, 1857, p. 89; Nevins, *Ordeal of the Union,* II, 199–200.

14. Taylor, *Transportation Revolution,* pp. 42–43; *ARJ,* June 30, 1855, p. 406.

15. *ARJ,* January 10, 1852, p. 22; March 7, 1857, p. 147.

16. Scheiber, *Ohio Canal Era,* pp. 258–59, 280.

17. *Ibid.,* pp. 295, 387–88, 390, 391.

18. *ARJ,* December 13, 1851, p. 797; January 29, 1859, p. 83.

19. Chase, "Foreign and Domestic Commerce of the United States," pp. 143–44.

20. *ARJ*, December 13, 1851, p. 785; March 17, 1855, p. 163; September 3, 1859, p. 565; Taylor, *Transportation Revolution*, p. 62.

21. Taylor, *Transportation Revolution*, p. 167; Johnson and others, *History of Domestic and Foreign Commerce of the United States*, p. 239; Fishlow, *American Railroads and the Transformation of the Ante-Bellum Economy*, pp. 263–66.

22. Nevins, *Ordeal of the Union*, II, 214–27; Taylor and Neu, *American Railroad Network*, map 2.

23. Hunter, *Steamboats on the Western Rivers*, p. 481.

24. Haites, Mak, and Walton, *Western River Transportation*, p. 120.

25. *Ibid.*, pp. 130–31.

26. Hunter, *Steamboats on the Western Rivers*, p. 482.

27. *Ibid.*, pp. 490–91; *ARJ*, June 27, 1857, p. 412.

28. Nichols, *Forty Years of American Life*, II, 6–8; Foster, *Way-Side Glimpses*, pp. 146–47.

29. *ARJ*, April 15, 1854, p. 237.

30. Hunter, *Steamboats on the Western Rivers*, pp. 500–501.

31. Fishlow, *American Railroads and the Transformation of the Ante-Bellum Economy*, p. 293; Nevins, *Ordeal of the Union*, II, 220; Hunter, *Steamboats on the Western Rivers*, pp. 493–94.

32. Hunter, *Steamboats on the Western Rivers*, p. 645; Belcher, *Economic Rivalry between St. Louis and Chicago*, p. 46.

33. Hunter, *Steamboats on the Western Rivers*, p. 645.

34. Chase, "Foreign and Domestic Commerce of the United States," p. 148; Belcher, *Economic Rivalry between St. Louis and Chicago*, pp. 118–38; Foster, *Way-Side Glimpses*, pp. 212–13.

35. Belcher, *Economic Rivalry between St. Louis and Chicago*, p. 109; Nevins, *Ordeal of the Union*, II, 223–26.

36. U.S., Congress, Senate, *Report of the Select Senate Committee on Transportation Routes to the Seaboard* no. 307, 43rd Cong., 1st sess. 1874, pp. 202, 847; Fishlow, *American Railroads and the Transformation of the Ante-Bellum Economy*, p. 278.

37. Mark Twain, *Life on the Mississippi*, pp. 474–75.

CHAPTER 7. TECHNICAL ADVANCES IN ANTEBELLUM RAILROADS

1. Emerson and Forbes, eds., *Journals of Ralph Waldo Emerson*, VIII, 504; Thornbrough and Riker, *Diary of Calvin Fletcher*, III, 409.

2. Foster, *Way-Side Glimpses*, pp. 119–20; Nichols, *Forty Years of American Life*, II, 9; Bunn, *Old England and New England*, p. 146.

3. Taylor and Neu, *American Railroad Network*, maps 1, 2, and 3.

4. *Ibid.*, pp. 8–14.

5. *Weekly National Intelligencer*, July 25, 1857; *Annual Report of the Illinois Central Railroad, 1854*, p. 1–7.

6. Fish, "The Northern Railroads, April, 1861," p. 786; Black, *Railroads of the Confederacy,* p. 13; Weber, *Northern Railroads in the Civil War,* p. 6.

7. *ARJ*, September 1, 1849, p. 550; August 5, 1854, pp. 481–82.

8. *Ibid.,* December 27, 1856, p. 828; September 3, 1859, p. 571.

9. *Ibid.,* May 6, 1854, p. 281; August 2, 1856, p. 490.

10. *Ibid.,* August 2, 1856, p. 490; December 19, 1857, p. 802; September 3, 1859, p. 568; Stover, *History of the Illinois Central Railroad,* p. 534; Fish, "The Northern Railroads, April, 1861," p. 786.

11. *ARJ*, August 2, 1856, p. 490; Fish, "The Northern Railroads, April, 1861," p. 786; Schotter, *Growth and Development of the Pennsylvania Railroad Company,* pp. 35, 42; Black, *Railroads of the Confederacy,* p. 14.

12. *ARJ*, February 4, 1854, p. 71; December 16, 1854, p. 797.

13. *Ibid.,* November 5, 1853, p. 717; March 4, 1855, pp. 187–88; June 30, 1855, p. 403; September 3, 1859, p. 566; Foster, *Way-Side Glimpses,* pp. 66–68.

14. *ARJ*, July 9, 1853, p. 437.

15. White, *American Locomotives,* pp. 20–21.

16. *Ibid.,* p. 486.

17. *Ibid.,* pp. 95–96, 456–57.

18. *Ibid.,* pp. 194–99, 206–10, 486; *ARJ*, October 29, 1853, p. 701.

19. *Ibid.,* June 10, 1854, p. 360; W. H. Osborn to J. Newton Perkins, October 30, 1856, October 21, 1856, Illinois Central Archives, Newberry Library, Chicago.

20. White, *American Locomotives,* pp. 20–23.

21. *Ibid.,* pp. 20–21, 449–50, 453, 456–57; *ARJ*, May 3, 1856, p. 280.

22. *ARJ*, September 16, 1854, p. 590; July 21, 1860, pp. 625–26; July 14, 1860, p. 601; February 11, 1860, p. 126, June 2, 1860, pp. 462–63; White, *American Locomotives,* pp. 83–86.

23. *ARJ*, August 27, 1853, p. 555.

24. Bell, *Early Motive Power of the Baltimore and Ohio Railroad,* pp. 56–57; *ARJ*, June 18, 1853, p. 391; July 3, 1855, p. 424.

25. White, *American Locomotives,* pp. 86–89.

26. *ARJ*, July 21, 1860, p. 625; July 14, 1860, p. 601; February 11, 1860, p. 126; July 14, 1855, p. 446.

27. *Ibid.,* December 12, 1857, p. 793; *Annual Report of the Illinois Central Railroad, 1860;* White, *American Locomotives,* p. 85.

28. *ARJ*, July 12, 1856, p. 437; February 26, 1859, p. 138; November 12, 1859, p. 59; October 20, 1860, p. 922.

29. Ringwalt, *Development of Transportation,* p. 163; *ARJ*, May 15, 1852, p. 308.

30. B. F. Johnson to W. H. Osborn, July 24, 1855, Illinois Central Archives, Newberry Library; *ARJ*, May 12, 1860, p. 406.

31. Ringwalt, *Development of Transportation,* p. 162; *ARJ*, July 16, 1853, p. 455; Mencken, *Railroad Passenger Car,* pp. 22–25; Nichols, *Forty Years of American Life,* I, 241–43; Beste, *The Wabash,* II, 349–50.

32. Beste, *The Wabash*, I, 110; Mencken, *Railroad Passenger Car*, pp. 42–54; *ARJ*, May 15, 1852, p. 308; Nichols, *Forty Years of American Life*, I, 241–43; Olmsted, *Journey in the Seaboard Slave States*, pp. 57, 104; Trollope, *North America*, I, 36–38.

33. Mencken, *Railroad Passenger Car*, pp. 14–15, 28, 118; Fish, "Northern Railroads, April 1861," p. 787; Alexander, *Pennsylvania Railroad*, p. 92; White, Jr., "Splendor and Gloom," pp. 38–47.

34. Mencken, *Railroad Passenger Car*, pp. 57–59.

35. *Ibid.*, pp. 59–64.

36. *ARJ*, August 16, 1856, p. 520; September 1, 1860, p. 771; Greeley, *Overland Journey from New York to San Francisco*, pp. 7–8; Cawley, ed., *American Diaries of Richard Cobden*, p. 163; Trollope, *North America*, I, 127–28.

37. *ARJ*, August 17, 1850, p. 516; Thompson, *Wiring a Continent*, pp. 206–9; Hungerford, *Men of Erie*, pp. 92–94.

38. Foster, *Way-Side Glimpses*, pp. 100–104; B. F. Johnson to W. H. Osborn, November 20, 1855, Illinois Central Archives, Newberry Library.

39. *ARJ*, January 14, 1860, p. 22; March 30, 1850, p. 197; January 28, 1854, p. 52; October 11, 1851, p. 648; Bunn, *Old England and New England*, pp. 147–49.

40. Griswold, *Train Wreck*, pp. 17–28; Mencken, *Railroad Passenger Car*, pp. 118–22.

41. *ARJ*, December 23, 1854, p. 801; Botkin and Harlow, eds., *Treasury of Railroad Folklore*, pp. 78–79; B. F. Johnson to J. Newton Perkins, December 31, 1855, Illinois Central Archives, Newberry Library.

42. *ARJ*, June 7, 1856, pp. 356–57; Chambers, *Things as They Are in America*, pp. 53–54.

43. *ARJ*, August 21, 1852, p. 530; September 3, 1853, p. 567; March 14, 1857, p. 163.

44. *Eighth Census, 1860*, "Population," pp. 672–73; Taylor, *Transportation Revolution, 1815–1860*, p. 291; *ARJ*, November 12, 1853, p. 733; Stover, *History of the Illinois Central Railroad*, p. 81.

45. *ARJ*, December 22, 1855, p. 802; August 1, 1857, p. 488; Hungerford, *Men of Erie*, p. 143; B. F. Johnson to J. Newton Perkins, December 17, 1855, Illinois Central Archives, Newberry Library; W. H. Osborn to J. Newton Perkins, November 20, 1856, Illinois Central Archives, Newberry Library; Stover, *History of the Illinois Central Railroad*, p. 83.

46. *ARJ*, June 25, 1853, p. 405; November 12, 1853, p. 733; March 15, 1856, p. 163; September 11, 1852, p. 587; September 1, 1855, p. 555; September 15, 1860, p. 817; Chambers, *Things as They Are in America*, pp.331–32; Beste, *The Wabash*, I: 109.

47. Roswell B. Mason to Robert Schuyler, April 18, April 22, 1853, Illinois Central Archives, Newberry Library.

48. *ARJ*, July 27, 1850, pp. 472–73; August, 1857, p. 484; June 11, 1859, p. 376.

49. Ringwalt, *Development of Transportation*, p. 166; Taylor, *Transpor-*

tation Revolution, 1815–1860, pp. 135, 442; B. F. Johnson to W. H. Osborn, November 1, November 21, 1855, Illinois Central Archives, Newberry Library.

50. *Eighth Census, 1860,* "Mortality and Property," pp. 325–31.

51. *ARJ,* June 11, 1853, p. 376.

52. *Ibid.,* September 15, 1855, p. 582; July 25, 1857, p. 470; November 5, 1859, pp. 710–11; November 12, 1859, p. 727; November 19, 1859, p. 743.

53. *Eighth Census, 1860,* "Mortality and Property," p. 331; Taylor, *Transportation Revolution, 1815–1860,* p. 347.

54. *ARJ,* October 27, 1855, pp. 673–74 Taylor, *Transportation Revolution, 1815–1860,* pp. 92–93; Boorstin, *The Americans,* pp. 250–56; see my chapter 4 "Uncle Sam and the Railroads."

55. Taylor, *Transportation Revolution,* pp. 97–100; John Murray Forbes to James W. Grimes, November 11, 1859, in Cockran, *Railroad Leaders,* p. 332; Chandler, *Henry Varnum Poor,* pp. 74–78.

56. Adler, *British Investment in American Railways,* p. 42.

57. *Ibid.,* pp. 23, 66; Cleveland and Powell, *Railroad Promotion and Capitalization in the United States,* p. 196; Taylor, *Transportation Revolution,* p. 347.

Chapter 8. Railroads on the Eve of War

1. Nevins, *Ordeal of the Union,* II, 194–95; Ringwalt, *Development of Transportation Systems,* p. 144.

2. *Historical Statistics of the United States, Colonial Times to 1957,* pp. 14, 72, 297.

3. Shannon, *America's Economic Growth,* pp. 256–57; Chase, "Foreign and Domestic Commerce of the United States," p. 148.

4. Nevins, *Ordeal of the Union,* II, 165; *Historical Statistics of the United States, Colonial Times to 1857,* p. 285; Schlebecker, *Whereby We Thrive;* pp. 103, 114–15.

5. Nevins, *Ordeal of the Union,* II, 169; John Murray Forbes to D. D. Williamson, September 30, 1846, in Cockran, *Railroad Leaders,* p. 326; Stover, *History of the Illinois Central Railroad,* pp. 72–73; Gates, *Illinois Central and Its Colonization Work,* p. 293; Sterling, *Letters from the Slave States,* p. 11.

6. *Historical Statistics of the United States, Colonial Times to 1857,* p. 14; Schlebecker, *Whereby We Thrive,* pp. 95–96; Nevins, *Ordeal of the Union,* II, 172–74.

7. Nevins, *Ordeal of the Union,* II, 248; North, *Economic Growth of the United States,* p. 258; Taylor, *Transportation Revolution, 1815–1860,* p. 247.

8. Nevins, *Ordeal of the Union,* II, 248–50; *Statistical History of the United States from Colonial Times to the Present,* pp. 580, 590, 593; Shannon, *America's Economic Growth,* p. 220.

9. *Historical Statistics of the United States, Colonial Times to the Present,*

p. 608; Nevins, *Ordeal of the Union,* II, 253–55; Nichols, *Forty Years of American Life,* I: 380–81.

10. *ARJ,* January 8, 1853, p. 27; *National Intelligencer,* November 11, 1854.

11. *DeBow's Review,* September 1852, p. 305; *Weekly National Intelligencer,* March 7, 1857; Nevins, *Ordeal of the Union,* II, 192.

12. *ARJ,* September 22, 1860, p. 839; December 22, 1860, p. 1124; August 31, 1861, p. 618; September 7, 1861, p. 633; Taylor, *Transportation Revolution,* pp. 397–98.

13. Catton and Catton, *Two Roads to Sumter,* p. 67.

14. Turner, *Victory Rode the Rails;* pp. 288–94.

15. Reid, *After the War;* p. 28.

Bibliography

PRIMARY WORKS

American Railroad Journal, 1848–61.

Basler, Roy P., ed. *The Collected Works of Abraham Lincoln.* New Brunswick, N.J.: Rutgers University Press, 1953.

Beste, J. Richard. *The Wabash or the Adventures of an English Gentleman's Family in the Interior of America.* London, 1855.

Bunn, Alfred, *Old England and New England.* London, 1853.

Chambers, William. *Things as They Are in America.* Philadelphia, 1854.

Chase, S. P. *Foreign and Domestic Commerce of the United States.* Senate Document 55, 38th Congress, 1st Session, 1864.

Commercial and Financial Chronicle, 1865–70.

DeBow's Review.

Eighth Census of the United States, 1860. "Mortality and Property." Washington, D.C., 1866.

Emerson, Ralph Waldo. *Journals of Ralph Waldo Emerson.* Edited by Edward W. Emerson and Waldo E. Forbes. Boston, Mass.: Houghton, 1909–14.

Foster, Lillian. *Way-Side Glimpses, North and South.* New York, 1860.

Greeley, Horace. *An Overland Journey from New York to San Francisco.* New York, 1860.

Historical Statistics of the United States, Colonial Times to 1957. Washington, D.C., 1960.

Illinois Central Archives, 1851–1906. Newberry Library, Chicago.

Johannsen, Robert W., ed. *The Letters of Stephen A. Douglas.* Urbana: University of Illinois Press, 1961.

National Intelligencer.

Nichols, Thomas Low. *Forty Years of American Life.* London, 1864.

Olmsted, Frederick L. *A Journey in the Seaboard Slave States.* New York: Putnam, 1904.

Poor, Henry V. *Manual of the Railroads of the United States.* New York 1868–1901.

Reid, Whitelaw. *After the War: A Southern Tour.* Cincinnati, 1866.

Report of the Select Senate Committee on Transportation Routes to the Seaboard. U.S. Congress, Senate, *Document* 307, 43d Congress, 1st Session, 1874.

Sterling, James. *Letters From the Slave States.* London, 1847.

The Statistical History of the United States from Colonial Times to the Present. New York, 1976.

Thornbrough, Gayle and Dorothy L. Riker, eds. *The Diary of Calvin Fletcher.* Indianapolis: Indiana Historical Society, 1972–74.

Trollope, Anthony. *North America.* Philadelphia, 1862.

Twain, Mark. *Life on the Mississippi.* New York, 1874.

Weekly National Intelligencer.

SECONDARY WORKS

Adler, Dorothy. *British Investment in American Railways, 1834–1898.* Charlottesville: University Press of Virginia, 1970.

Alexander, Edwin P. *The Pennsylvania Railroad.* New York: Norton, 1947.

Baringer, William E. and Earl S. Miers, eds. *Lincoln Day by Day: A Chronology, 1809–1865.* Washington, D.C., 1960.

Belcher, Wyatt W. *The Economic Rivalry between St. Louis and Chicago, 1850–1880.* New York: Columbia University Press, 1947.

Bell, J. Snowden. *The Early Motive Power of the Baltimore and Ohio Railroad.* New York, 1912.

Black, Robert C. III. *The Railroads of the Confederacy.* Chapel Hill: University of North Carolina Press, 1952.

Boorstin, Daniel J. *The Americans: The National Experience.* New York: Random House, 1965.

Botkin, B. A. and Alvin F. Harlow. *A Treasury of Railroad Folklore.* New York: Crown, 1953.

Burgess, George H., and Miles C. Kennedy. *Centennial History of the Pennsylvania Railroad.* Philadelphia; Pennsylvania Railroad Company, 1949.

Casey, Robert J., and W. A. S. Douglas. *Pioneer Railroad: The Story of the Chicago and North Western System.* New York; McGraw-Hill, 1948.

Catton, William, and Bruce Catton. *Two Roads to Sumter.* New York; McGraw-Hill, 1963.

Cawley, Elizabeth H., ed. *The American Diaries of Richard Cobden.* Princeton, N.J., Princeton University Press, 1952.

Chandler, Alfred D., Jr. *Henry Varnum Poor: Business Editor, Analyst, and Reformer.* Cambridge, Mass.: Harvard University Press, 1956.

Chronology of American Railroads, Including Mileage by States and Years. Washington, D.C., 1957.

Cleveland, Frederick A. and Fred W. Powell. *Railroad Promotion and Capitalization in the United States.* New York, 1909.

Cockran, Thomas C. *Railroad Leaders, 1845–1890.* Cambridge, Mass.: Harvard University Press, 1953.

Corliss, Carlton J. *Main Line of Mid-America: The Story of Illinois Central Railroad.* New York; McClelland, 1950.

Cotterill, Robert S. "Southern Railroads, 1850–1860." *The Mississippi Historical Review,* March 1924, pp. 396–405.

—— "Southern Railroads and the Western Trade." *The Mississippi Historical Review,* March 1917, pp. 427–41.

Couper, William. *Claudius Crozet: Soldier, Scholar, Educator, Engineer.* Charlottesville, Va., Historical Publishing Co., 1936.

Derleth, August. *The Milwaukee Road: Its First Hundred Years.* New York; McClelland, 1948.

Donaldson, Thomas. *The Public Domain.* Washington, D.C., 1884.

Durrenberger, Joseph A. *Turnpikes: A Study of the Toll Road Movement in the Middle Atlantic States and Maryland.* Valdosta, Ga., 1931.

Fish, Carl R. "The Northern Railroads, April, 1861." *The American Historical Review,* July 1917, pp. 778–93.

Fishlow, Albert. *American Railroads and the Transformation of the Ante-Bellum Economy.* Cambridge, Mass.: Harvard University Press, 1965.

Gates, Paul W. *The Farmer's Age: Agriculture, 1815–1860.* New York: Holt, 1960.

—— *The Illinois Central Railroad and Its Colonization Work.* Cambridge, Mass.: Harvard University Press, 1934.

Griswold, Wesley S. *Train Wreck.* Brattleboro, Vt.: Stephen Greene, 1969.

Haites, Erik F., James Mak, and Gary M. Walton. *Western River Transportation.* Baltimore, Md.: Johns Hopkins University Press, 1975.

Hargrave, Frank F. *A Pioneer Indiana Railroad.* Indianapolis, Ind., Burford, 1932.

Harlow, Alvin F. *The Road of the Century.* New York; McClelland, 1947.

—— *Steelways of New England.* New York: McClelland, 1946.

Havighurst, Walter. *Voices on the River: The Story of the Mississippi Waterways.* New York: Macmillan, 1964.

Hayes, William E. *Iron Road to Empire: The History of 100 Years of the Progress of the Rock Island Lines.* New York: Simmons-Boardman, 1953.

Hibbard, Benjamin H. *A History of the Public Land Policies.* New York: Macmillan, 1924.

Hirschfeld, Charles. *The Great Railroad Conspiracy: The Social History of a Railroad War.* East Lansing: Michigan State College Press, 1953.

Hungerford, Edward. *Men of Erie.* New York: Random House, 1946.

—— *The Story of the Baltimore & Ohio Railroad, 1827–1927.* New York: Putnam, 1928.

Hunter, Louis C. *Steamboats on the Western Rivers.* Cambridge, Mass.: Harvard University Press, 1949.

Jackson, W. Turrentine. *Wagon Roads West.* Berkeley: University of California Press, 1952.

Johannsen, Robert W. *Stephen A. Douglas.* New York: Oxford University Press, 1973.

Johnson, Arthur M. and Barry E. Supple. *Boston Capitalists and Western Railroads.* Cambridge, Mass.: Harvard University Press, 1967.

Johnson, Emory R. and others. *History of Domestic and Foreign Commerce of the United States.* Washington, D.C., 1915.

Kirkland, Edward Chase. *Men, Cities and Transportation: A Study in New England Transportation, 1820–1900.* Cambridge, Mass.: Harvard University Press, 1948.

Klein, Maury. *History of the Louisville & Nashville Railroad.* New York; Macmillan, 1972.

Lefler, Hugh T., and Albert R. Newsome. *North Carolina.* Chapel Hill: University of North Carolina Press, 1963.

Mac Gill, Caroline E. *History of Transportation in the United States before 1860.* Washington, D.C.: Carnegie Institute, 1917.

Mencken, August. *The Railroad Passenger Car.* Baltimore, Md: Johns Hopkins University Press, 1957.

Neu, Irene D. *Erastus Corning, Merchant and Financier, 1794–1872.* Ithaca, N.Y.: Cornell University Press, 1960.

Nevins, Allan. *Ordeal of the Union.* 2 vols. Vol. II: *A House Dividing, 1852–1857.* New York: Scribners, 1947.

North, Douglass C. *The Economic Growth of the United States, 1790–1860.* New York: Prentice-Hall, 1966.

Overton, Richard C. *Burlington Route: A History of the Burlington Lines.* New York: Knopf, 1965.
—— *Burlington West: A Colonization History of the Burlington Railroad.* Cambridge, Mass.: Harvard University Press, 1941.
Paxson, Frederick L. *The History of the American Frontier, 1763–1893.* Boston: Houghton, 1924.
—— "The Railroads of the Old Northwest before the Civil War." *Transactions of the Wisconsin Academy of Science, Arts and Letters* XVII (1911): 243–67.
Phillips, Ulrich B. *A History of Transportation in the Eastern Cotton Belt.* New York: Macmillan, 1913.
Riegel, Robert E. *The Story of Western Railroads: From 1852 Through the Reign of the Giants.* New York: Macmillan, 1926.
Ringwalt, J. L. *Development of Transportation Systems in the United States.* Philadelphia, 1888.
Rowland, Dunbar, ed. *Jefferson Davis, Constitutionalist: His Letters, Papers and Speeches.* Jackson, Miss., 1923.
Salsbury, Stephen. *The State, the Investor, and the Railroad.* Cambridge, Mass.: Harvard University Press, 1967.
Sanborn, John B. *Congressional Grants of Land in Aid of Railways.* Madison, Wisc., 1899.
Scheiber, Harry N. *Ohio Canal Era: A Case Study of Government and the Economy, 1820–1861.* Athens: Ohio University Press, 1969.
Schlebecker, John T. *Whereby We Thrive: A History of American Farming, 1607–1972.* Ames: Iowa State University Press, 1975.
Schotter, H. W. *The Growth and Development of the Pennsylvania Railroad.* Philadelphia: Allen, Lane, and Scott, 1927.
Searcher, Victor. *Lincoln's Journey to Greatness.* Philadelphia, Pa.: Winston, 1960.
Shaw, Robert B. "The Profitability of Early American Railroads." *Railroad History,* Spring 1975, pp. 56–69.
Shaw, Ronald E. *Erie Water West: A History of the Erie Canal, 1792–1854.* Lexington: University of Kentucky Press, 1966.
Starr, John W., Jr. *Lincoln and the Railroads.* New York: Dodd, 1927.
Stover, John F. *History of the Illinois Central Railroad.* New York: Macmillan, 1975.
—— *American Railroads.* Chicago: University of Chicago Press, 1961.
Taylor, George Rogers. *The Transportation Revolution, 1815–1860.* New York: Holt, 1951.
Taylor, George Rogers, and Irene Neu. *The American Railroad Net-*

work: 1861–1890. Cambridge, Mass.: Harvard University Press, 1956.

Thompson, Robert L. *Wiring a Continent.* Princeton, N.J.: Princeton University Press, 1947.

Turner, Georgia Edgar. *Victory Rode the Rails: The Strategic Place of the Railroads in the Civil War.* Indianapolis, Ind.: Bobbs, Merrill, 1953.

Waggoner, Madeline S. *The Long Haul West: The Great Canal Era. 1817–1850.* New York: Putnam, 1958.

Ward, James A. "J. Edgar Thomson and the Georgia Railroad." *Railroad History,* Spring 1976, pp. 4–33.

—— *That Man Haupt: A Biography of Herman Haupt.* Baton Rouge: Louisiana State University Press, 1973.

Weber, Thomas. *The Northern Railroads in the Civil War, 1861–1865.* New York: Kings Crown Press, 1952.

White, John H., Jr. "Splendor and Gloom: The Decoration of Victorian Railroad Cars." *Nineteenth Century,* Spring 1977, pp. 38–47.

—— *American Locomotives: An Engineering History, 1830–1880.* Baltimore, Md.: Johns Hopkins University Press, 1968.

Index

Construction (*Continued*)
northern and southern, 90; cost of in 1850s, 190-92; workers, 214; daily wages paid, 214
Container freight in 1850s, 34
Coolbaugh, William F., 164
Cooper, Peter, 8
Copperheads, 229
Cornell, Ezra, 207
Corning, Erastus, 45-48, 163
Couplers, link-and-pin type, 23, 207
Cowcatcher, invention of, 20
Crocker, Alvah, 33
Crops: increase of in West in 1850s, 158, 184-85; western crops go to market via canals, 168-70; to eastern markets via Great Lakes, 176; increased prices for, 220
Crowninshield, F. B., 34
Crystal Palace Exhibition (London, 1851), 226
Cumberland, Md., 1, 55, 98
Cutler, William Parker, 134
Cuyler, Richard R., 74, 76

Daniel Nason (locomotive), 4
Davis, Jefferson, 100, 107, 109, 110, 111, 112, 157
Dayton & Michigan R.R., 120, 133, 135-36
Dearing, William, 73
De Bow, James D. B., 17, 60, 82, 227
De Bow's Commercial Review of the South and West, 17, 82
Deere, John, 221, 226
Delaware: first railroad, 7; rail mileage in 1840, 7; rail mileage in 1850, 7, 26; rail mileage in 1860, 26; investment per mile, 26
Delaware & Cobb's Gap R.R., 57
Delaware & Hudson Canal & R.R., 6, 166
Delaware, Lackawanna & Western R.R., 44, 57, 104, 196-97
Delaware R.R., 44, 54

Denver (Steamboat), 169
Depots: lack of "union" stations in 1850, 22; mentioned, 67, 108, 229
Derby, Elias H., 33, 34
Detroit, Mich., 14
Detroit & Milwaukee R.R., 149, 151
Detroit & Pontiac R.R., 151
De Witt Clinton (locomotive), 8
Dining service (railroad), lacking at mid-century, 21, 186
Dinsmore's American Railroad Guide, 212
Dividends (railroad): paid by northeastern lines in 1850s, 27, 29; by southern lines in 1850s, 62, 68, 72, 73, 74, 76-77, 87; portion of lines paying dividends in 1850s, 215-16; mentioned, 47, 52, 131, 140, 143
Dix, Thomas A., 154
Dodge, Grenville M., 42
Double trackage, 193
Douglas, Stephen A.: and first federal land grant for railroads, 80, 94, 99-101, 102; and Kansas-Nebraska Bill, 111-12; mentioned, 50, 106, 107, 111, 113, 157, 184
Drew, Daniel, 19, 47, 50-51
Dripps, Isaac, 20
Dubuque (locomotive), 155
Dubuque & Pacific R.R., 149, 153, 154-55
Dunkirk, N.Y., 49, 50
Dunn, George H., 139
Durant, Thomas C., 42

East Tennessee & Georgia R.R., 79, 87-88, 219
East Tennesse & Virginia R.R., 79, 87-88
East Tennessee, Virginia & Georgia R.R., 88
East-West railroad traffic: gains over north-south river traffic in 1850s, 177, 219-20; exchange of western

food for eastern manufactured goods, 222, 227, 229, 232

Effie Afton (steamboat), 146-47

Ellicot's Mills, Md., 6

Ellis, Abner T., 137

Emanuel, Morris, 86

Emerson, Ralph Waldo, 186

Employees, rail: North and South compared, 92; accidents kill more employees than passengers, 210; awards to employees for no accidents, 210; number of in 1850s, 212-13; no labor unions in 1850s, 212

Engineers, locomotive, 213-14

English investment in American railroads, 84, 85, 88, 93, 190, 218

English railroads, 16

Equinox (locomotive), 200

Erie, Pa., and trouble with Ohio, 129-30

Erie Canal: and competing railroads, 46, 167-70; construction of, 164, 166; most common types of freight carried, 167-68; rates on, 168; gives better service than Pennsylvania Canal, 171; mentioned, 9, 17, 45, 176

Erie R.R.: early construction, 49; completion in 1851, 49-50; problems in 1850s, 50-51; competition with Erie Canal, 167-70; and telegraph usage, 207-8; and shipment of milk, 222; mentioned, 9, 25, 44, 45, 46, 51, 90, 129, 177, 194, 211, 213, 214, 215, 218, 227

Evansville & Crawfordsville R.R., 120, 140

Everett, Edward, 30

Fairbanks, Erastus, 38, 211

Fairs, agricultural (in Illinois), 222

Farley, Jesse P., 155

Farm implements, increased use of, 221

Farmers: aided by new railroads, 219-22; most in Ohio, Indiana and Illinois had rail service by eve of Civil War, 221-22; in northeast shift from grain to truck, dairy and orchard production, 222

Farm-mortgage stockplans aid railroad construction, 152-53

Farnum, Henry, 114-15, 146-47, 154, 196

Federal government, and railroads, 94-96, 99-105, 109-13

Fencing of railroad routes, not too common in 1860, 189

Ferry, railroad, 194

Fillmore, Millard, 25, 50, 80, 94, 100, 102, 105

Finance: of railroads by eastern cities, 58, 217-18; southern state investment in railroads, 63, 66; sources of railroad capital, 217-18

Fink, Albert, 88-89, 92

Firemen, locomotive, 213

Fisk, Jim, 51

Five-foot (Southern) gauge, 187-89

Fletcher, Calvin, 159, 180, 186

Florida: first railroad, 11; rail mileage in 1840, 11; rail mileage in 1850, 11, 61; rail mileage in 1860, 61; investment per mile, 61; mentioned, 103

Florida R.R., 64, 78

Follett, Timothy, 39

Fontaine, Edmund, 66

Forbes, John Murray: and western railroads, 145-46; 150-51, 155, 156, 222; mentioned, 43, 217

Foreign investment in American railroads, 218

Forrest Queen (Ohio River steamboat), 139

Fort Wayne & Chicago R.R., 124

Foster, Lillian, 208

Franklin & Ohio R.R., 134

Franklin Canal Company, 129

Headlight (locomotive), 20-21
Helm, John L., 88
Hinkley, Holmes, 199
Holcombe, F. P., 72
Hoosac Tunnel, 33, 52
Hopkinson, Thomas, 33
Horseshoe Curve, 52
Howe, William, 194
Howe truss bridge, 194
Hudson River R.R., 19, 44, 47-48
Hudson River steamboats. 19
Hunter, Louis C., 177-78
Huntington, Collis P., 42
Hunt's Merchants' Magazine and Commercial Review, 17

Illinois: first railroad in, 13; mileage in 1840, 13; mileage in 1850, 13, 116; and first railroad land grant, 94, 99-101; mileage in 1860, 116; investment per mile, 116; construction during the 1850s, 141-48; by 1860 leads in corn and wheat production, 221; and promotion of agriculture, 222; mentioned, 3, 5, 159-60
Illinois & Michigan Canal, 146
Illinois Central R.R.: receives land grant, 99-101, 141-42; construction of, 141-43; longest railroad in the world, 142; sale of land, 142; cost of original construction, 190; cost of original rails from England, 192; experiments with coal and wood for fuel, 203; number of employees, 213; promotes agriculture, 222; mentioned, 43, 80, 85, 90-91, 108, 121, 122, 139, 150, 154, 177, 193, 194, 198-99, 200, 204, 210, 211, 218
Immigrants: help build western railroads, 142, 214; increase population in Mississippi Valley, 220
Indiana: first railroad in, 13; mileage in 1840, 13; mileage in 1850, 13, 116; mileage in 1860, 116; investment per mile, 116; construction during the 1850s, 136-41, 160; mentioned, 5, 98, 159
Indianapolis & Bellefontaine R.R., 133
Indianapolis & Cincinnati R.R., 120, 139-40, 200
Industrial production: growth of in mid-century, 222-29; concentrated in Northeast, 222; increase in industrial investment, 224; variety of, 226
Inness, George, 104
Investment (railroad): in 1850, 6, 14-15; in 1860, 26, 27, 62, 69, 72; northern and southern lines compared, 89; western line investment compared with rest of nation, 117-19; growth of, 217; mentioned, 46
Iowa: first railroad in, 13; mileage in 1860, 116; investment per mile, 116; construction during the 1850s, 153-55; mentioned, 102, 148
Iron, production of increased, 224

Jackson, Andrew, 98
Jackson County (Mich.) "railroad war," 150
James River & Kanawha Canal, 166, 172
Jefferson, Thpmas, 98
Jervis, John B., 47, 115, 149, 166
Jesup, Morris K., 198
Jewett, Hugh J., 134
Johnson, Andrew, 94, 103
Johnson, Herschel V., 77
Joliet & Chicago R.R., 147
Jones, George Wallace, 99, 102
Joy, James F., 43, 145, 150, 156
Junction R.R., 130

Kansas-Nebraska Act, 111-12
Keep, Henry, 48

Louisville, New Albany & Chicago
R.R., 120, 140-41
Lucas, James H., 184
Lumpkin, Wilson, 59, 77

McCallum, Daniel C., 50
McClellan, George B., 110, 139, 143, 213
McClernand, John A., 99
McCormick, Cyrus, 221
McLane, Lewis, 55
McLean County Tax Case, and Illinois Central, 143
Macon & Western R.R., 12, 59, 64, 74, 76, 77
Madison, James, 164
Madison & Indianapolis R.R., 120, 139
Mad River & Lake Erie R.R., 131, 133
Maine: first railroad, 7; rail mileage in 1840, 7; rail mileage in 1850, 7, 26; rail mileage in 1860, 26; investment per mile, 26
Mak, James, 178
"Manifest Destiny," and railroads, 95
Mann, C. M., 206
Manufactured goods: increase in production of, 222-29; increased value of, 224, number of factories, 224; variety of, 226; use of automatic machinery, 226
Marietta and Cincinnati R.R., 5, 120, 133-35
Maryland: first railroad, 7; rail mileage in 1840, 7; rail mileage in 1850, 7, 26; rail mileage in 1860, 26; investment per mile, 26; mentioned, 56
Mason, Roswell B., 142, 214
Mason, William, 28, 198
Massachusetts: first railroad, 7; rail mileage in 1840, 7; rail mileage in 1850, 7, 26; early construction of railroads, 8; rail mileage in 1860, 26; investment per mile, 26; di-

vidend paying lines, 29; construction in the 1850s, 30-37; mentioned, 116
Maury, Matthew F., 227
Memphis & Charleston R.R., 79, 85, 86-87
Memphis & Little Rock R.R., 89
Memphis & Ohio R.R., 79, 87
Memphis Railroad Convention (1845), 107
Merchandise, moves more by rail than canal, 170
Merchant capitalism, shifts to a modern national economy, 227-29
Merrick, Samuel V., 51
Miami & Erie Canal, 173
Michigan: first railroad in, 13; mileage in 1840, 13; mileage in 1850, 13, 116; mileage in 1860, 116; investment in, 116; construction during the 1850s, 148-51; mentioned, 103
Michigan Central R.R., 43, 145, 148, 150-51, 208
Michigan Southern & Northern Indiana R.R., 148-150
Michigan Southern R.R., 148-49, 210
Mid-Atlantic railroads: in 1850, 5, 7, 9-10; construction during the 1850s, 23, 26, 43-58; investment per mile in 1860, 26; number of, 215
Mileage, railroad: in 1840, 7; in 1850, 3, 5, 6, 7; compared to population, 7, 11-14, 60; compared to area, 7, 11-14, 26-27, 60; in 1860, 16; in the rest of the world, 1860, 16; increase during 1850s, 23-24
Milk, moved to cities by rail, 222
Milwaukee, and railroads, 151-53
Milwaukee & Mississippi R.R., 149, 151-52
Minnesota: first railroad in, 13; mentioned, 103, 115-16
Minot, Charles, 50, 207-8

Mississippi: first railroad, 11; rail mileage in 1840, 11; rail mileage in 1850, 11, 61; rail mileage in 1860, 61; investment per mile, 61; mentioned, 101, 103

Mississippi & Missouri R.R., 149, 153-54

Mississippi Central R.R., 79, 85

Missouri: first railroad in, 13; mileage in 1860, 116; investment per mile, 116; construction during the 1850s, 155-57; mentioned, 102, 148

Missouri Democrat (St. Louis), 227

Missouri Pacific Ry., 157

Mitchell, Alexander, 153

Mobile, Ala., and railroads, 80

Mobile & Ohio R.R., 79, 80-81, 84, 85, 86, 90-91, 100, 194

Mohawk & Hudson R.R., 45

Monon R.R., 120-21

Monroe R.R., 76

Montgomery & West Point R.R., 79, 80, 81-82, 92

Montreal, and rail connection through Maine, 40, 42

Moran, Charles, 213

Morehead, John M., 66

Morgan, Charles, 43

Motive power (railroad): at mid-century, 20-21, 196-203; northern and southern compared, 90-91

Myer, Henry B., 206

Nashville & Chattanooga R.R., 79, 87, 193

National Road, 2, 98, 134, 160, 163

Neu, Irene D., 187

New England railroads: in 1850, 5, 7, 8-9; construction during 1850s, 24, 26-42; investment per mile in 1860, 26; number of, 215; mentioned 25, 44, 61

New Hampshire : first railroad, 7; rail mileage in 1840, 7; rail mileage in 1850, 7, 26; rail mileage in 1860, 26; investment per mile, 26

New Haven R.R., 29, 34, 36

New Jersey: first railroad, 7; rail mileage in 1840, 7; rail mileage in 1850, 7, 26; rail mileage in 1860, 26; investment per mile, 26; dividend paying lines, 27, 29

New Jersey R.R., 27, 200, 202

New Orleans: and railroads, 82, 84; and steamboat traffic in 1850s, 183

New Orleans, Jackson & Great Northern R.R., 79, 82, 84, 85

New York (State): first railroad, 7; rail mileage in 1840, 7; rail mileage in 1850, 7, 26; leading railroad state by 1850, 9; rail mileage in 1860, 26; investment per mile, 26; dividend paying lines, 29; canals in, 164-65; state law favors canals over railroads until 1851, 171; mentioned, 25, 116

New York & Harlem R.R., 44, 47-48, 222

New York & New England R.R., 36

New York & New Haven R.R., 36, 210

New York Central & Hudson River R.R., 48

New York Central R.R.: predecessor lines, 45; creation in 1853, 45-46; growth during 1850s, 45-47; expansion in Ohio, 128-33; expansion in Indiana, 139-40; expansion in Michigan, 148-50; competition with Erie Canal, 167-71; right-of-way "railroad farms," 189-90; freight rates, 215; mentioned, 9, 17, 44, 48, 50, 90, 120-21, 122, 129, 141, 177, 192, 200, 202, 204, 211, 212, 213, 225, 227, 228

New York City, 49

New York Stock Exchange, and rail shares, 215-16

Niagara Bridge & Canandaigua R.R., 44, 48

general use, 190; steel rail rare, 190; import duties on rail, 190; weight of rail in 1850s, 190

Ramsdell, Homer, 213

Rates (railroad): well below turnpike rates, 161; compared to canal, 167-68; freight rates of 1850s, 214-15

Reading R.R., 44, 58, 213

Reapers: number of in use grows as does wheat production and rail mileage, 221

Redfield, William C., 49

Refrigerator cars, 204

Reid, Whitelaw, 232

Relay House, 1

Republican Party, 229

Revenue (railroad): passenger and freight compared, 17; in 1850s, 167-68

Reynolds, L. O., 76

Rhode Island: first railroad, 7; rail mileage in 1840, 7; rail mileage in 1850, 7, 26; rail mileage in 1860, 26; investment per mile, 26

Richmond, Dean, 46

Richmond & Danville R.R., 64, 65, 90, 91

Richmond, Fredericksburg & Potomac R.R., 10

Right-of-way, from public domain, 95

Roadbed, 205

Robb, James, 82, 84

Robert Hanna (steamboat), 180

Robinson, William, 122-24

Rochester & Buffalo R.R., 214

Rock Island (Ill.) Bridge, 114, 146-47, 162, 194, 196

Roebling, John A., 48, 134, 196

Rogers, Thomas, 21, 197-99

Rogers Locomotive Works, 199

Rose, Chauncey, 43

Rutland R.R., 30, 44

Rutland & Burlington R.R., 30, 38-39

Sacramento Valley R.R., 175

St. Johnsbury & Lake Champlain R.R., 211

St. Lawrence & Atlantic R.R., 40

St. Louis, Mo.: and Ohio & Mississippi R.R., 137; and steamboat traffic in 1850s, 183; compared to Chicago, 183-84, 227; mentioned, 2, 15, 147, 156, 227

St. Louis Railroad Convention (1849), 107, 157

Salaries, of railroad presidents, 213

Sandusky (locomotive), 126

Sandusky, Dayton & Cincinnati R.R., 120, 131

Sandusky, Mansfield & Newark R.R., 120, 133, 135-36

Sangamon & Morgan R.R., 147

Santa Fe Trail, 106

Savannah, Ga., 74, 76

Scandals (railroad), 36, 38, 153

Schuyler, Robert, 36, 47, 142

Scott, Isaac, 76

Scott, Thomas A., 52, 214

Seaboard Air Line, 63, 64

Seaboard & Roanoke R.R., 10

Securities, railroad, 62, 73, 88, 143

Seward, William H., 50, 100, 150

Sheffield, Joseph E., 114

Shields, James, 99

Shreve, Levin L., 88

Sidings: northern and southern compared, 90; amount of in 1860, 193

Signals, railroad, 195

Slaves, used by railroads, 65, 85, 92

Sleeping cars: first operated, 205-16; many experiments with in 1850s, 206-7; designs of, 206; charge per night, 206; lack of good ventilation in, 206-7; cost to build, 206; mentioned, 22, 186

Slidell, John, 82

Smith, John, 39

Smith, John Gregory, 39

vania R.R., 51-53, 54, 124, 125, 171, 190, 194; mentioned, 12, 59, 73, 87

"Through rail traffic" (in modern sense) non-existent in 1860, 189

Tickets, railroad, in late 1850s, 214

Tidewater canals, 165

Ties, railroad, 193

Tilden, Samuel J., 144

Toledo & Illinois R.R., 136

Toledo, Norwalk & Cleveland R.R., 130

Toledo, Wabash & Western R.R., 120, 136, 147

Tom Thumb (locomotive), 6

Trade (foreign and domestic), increasing in 1850s, 96, 229

Traffic, railroad: northern and southern traffic compared, 88-89; compared to that on Erie Canal, 167-68

Trans-Allegheny Canals, 164-66

Trollope, Anthony, 205, 207

Troop movement, during Civil War, 142, 230

Troy & Greenfield R.R., 33

Turnpikes: badly hurt by appearance of railroads, 15, 160-63; losing out to railroads in 1850s, 96; fail to be profitable, 161; freight rates on, 161

Tunstall, W. P., 65

Twain, Mark, 185

Twichell, Ginery, 33

Two Roads to Sumter, 229

Tyler, Daniel, 76

Tyson, Henry, 97

Uniforms, for railroad crews, 213-14

Union Pacific R.R., 42

U.S. Army survey of routes to the Pacific, 109-11, 113

U.S. Mails, and Sunday trains, 212

U.S. Patent Office, 226

Urban population, at mid-century, 224

Utica & Schenectady R.R.: 27, 45, 46

Vanderbilt, Commodore Cornelius, 19, 47, 48, 50, 163

Vermont: first railroad, 7; rail mileage in 1850, 7, 26; rail mileage in 1860, 26; investment per mile, 26

Vermont & Canada R.R., 39

Vermont Central R.R., 30, 38-39

Vicksburg & Jackson R.R., 86

Vicksburg & Meridian R.R., 86

Virginia: early railroads, 10-12; rail mileage in 1840, 11; rail mileage in 1850, 11, 61; rail mileage in 1860, 61; rail investment in 1860, 61; mentioned, 60, 63-66

Virginia & Tennessee R.R., 64, 65, 88, 193

Virginia Central R.R., 10, 64, 65, 66

Wabash & Erie Canal, 98, 136, 159-60, 166, 174

Wabash R.R., 120-21, 136, 147, 157

Wadley, William, 77, 86, 92

Wages and salaries, paid rail workers, 213-14

Wagner, Webster, 206

Wagner sleeping car, 228

Wale, Thomas B., 161

Walker, Amasa, 30

Walter, Harvey W., 85

Walton, Gary M., 178

Washington, D.C., 1-3

Water, consumption by a locomotive, 200

Watertown & Rome R.R., 44, 48

Webster, Daniel, 25, 33, 37, 50, 100

Weed, Thurlow, 46

Weld, Charles R., 210-11

Wentworth, John, 99, 184

West, Thomas, 37

Western & Atlantic R.R., 12, 35, 59, 64, 72, 77-78

Western canals, 165, 172-76
Western R.R. (Mass.), 4, 8, 30, 31-33, 47, 149, 161-63, 218
Western railroads: construction during 1850s, 24, 115-19; mileage in 1860, 116; investment per mile, 116; number of, 215
Western River Transportation, 178
Western steamboats: increase in tonnage in 1850, 157; loses to railroads in 1850s, 176-85; inferior to rail service in distance, speed, area of service, and lack of year-round service, 179-83; more comfortable than rail travel, 182; accidents on, 182; lower freight rates, 183; mentioned, 160
Wheeling, Va., 2, 55, 98
Whipple, A. U., 110
Whistler, George W., 31
Whitney, Asa, 42, 105-7, 157

Whitney Memorial to Congress, 106
Wilmington, N.C., 68-69
Wilmington & Manchester R.R., 64, 68-69, 71
Wilmington & Weldon R.R., 64, 68
Wilmington, Charlotte & Rutherfordton R.R., 64, 68-69
Winans, Ross, 20, 75, 202
Wisconsin: first railroad in, 13; mileage in 1850, 13, 116; mileage in 1860, 116; investment per mile, 116; construction during the 1850s, 151-53; mentioned, 103, 148
Wood, as locomotive fuel, 123, 199-203
Woodruff, Theodore T., 206
World railroad mileage, 16

Yulee, David L., 78